The
Story Cycle
Method

Additional Publications by Sascha Brown Rice

The Companion Journals:

The Compass Notebook: A Story Cycle Guided Journal

The Field Notes Writing Tracker: A Story Cycle Process Journal

The Story Cycle Companion Workbook: Writing Prompts and Activities

MUSE & MOON
PUBLISHING

The Story Cycle Method

A Practical Playbook for Writers and Dreamers

Sascha Brown Rice

The Story Cycle Method:
A Practical Playbook for Writers and Dreamers

Copyright © 2023 by Sascha Brown Rice

First Edition
Printed in the United States of America.

ISBN: 979-8-9873195-8-1, paperback
ISBN: 979-8-9873195-1-2, ebook

Book design & typesetting by HR Hegnauer

MUSE & MOON
PUBLISHING

Muse & Moon Publishing
Los Angeles, California
www.museandmoonpublishing.com

For my students.

Table of Contents

Part IV: Craft

Part V: Dream to Draft

Part VI: That's a Wrap

Introduction

Introduction

A creative journey rarely follows a neat, linear path. The writing process takes us into unfamiliar territory and even with careful planning, we hit detours and get turned around. When we're disoriented, momentum slows and motivation recedes. Gloom descends and a storm of doubt clouds the mind. It's no wonder that inspiration can feel like the weather, but productivity doesn't need to be ruled by illusive forces. The creative process moves through predictable cycles—what we'll refer to as Story Cycles. When we accept this organic ebb and flow, we build momentum and find the resilience to finally reach the finish line.

There are four distinct Cycles: Calibrate, Cultivate, Collaborate, and Craft. Each phase is essential, and flux is normal. It's natural to experience periods of expansion and contraction, renewal and release. We can weather these changes when we survey the landscape through the Story Cycle lens. Following the Story Cycles Method empowers us to enjoy the journey.

The cycles have the familiar characteristics of seasons and the elemental forces. Tapping into these recognizable energies demystifies the process and makes writing more intuitive.

You've likely heard the advice to be more disciplined, but muscling your way through often backfires, erodes confidence, and leaves a writer feeling worse than before. Imposing discipline fails to address the root problem and doesn't factor in the demands of the cycle the writer is moving through. Instead, when you feel lost, stuck, or overwhelmed, pause and calibrate. Assess the prevailing conditions and adapt to the cycle you're currently in.

With the Story Cycle mindset, we can weather the seasons of creativity.

Winter is an opportunity to *calibrate:* to listen, reflect, and dream. The *airy* stillness gives us permission to pause and reflect.

The spring season is when we *cultivate:* plant and prepare. *Water* invigorates the process of discovery and development.

The summer cycle is an invitation to play, improvise, and *collaborate.* In this cycle, *fire* sparks joy and ignites inspiration.

The *Craft* Cycle is anchored in autumn: fall heralds the harvest. The *earthy* pragmatics help us revise, refine, and complete.

WHO IS THIS BOOK FOR

The rugged design of the Story Cycle Method makes the concepts and techniques relevant for creatives of all stripes: the dreamer, the rebel, the independent-minded leader, the perfectionist, the workhorse, the procrastinator—and even those who don't yet know what they are. While the book is especially geared toward writers, the Story Cycle Method works for filmmakers and a wide range of other creatives. We focus on the written word and putting pen to page, but the Story Cycle Method can serve musicians, editors, video game designers, and painters. The tools and techniques in the book will accommodate new authors and seasoned writers alike. Even the most experienced writer can get stuck in a rut.

SEASONS ARE A STATE OF MIND

The seasons of Story Cycles are a state of mind. Writers can access any of the four cycles, no matter the time of year, and just as seasons manifest differently around the globe, we each have our own rhythms. My ecosystem differs from yours. When Californians are pulling out flip-flops and swimming suits, winter weather arrives in Australia. Yet, all writers experience fluctuations. The seasonal metaphor helps you navigate the ebb and flow of inspiration.

Anchoring your writing practice in the logic of nature insulates you from the crosswinds of culture and protects us from the battering noise of awards season, pilot season, fire season, election season, and the seasonless churn of demands in our nonstop, tech-charged world. Just as a new season heralds changes in climate, temperature, weather, and light, Story Cycles influence our pace and needs.

As a resident of sunny southern California, it's sometimes hard for me to tap into the seasons. In fact, no matter where you live, the distractions and comforts of modern life often disconnect us from nature's rhythms. Many of us have become accustomed to swaddling ourselves in climate-controlled cocoons and disrupting our organic biorhythms by powering up lights at night and chugging caffeine during the day. And with the trick of technology, we can zoom around the world without leaving home.

As a city dweller, connecting with nature requires effort. When I look up to the night sky, I see a constellation of air traffic and city lights. Yet, when I focus on the moon, the shimmering celestial wonder works magic on my soul. Like the lunar cycles, the seasons reconnect me to the pulse of the planet.

Our intimate relationship with seasons permeates language. Spring (the show-off of the quartet) has inspired countless expressions: spring fever, spring cleaning, spring chicken, spring to mind, spring into action, and spring in your step. Summer, fall, and winter show up in familiar phrases like autumn years, summer fling, dog days of summer, lion in winter, and turning over a new leaf.

When a season arrives, you know it. You feel it whether it's tourist season or holiday season, wedding season or football season, back-to-school season or mating season. It's obvious when it's flu season or the rainy season. You jump into action when it's growing season and peak season. You know it will be delicious when it's in season and distasteful when out of season.

Everything has its season.

The creative process moves through seasons, and the Story Cycle Method will help you negotiate limits and seize opportunities. Productivity ebbs and flows; clarity waxes and wanes. But the Story Cycle mindset gives writers a way to adapt and move forward. Once you're able to discern what Story Cycle you're moving through, you can angle in the right direction and identify the next right action: suit up, strip down, roll up your sleeves, hibernate, or migrate to a more hospitable zone. Don't get mad at the rain—get an umbrella or move indoors. When you calibrate your creative compass, you can make progress no matter the weather or terrain.

Stop waiting for more favorable conditions. It's time to begin.

THE ORIGIN OF STORY CYCLES

The Story Cycle Method originated out of a need for a kinder, gentler mindset. It began as a loose set of ideas and informal practices to help me work through creative challenges. Then people started coming to me for advice. Being a teacher wasn't my goal, but I fell in love with helping others find and shape their stories.

Whether I was making a movie, drafting a novel, or helping a student write a memoir, I noticed a recurring ebb and flow of productivity and inspiration. The Story Cycle framework began to coalesce, and I realized these concepts didn't just make sense to me. My students told me our work together was making transformational shifts in their process.

In the midst of winter, I found there was, within me, an invincible summer.

And that makes me happy. For it says that no matter how hard the world pushes against me, within me, there's something stronger—something better, pushing right back.

—Albert Camus

I began offering courses and workshops. When I discovered that my students hadn't encountered this method elsewhere, I put the draft of my novel aside, pushed my script to the back burner, and turned my focus to wrangling my teaching materials into a book.

The Story Cycle Method isn't a formula but a practice. I still face challenges and experience feelings of self-doubt. Some days I feel like my modest body of work doesn't qualify me to author a book on writing. I haven't smashed box office records with Oscar-winning scripts, and the sole Emmy nomination I received didn't result in a win (and it was regional, not prime time.) Yet, rather than getting stuck in a swamp of compare and despair, I observe these thoughts and let them go.

There will always be someone else who has achieved more. I haven't sold millions of copies of a *New York Times* best-selling novel, but I feel proud of my accomplishments, and most of all I believe my voice matters and so does yours. It's natural to compare ourselves to others, but when that less-than feeling strikes, I now know it is just a sign that my journey isn't over. Like you, I am very much a work in progress, and my story is still unfolding.

What follows is an introduction to the Story Cycle Method and a distillation of lessons learned. We'll go behind the scenes into the real experience of my clients, and rather, than dazzling you with tales of my wild success, I'll give you a front-row seat to my messy, imperfect journey.

HOW TO USE THIS BOOK

While you can read the book nonsequentially, start on page one if you want the scaffolding of a step-by-step guide. Parts One, Two, Three, and Four take you through each of the four Story Cycles. In Part One, we navigate the wintry chill of the Calibrate Cycle; in Part Two, we swim through the invigorating springtime of the Cultivate Cycle; in Part Three, we move through the summery abundance of the Collaborate Cycle; and in Part Four, we settle into the Craft Cycle, the demanding phase of finishing.

Each chapter includes practical tools and techniques and at least one behind-the-scenes story that illustrates the concepts presented. My students and colleagues generously granted permission to share their experiences. Some names have been changed to protect the writers' identities.

Don't get caught up in the terminology. Instead, put pen to page and try the exercises. When you reach an activity, you will be prompted to jump to the end of each chapter where you'll find step-by-step instructions. You'll want two companion journals. One notebook will be a workbook for tackling the exercises, and the other will be a place to reflect on the process.

If you're hungry for homework, you can speed through the exercises, but embedded within each chapter I've highlighted an activity you don't want to miss. It's fine to save prompts for later or to opt out of assignments, but don't skip over the ones highlighted within the chapter. These are the most important ones—like this one here.

ACTIVITY: Compass Notebook

Dedicate a journal to tackling the exercises in the book.

- ☐ Any old notebooks will do, but consider using
     The Compass Notebook: A Story Cycle Guided Journal
- ☐ Once you have your notebook, you'll be ready to tackle the
     exercises in Chapter One.

Purchase:
The Compass Notebook

This isn't a race. Savor the journey. There are six parts, so you might give yourself two months to work through the book. Or you might take a year to work your way through the whole book. There's no need to rush. If you're like most people, you have responsibilities. Start by devoting ten minutes a day to your writing.

Tip: If you are juggling a busy schedule, simply start with the time you have.

CONTENTS OVERVIEW

PART I: CALIBRATE

We begin with the Calibrate Cycle. The winter cycle is a time to step back from the front lines, to cocoon, hibernate, and look within. Chapter One unpacks the pause. When we activate this season, we make space to clarify and set intentions. This chapter is the perfect launching pad for a new project and the place to return when you feel lost.

In Chapter Two, we introduce a foundational practice: radical self-care. Our physical bodies require maintenance and attention. We can calibrate with a body check-in and the gratitude list. We expand our understanding of self-care by tending to the eight realms of radical self-care.

Next, we embrace the concept of wonder and adopt the mindset of the explorer. At the heart of this cycle is the practice of tracking your process or keeping field notes. In Chapter Three, we learn the concept of The Bridge, a simple technique to facilitate your way into creativity.

To calibrate your creative compass, we find our *why* and revisit why we want to bring a story into the world. In Chapter Four, we reconnect to purpose and reset intentions. We wrap up this section with the ultimate calibration: The Story Cycle Survey.

PART II: CULTIVATE

Next, we move into the spring cycle, the time for planting and planning. In Chapter Five, we focus on capacity. This concept helps us consider the weather and terrain so we can navigate the demanding process of development.

The Cultivate Cycle is a fertile time ripe with possibilities, so in Chapter Six, we set markers and milestones to chart the course forward. These measurable steps will be anchors when you experience the creative ebb and flow. We will reimagine what "writing" looks like and unpack the benefits of discovery writing.

In Chapter Seven, we cultivate with the improvisation technique: explore and heighten. We lean into the concept of "Yes, and . . ." and nourish the process by digging into senses and emotions. Finally, we'll unveil one of the most liberating tools: the question list.

Next, we'll pivot to the inner workings of your story. We'll dig into the character's inner world and make their journey more difficult by adding obstacles. Regardless of the medium or genre, writers need to create conflict. In Chapter Eight, we'll develop tension by exploring secrets, fears, and the desires. This cycle requires patience and persistence, so we'll return to milestones and markers with an eye toward celebrating.

PART III: COLLABORATE

As the cycle's name suggests, the core feature of this phase is connection. The Collaborate Cycle is the time to connect and play. Even a solo writer who hides out in a remote cabin must learn to collaborate, even if it's with their own subconscious. Just as improvisation helps us during development, the mercurial summer cycle demands a willingness to let go of control. Chapters Nine, Ten, Eleven, and Twelve highlight the virtues of play.

We learn nonlinear techniques like using word clouds to generate material. We rekindle creative connection by injecting whimsy into the process. We'll take inspiration from the surrealists and stir up some serendipity with a brief foray into tarot. We make friends with the inner critic and call the muse.

To handle the heat of the summer cycle, we'll scaffold the process with radical self-care and activate the warmth of the Collaborate Cycle by finding connection. We'll consider when and how to present work for feedback. Even constructive criticism can be destabilizing, so instead of slipping into an abyss of despair, we'll practice the art of listening, and we'll rekindle the creative fire with the kind critic and the love list.

PART IV: CRAFT

Next, we move into the most revered and misunderstood phase: the Craft Cycle. The autumnal season is when we harvest, but it is also a time to clear away the dead and prepare for winter.

In Chapters Thirteen, Fourteen, and Fifteen, we'll stay grounded in pragmatics and rethink the fundamentals.

We crack open the Craft Cycle with a more intuitive approach to structure. To liberate ourselves from the conventional constraints of outlining, we work with the beating heart and the narrative spine of the story. We look at drafting and unpack the different types of revision. We use voice and point of view to shape the reader's experience, then turn to the masters for models that can instruct and inspire.

How do you know when you're done and ready to move on? In Chapter Sixteen, we look at one of the most elusive aspects of the writing process: finishing. Even if you've carefully calibrated, enthusiastically cultivated, thoughtfully collaborated, and diligently crafted, your project still may not be ready to harvest.

More often than not, projects take longer than planned and unexpected obstacles materialize. When you find yourself in the messy middle, it's natural to look for a shortcut. Instead of looking for a way around, look for a way through. As we refine and polish, we also must let go. The defining characteristic of this season is transformation. Before we move out of the Craft Cycle, we must navigate the mists of maybe.

PART V: DREAM TO DRAFT

After we've moved through all four Story Cycles, it's time to put it all together. In this section, we'll combine the distinctive features of each cycle. To move from dream to draft, we must spiral through the Story Cycles again and again.

In Chapter Seventeen, we break through blocks by pulling techniques from one Story Cycle into another. We lighten the sometimes-stuffy craft phase with playful exercises from the Collaborate Cycle. We wake up our emotions by invoking the invigorating energy of the Cultivate Cycle.

Next, we activate the power of Story Cycles by wielding the potent forces of air, water, fire, and earth. We break down the essential properties of each element and identify its corresponding Story Cycle. This intuitive framework helps us calibrate no matter what season we're cycling through. When you're unable to move forward, tune into the elemental forces.

In Chapter Nineteen, we collaborate with the critic. Crossing the finish line can be wonderfully satisfying, but even just the prospect of sharing work may trigger fear and self-doubt. We uncover what the critic's rants really mean and learn how to reframe their toxic narratives.

PART VI: THAT'S A WRAP

To wrap up, we embrace the in-between time. Letting the ground lie fallow is a vital part of the process. Sometimes a project just needs to mulch more. We'll revisit the revitalizing power of radical self-care and return to Markers and Milestones with a specific eye toward celebrating.

When we arrive at Chapter Twenty-One, we gather our favorite exercises, concepts, and tools. We review how to use the Story Cycle framework to triage common challenges, and we'll identify the tools and techniques that best serve each creative phase. We pack our backpacks, so we are prepared to maneuver the finicky final stages of completion.

We're at the end of the book—but perhaps at the beginning of the writing journey.

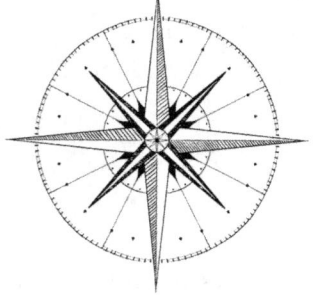

PART I

Calibrate

THE WINTER CYCLE

Energy wanes; activity lags.

The sun's ebbing presence makes the days shorter and darker.

Slow down. Ration the reserves.

Indulge the urge to hibernate.

This season is a time to pause and reflect . . .

(before you begin again).

The Pause

Winter: It's time to calibrate: to reflect and listen. Settle into stillness.

The airy quiet of the winter cycle may feel uncomfortable, but it's important to periodically step back from the front lines and look within. No matter what Story Cycle you're moving through, pause and calibrate. Simple practices like journal writing and using a timer help you anchor yourself in the now. By pairing the timer with freewriting, we'll build a writing practice bit by bit, word by word.

FIRST THINGS FIRST: Practice

Many of my students want to know how long it will take to finish. The timeline depends on your unique circumstances, your experience, the specific demands of the project, and how much time you're able to dedicate to writing. The best way to move forward on your writing journey is to work with the time you have.

Many people think they'll begin writing when they have more time. It's a mistake to wait until a "better" time or until you have "enough" time. If you wait for the ideal conditions, you may never start at all. Even if you are retired, rich, or on a retreat, there will always be demands on your time. Life inevitably throws us curveballs: fun opportunities, family responsibilities, health troubles, life changes, and emotional highs and lows.

Seize the day. Build a writing practice one minute at a time. The sooner you begin, the sooner you will arrive.

The sooner you begin, the sooner you will arrive.

Time To Write

The first step of your writing journey is to set aside time to write. It's not necessary to write every day but make writing a habit. It's a myth that to be a writer you need to spend eight hours a day banging away at the keyboard. You can make progress even if you can only scrape together two hours a week. It's worthwhile to stay connected to the material even if you can only "touch" the work for ten minutes a day.

How long should your writing session be? Experiment and discover what works for you. I find that two-hour blocks provide a solid container, but three or four hours help me build more momentum. On the other hand, an hour might feel like an overwhelming swath of time. Different cycles, circumstances, and projects demand different levels of attention.

ACTIVITY: Make a Writing Date　　　　　🕗 10 minutes

- ☐ Look at the next week and assess how much time you have available.
- ☐ Schedule two to five writing sessions in your calendar.
  - The sessions may be anywhere from three minutes to three hours.
  - If you have only one hour in the week to work with, then I recommend starting with three twenty-minute blocks.

THE JOURNAL

In the introduction, you were tasked with choosing two notebooks, but if you haven't already, get yourself a journal. This will be a place where you can tackle exercises and explore ideas with freewriting. Any old notebooks will do. While writing on a digital device is a convenient way to record memories and ideas, it's worthwhile to dedicate some time to writing in a journal.

Many students prefer typing on a device, but before you decide to play exclusively for Team Digital, consider the benefits of an analog approach. First, the beauty of writing by hand is that you remove potential friction. You don't need fancy equipment, chargers, or outlets. Instead of waiting to boot up your device, you simply need to open your notebook and begin. The blank page also provides an expansive canvas. You can organize the page how you like, make notes in the margins, and doodle. Writing by hand connects us to our bodies, forces us to slow down, and anchors us in the present moment. It might seem painfully slow and outdated, but creativity is not about being faster.

In a world where immediate gratification dominates, the laborious task of writing by hand might seem tedious, but decades of research have proven there's value in putting pen to page. The repetitive motion of marking characters on the page increases activity in the same sections of the brain activated in meditation. Writing cursive especially stimulates synchronicity between the left and right brain. In fact, "graphotherapy," a therapeutic treatment involving the daily practice of putting pen to page, is used to calm and retrain the brain. The prescription: regular sessions of scribing a simple sentence like, "I will be more peaceful." Writing by hand has even been shown to lower blood pressure, improve liver function, lessen symptoms of asthma, and boost the immune system.

While I'm not suggesting you ditch your laptop, try to incorporate writing by hand into your writing practice. Working with pen and paper also encourages the writer to find inspiring surroundings. Instead of lugging a laptop around, curl up on the couch or venture into nature. Stepping away from the computer also reduces the risk of succumbing to digital distractions like email, texts, entertaining videos, and the research rabbit hole.

THE TIMER

No matter how long you plan to write in a given session, I recommend using a timer. In my own experimenting, I've learned that working with a timer has many benefits. A finite window of time creates a sense of urgency and helps me to stay focused. The timer gives me a sense of control as I wade into the unknown. The timer cues me when it's time to move on. I might decide not to move on to the next action item, but the timer helps me make a conscious choice about how I allocate my energy. Our access to the internet makes it especially easy to fall down the research rabbit hole, so the timer keeps me on track and prevents me from wasting time on a low-priority task.

The timer is also a great reminder to get up, move around, stretch, or get a glass of water. If we fail to take breaks, we may end up with achy backs, headaches, and eyestrain. Before discovering the timer, I spent an entire summer banging out a first draft of a novel. I pounded on the keyboard for five, six, even seven hours at a time, day after day, week after week. I completed the draft, but I gave myself carpal tunnel syndrome. The pain was so debilitating that for weeks I could barely even turn a doorknob, and for several months I was unable to hold a pen or type. When we experience a creative rush, it's hard to stop. But to go the distance, one needs to take breaks. The timer helps us calibrate.

I often break my writing session into twenty-minute intervals. Then, rather than feeling defeated if my writing session is cut short, I feel a sense of progress because I know I've completed one or two twenty-minute bursts.

FIVE JOURNAL PRO TIPS

1. TAKE UP SPACE: Don't limit yourself to one journal. Dedicate notebooks to specific projects. For example, use one notebook for all activities. Start each new question or prompt on a fresh page. This gives you space to continue a freewrite in case you'd like to return to it. Give your writing room to grow.

2. NAME IT: Make a habit of assigning titles to all journal entries. The practice of naming is a way to honor your writing. While the material is still fresh in your mind, jot down a word or phrase at the top of the page. Even title freewrites and exercises. A label will help you find material, and over time this practice will demystify your process. Even if you feel that what you wrote is terrible or insignificant, honor your effort. (You may realize later that you made an important discovery.)

3. BE MESSY: Your journal is for your eyes only. Give yourself permission to be imperfect. Don't worry about handwriting, grammar, spelling, or punctuation.

4. INCLUDE THE DATE, TIME, AND PLACE. These details may seem obvious and unnecessary now, but later this information may provide important insights about productivity and help jog your memory so you can reconnect to what you discovered.

5. STAR IT: Use highlighters, stars, and sticky notes to mark special pages. This will help you find the gems even after the brilliant light of inspiration fades. Assign a page for future ideas and a place for notes on projects on the back burner.

First, forget inspiration. Habit is more dependable.

–Octavia Butler

FREEWRITING

Freewriting, sometimes called "wild writing," is one of the best ways to activate the pause. This practice allows the writer to tap into the subconscious, warm up, and drop into the now.

Like stream-of-consciousness writing, when you freewrite, let go of the idea of "good writing." Write anything that comes to mind; give yourself a place to be imperfect, silly, or even stupid. Throw out the rules and embrace the messy process of creating. Give yourself a safe space for bad ideas.

A good length of time for a freewrite is one to five minutes. Beyond seven minutes, the brain often wants to get involved. By containing freewrites to short bursts, you can sneak past the inner critic and access your subconscious.

It's essential to keep the pen moving. Don't stop to think—that's stalling and trying to control. Rather than contemplating the value of an idea, turn your focus to the simple act of putting words on the page. Thinking comes in handy for editing, crafting, and shaping your story. Revising will come later. It's nearly impossible to generate and edit at the same time, so during a freewrite, don't edit—just let it flow. For this activity, it doesn't matter if the sentences are bad, good, crazy, or brilliant. It doesn't need to make sense. Just keep going.

It is tempting to stop to ponder, but during a freewrite, focus on putting the pen to page. Drop into the present moment; connect to your senses. The most important rule of freewriting is to keep the pen moving. Stay with it and ideas will percolate.

So, grab a pen, set a timer, and allow words to flow onto the page. If you get stuck, keep the pen moving. You may repeat the guiding prompt, and something will come to mind. Do not stop moving your pen or tapping the keyboard. You may simply write, *What's next? What's next? What's Next?*

ACTIVITY: Freewrite 4 minutes

Use freewriting to explore the prompts.

* See the end of the chapter for step-by-step instructions.

RECAP: Honor the Pause

The creative process spirals through the Story Cycles, so make it a habit to pause and calibrate. If you feel restless, it may be because you are ready to migrate to the next cycle, or it might just be a case of spring fever. Before you move from winter to spring, consider this quick calibration.

We can invoke the pause by using the foundational tools: the timer and freewriting. No matter what cycle you are moving through, it's important to make time to calibrate.

Calibrate Your Compass

Snow day: If energy wanes, indulge the urge to hibernate and cocoon.
☐ Spend Sunday morning in bed, make a pot of tea, or cozy up with a book.

Tools and Techniques

◎ The pause
◎ Timer
◎ Freewriting

Chapter One Activities

Freewrite

⏰ 4 minutes

Use freewriting to explore the prompts below. Don't stop writing. Keep the pen moving. Let a stream of consciousness flow on the page. When you get stuck, return to the guiding prompt and rewrite the prompt until a new idea presents itself. You can even write and rewrite "what's next" until a new idea pops up. Keep going. What's next, what's next, what's next, what's next ...

Remember: this is a way to warm up, so lower the stakes and have fun. (Dedicate two minutes to each prompt.)

Prompts:
- ☐ I feel ...
- ☐ I want ...

BEHIND THE SCENES: Corner Turn

Karen and I sat on the floor watching our sons play with blocks. Wordlessly, the boys stacked and sorted. Their peaceful collaboration and Karen's characteristic equilibrium made me acutely aware of the turmoil brewing inside me. I was feeling out of balance and overdue for a calibration. I hadn't yet learned to apply the principles of Story Cycles to everyday life.

We heard the booming voices of our husbands as they gave a loud bro-welcome to Dad #3. The dudes were best friends from college, and our three families were meeting up to vacation together for spring break. Their families had specially flown into town because, in a few hours, we'd all be leaving Los Angeles and caravanning out to Palm Springs. Actually, they'd be going to the desert. I was going to London.

The indie feature that I had written and directed, *Mango Kiss*, had been selected to screen at a prominent London film festival. I was scheduled to fly out the next day. I had been looking forward to the trip. For the last year, *Mango Kiss* had been screening around the world, but I had missed nearly all the out-of-town showings. I'd stayed home while the film zipped all over the globe to far-flung venues in Hawaii, Atlanta, DC, Johannesburg, Paris, Barcelona, Helsinki, Italy, Germany, Hungary, Portugal, Australia, Canada, Brazil, and Tokyo.

I told friends I wasn't traveling with the film because it was cost prohibitive. That was true, but mostly I didn't want to be away from our son, who was still just a toddler. Even though I had only attended a handful of screenings, it was thrilling to know we were selling out theaters, winning awards, and even being booked in the coveted opening-night headlining feature spot.

Going to this festival had taken on special significance because I knew my window for traveling on my own was rapidly closing. I was now pregnant with our second child, and I knew I'd soon be too pregnant to feel comfortable flying. Once our daughter was born, I would be nursing and wouldn't want to take her on the road, nor could I imagine leaving her behind. I figured it would be years before jet setting would be in the realm of the possible.

Since the London festival coincided with spring break, my husband had taken the week off and was fully capable of being a full-time dad. He was bummed I would miss the three-family vacay, but he was supportive of my choice to go. The festival had paid for airfare, booked me in a posh hotel, and hooked me up with an all-access pass. I didn't want to miss the family trip, but I had been looking forward to going to the UK. I relished the opportunity to watch other films, meet other writer-directors, and connect with audiences. But about two weeks before my departure date, I found myself crying in mundane situations like driving the car, doing dishes, or pushing my son on the swing.

As Karen sorted Legos, I told her how excited I was about the trip and the red carpet experience ahead, but once again, I started crying for seemingly no reason. The pregnancy hormones had heightened my emotions, but my friend sensed there was more to it than that.

She watched the tears flow as I detailed the itinerary. When I stopped to blow my nose, she asked, "Do you want to go?"

Of course, I wanted to go, but I heard myself blurt out, "No."

Without missing a beat, she said, "Then don't go!"

I blew my nose again and explained that the festival was counting on me. They had promoted my attendance and arranged for media interviews, and I didn't want to let them down.

"In ten years, who will remember? What will you remember?"

In an instant, everything became crystal clear. I did not want to go. The tears stopped. I hadn't been able to admit it to myself, but I realized I did not want to be away from my family.

I hadn't known how conflicted I was. It had seemed preposterous to even contemplate passing up this opportunity, but Karen's serene inquiry had penetrated my denial and triggered a quick calibration. Since she is a fellow working mom, I knew she hadn't judged my decision to be leaving my family for the week.

I was only three months pregnant, and I hadn't wanted to admit to myself that my life was rapidly changing. I felt that the days with our young son were rushing by too fast, and while the doctor said it was safe to travel, it didn't feel right.

I emailed the festival and explained I wouldn't be able to attend. One of the cast members was already planning to be in London for the screening, so I arranged for her to get my VIP pass and all the royal treatment. The festival was a little annoyed but ultimately satisfied to have one of the movie's beautiful actresses take my place.

Twenty years later, I still remember that week in Palm Springs: the hours playing in the water with our son, floating in the pool, enjoying long chats, sharing laughs, and spending blissful afternoons reading on the chaise lounge. We don't always have the luxury of the pause, but that time I realized I could seize the opportunity I'd actually wanted, and it sticks with me as one of the smarter calibrations I've made along the way.

Over the following week, I explored my feelings with freewriting. I contemplated what was next. I still dreamed about making more movies. Since the film had wrapped, I had written a new screenplay and hadn't for a second entertained the idea of slowing down. As I journaled, I began to question the next moves on my career path. I realized my priorities had changed. What I wanted most was to be at home with my kids. I wanted to pause.

I deeply respect and admire women who can manage careers in the entertainment business and motherhood, but at that moment, I was more interested in finger painting with my son than pounding the pavement with my new script. My creative drive was still very much alive, but I decided that soon enough I'd make another film and there'd be another festival, another party, and another opportunity.

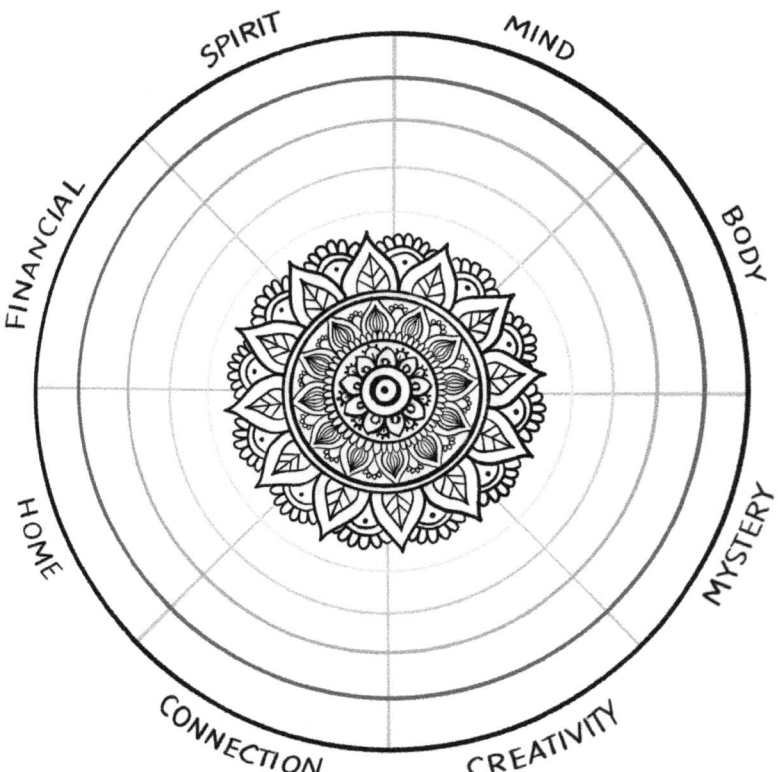

SPIRIT MIND

FINANCIAL BODY

HOME MYSTERY

CONNECTION CREATIVITY

Radical Self-Care

Winter: The Calibrate Cycle reminds us to rest and refill the well.

As we move through the creative process, taking time to calibrate helps us seize opportunities and respect our limits. Simple techniques like list making and checking in with our bodies are quick ways to calibrate. No matter where we are in the journey, radical self-care ensures we build a sustainable writing practice. Tending to the eight realms of self-care helps us weather the seasons of creativity.

FIRST THINGS FIRST: Calibrate with Care

Radical self-care is about taking time to pause and recharge. This practice is radical not because it demands an extraordinary act, but because setting boundaries around one's time requires us to stand up to a world of obligations, distractions, and possibilities.

The most important element of this practice is rest. It does not require fancy products or expensive treatments. Radical self-care can be as simple as remembering to take a lunch break or going on a walk. For me, radical self-care is getting on the yoga mat, even if only for just ten minutes. I need more sleep than the average bear, so another way I practice self-care is by going to bed early. Sleep may not seem like a revolutionary act, but rest and dreamtime fuel the imagination. Calibrate and refill the well.

RADICAL SELF-CARE

Radical self-care is an intentional rebellion against tradition and expectations. It's hard to break old habits. These patterns can be generational and may be born of inherited trauma. The poet and activist Audre Lorde pioneered the concept that self-care is a radical act. She wrote, "Caring for myself is not self-indulgence, it is self-preservation, and that is an act of political warfare." Lorde recognized the fundamental necessity of self-care for her survival as a Black woman in the face of systemic oppression and present-day racism. Prioritizing self-care became even more critical as she battled cancer.

Radical self-care is important for everybody, but for my students who are women of color, the imperative is often especially glaring. One of my clients is a television writer and often finds herself as the only person of color and the only Black woman in the writer's room. Not only is the lack of diversity isolating, but it also adds pressure and drains life force. For her, radical self-care means making time to practice yoga, talking about her experience with a trusted friend, and dedicating time to her passion projects. These actions renew her spirits so she can return to the writer's room ready to collaborate even in the face of active discrimination. A self-care practice doesn't eliminate the challenges, but it does help to mitigate the harm and restore energy.

Word of caution: Access to self-care is a privilege. It isn't always simply a matter of choice. The self-care proposition should not be used to minimize experience. While self-care enhances an individual's well-being, it is not a substitute for social consciousness. Specifically, as a white person, I must not turn a blind eye to the very real systems of oppression and the brutal history of racism in the United States. The power of storytelling amplifies the writer's responsibility to engage in complicated issues.

When I dare
to be powerful—
to use my
strength in the
service of my
vision, then it
becomes less and
less important
whether I am
afraid.

—Audre Lorde

What's Radical Self-Care For You?

The word "radical" is derived from "root." This reminds us that habits are deeply embedded, so to build new habits, we often must dig deep. There isn't a magic formula, and each person is different. You might need more time in nature, a greener diet, or more time alone. One of my clients is immune to criticism but prone to overworking. Another is impervious to defeat, but too often she puts others before herself. It can feel impossible, but protecting your energy is key to building creative momentum.

As an early riser, I am most productive in the morning, so while it's sometimes necessary (and fun) to stay up late, it's essential that I hit the hay at a reasonable hour most nights. Of course, there are times when I feverishly chisel away at a rewrite into the wee hours or succumb to late-night temptations to binge a new series. But when I get more rest, I am not only happier—I am also more creative. When I was younger, I could burn the midnight oil and then recover by sleeping late, but pulling all-nighters is not sustainable.

The Body Check-In

The body check-in is a quick way to calibrate. Writers need to access the inner world, so this centering exercise trains you to notice even the quieter thoughts and feelings. The body check-in is like an X-ray.

LIST MAKING

List making is a quick way to calibrate. This versatile tool helps us gather our thoughts and generate. It's the perfect warm-up because the act of making quick notes creates momentum. It also frees us from needing to know why something matters or how ideas connect.

ACTIVITY: The Body Check-In

 3 minutes

No one knows you like you. Tap into your inner world. What do you notice?

- ☐ Settle into a comfortable seated position, then set a timer for two minutes.
- ☐ Close your eyes and observe your breath.
- ☐ Turn your attention inward.
- ☐ Notice the sensations in your body and the chatter in the mind, then come back to your breath.
- ☐ When the timer goes off, open your eyes, pull out your journal, and set the timer for one minute.
- ☐ *Jot down your observations.*
- ☐ *What did you notice?*
- ☐ *What's on your mind? How is your body?*
- ☐ *Do you need to calibrate with self-care?*
- ☐ *Did something come up about your writing project?*

Download:
The Body Check-in Guided Meditation

Making a list also liberates the writer from the rules of composition. By decoupling the thought process from "writing," we amplify the connection to the unconscious, so we can capture slivers of inspiration. This practice is especially helpful in memoir writing because it's easy to get lost in the soup of life. One of my clients was writing about a wild year she spent hitchhiking and working odd jobs. The first wave of material flooded out and she generated over forty thousand words, but then she hit a wall. She didn't know what to do next. I suggested she make a list of the places and people that stood out from the adventure. The list provided topics to explore and helped us identify themes and connections.

Making time for self-care is radical because setting boundaries around one's time requires us to stand up to a world of obligations, distractions, and possibilities.

List of Lists

There are many types of lists: a pro/con list, a gratitude list, a list of questions, a list of *what I know for sure*, a list of ways to die, or the classic "to-do list." The simple act of writing something down often brings clarity. Penciling out the pros and cons usually reveals what makes sense or which path to pursue. Rather than daydreaming about ideas, make a list.

Action lists are invaluable, but sometimes before trying to figure out what's next, it's helpful to claim the wins. The creative process can be difficult to track, so it's worth taking stock of the victories. In addition to words written, note internal shifts, new habits, fresh perspectives, lessons learned, or discoveries. Sometimes what's most important stays hidden because it's so familiar.

List making can also quiet external noise and build a connection to the page. Emotions can drive the creative process, or they can lock us into distracting despair. When you can't snap out of a funk, calibrate by making a gratitude list. Take a moment to acknowledge the good all around: oxygen, clean drinking water—or, as Thich Nhat Hanh suggested, appreciate the non-toothache. It's important to honor where we are and acknowledge our blessings.

By pausing to reclaim gratitude, we understand our landscape. We can adjust our focus and how we approach a task, modulating our pace for the journey ahead.

ACTIVITY: Count Your Blessings: Make a Gratitude List   7 minutes

* See the end of the chapter for step-by-step instructions.*

> Keeping your body healthy is an expression of gratitude to the whole cosmos—the trees, the clouds, everything.
>
> —Thich Nhat Hanh

THE REALMS OF SELF-CARE

Radical self-care requires that we make time to renew creative energy. If writing is the exhale, filling the well is the inhale. A sustainable practice must include rest. Often, insights happen when we are off the clock. Have you ever had an idea come to you when you're taking a shower, walking your dog, or drifting off to sleep? Carving out space for radical self-care is part of the writer's job.

To facilitate the process of building a self-care practice, I've identified eight realms of radical self-care. These categories help us find balance in the ever-changing landscape of life. This framework was inspired by the "wheel of life" used by life coaches. When I looked into the origins of the wheel of life, it was no surprise that countless traditions employ the wheel as a symbol to make sense of the cyclical nature of life.

The Buddhist bhavacakra, or "wheel of becoming," is one of the oldest versions of this potent symbol. The bhavacakra is a symbolic representation of the endless cycle of life, birth, and death. Intricate mandalas often adorn monasteries to show Buddhist teachings and the path to enlightenment. Similarly, Native Americans employ the medicine wheel or Sacred Hoop. Interpretations vary, but across the many diverse indigenous tribes, this sacred symbol is used for healing.

I've identified core areas that feel right to me, but it's important the realms feel comprehensive to you. I encourage you to fashion your own definition of radical self-care. You may want to use the eight realms as a starting point to clarify your priorities and point of view.

Just as the Story Cycles are designed to help you navigate your creative journey, the eight realms of self-care can support you on your path to inspiration. Periodically revisit and reassess your needs. Self-care is a dynamic practice because we change and evolve as we move through different life stages.

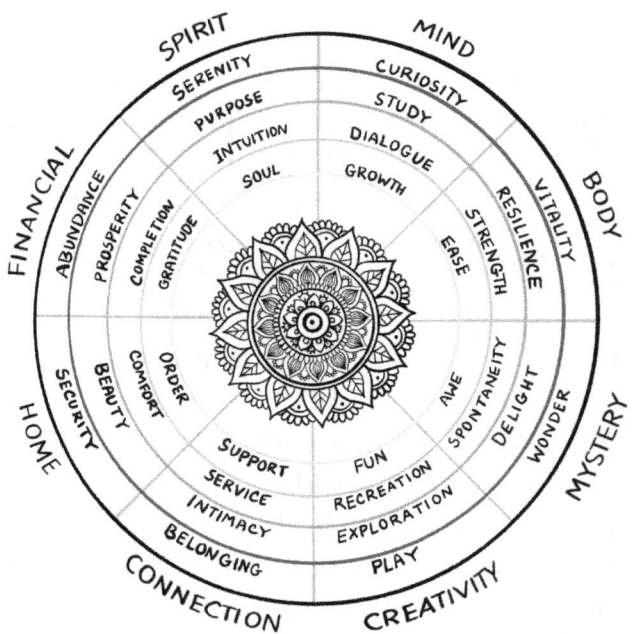

THE EIGHT REALMS

MIND: A healthy mind grows out of an active curiosity about the world, people, and ideas. The mind is nourished by engaging in study, inquiry, and dialogue.

BODY: The hallmarks of wellness are strength, resilience, and ease. As we move through the different cycles of life, our definition of health changes. Health also includes feeling comfortable in and appreciating our bodies, as well as dedicating time to grooming.

MYSTERY: An important part of life is feeling a sense of wonder and awe. Not everything can be neatly categorized, so it's important to allow space for surprise and delight. This fundamental human need can be found by connecting to nature and spending time outdoors.

CONNECTION: An essential part of happiness is feeling a sense of belonging. There are many ways to create meaningful relationships, but it's important to feel supported and a part of a tribe, family, team, or community. Relationships are a collaboration, a give-and-take, and they require nurturing and attention.

CREATIVITY: A critical part of experiencing fulfillment is making time to play, goof off, explore, have fun, enjoy hobbies, and engage in recreation. There are countless ways to experience creativity, but at the heart is being at ease with improvisation, experimentation, and collaboration.

FINANCIAL: Prosperity comes in many forms, so financial health will look different for everyone. The harvest is a time for completion, delivery, and honoring commitments. Wealth is experienced only when we feel grateful for what we have.

HOME: Having a place to call home helps us feel safe and secure. Claiming one's space is a continuous practice of feathering one's nest and tending one's garden.

Five Tips for Building a Radical Self-Care Practice

1. Make it early, easy, and free: It's not always possible, nor is it necessary, to splurge on activities that require lots of money or time. Build a buffet of bite-sized actions. Often the most nourishing actions don't cost money.
   - ☐ Work it in early in the day.
   - ☐ Self-care is a daily practice: Start by spending three minutes a day.

2. Body and soul: Self-care isn't only about tending to the body; it also means caring for spiritual, creative, and social needs. Meditation works, but also consider just having fun. What feels nourishing? What do you crave?
   - ☐ Legitimate self-care includes singing, dancing, reading, walking, cooking, laughing, being in nature, or simply staying in pajamas all day.

3. Be in the world and on planet Earth: We are human, so remember to connect to nature, friends, and the world. Unplug and reconnect.
   - ☐ Take a two-hour "retreat." Turn off electronics and sit outside with a book and a yummy beverage.

4. You are the expert: There are books, brilliant healers, and lots of resources out there, but no one knows you like you do. Each person has different sensitivities and strengths.
   - ☐ Use the body check-in technique to connect with your needs.

5. Have an attitude of curiosity: No need to obsess over getting self-care "right" or figuring it out. Give yourself time to find what works. There are infinite ways we can love, cherish, and care for ourselves.
   - ☐ Experiment and play.
   - ☐ Begin anew each day.

Reminder: Start small. Not only will this set you up for success, but also each time you achieve your goal, you build more trust in yourself and faith in the process.

Make the Realms Real

To survive, we must rest, eat well, hydrate, and connect with other human beings. To thrive, we need to go beyond the necessities of survival. We must tend all the realms. Be sure your self-care practice includes a wide range of actions: small and large, free and fancy, alone and together, inside and outside, nourishing to the mind and to the body.

ACTIVITY: Make a Self-Care Cheat Sheet   30 minutes

When we need it the most, it can be hard to remember what to do to refuel. So, before your energy wanes, identify ways to support your well-being.

See the end of the chapter for step-by-step instructions.

RECAP: Protect your Practice

Practicing radical self-care helps us protect our writing practice. Without regular self-care, the stresses of everyday life will erode your writing practice. Calibrating with radical self-care helps the writer weather the seasons of creativity. Techniques like the body check-in and the gratitude list are accessible ways to calibrate. These practices provide a reliable way to get centered and give us access to our inner world. We expand our understanding of self-care by tending to the eight realms of radical self-care.

Calibrate Your Compass

Less is more: Divide your daily to-do list into two categories: must-do and may-do.
- ☐ Include only one action in the must-do section.
    Make sure the must-do action is very small and one hundred percent achievable within the amount of time you have today.
- ☐ Move the rest of the action items to the may-do section.

Tools and Techniques

- ◎ The body check-in
- ◎ List making
- ◎ Radical self-care
- ◎ Eight realms

Chapter Two Activities

Count Your Blessings: Make a Gratitude List　⏰ 7 minutes

Make a gratitude list. Try to identify twenty blessings.

- ☐ Use list making to give thanks.
  - – Nothing is too small to be on the list: oxygen, clean drinking water, apples, water, socks.
  - – Consider the eight realms.

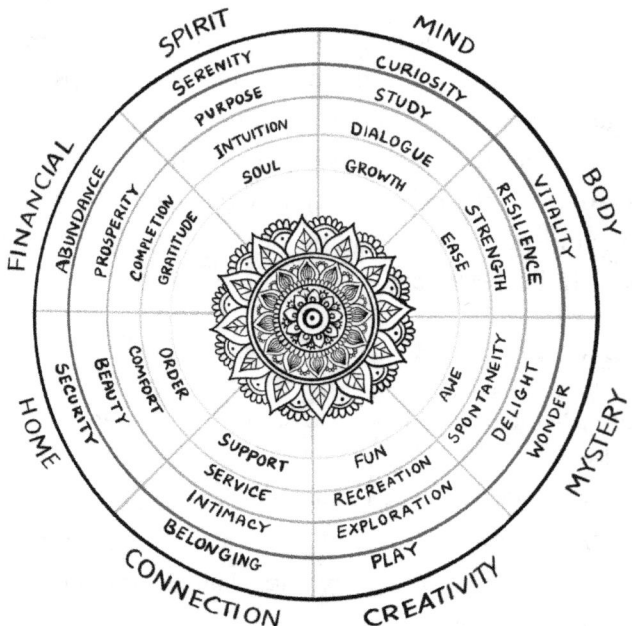

Make a Self-Care Cheat Sheet  30 minutes

Make a list of actions that support your physical, emotional, social, and spiritual well-being. Look for ways to nourish your body, mind, and spirit. Try this five-step process.

Step 1: Freewrite. 7 minutes
Muse on what radical self-care means to you.
PROMPT: *Radical self-care is . . .*

Step 2: Make a list. 7 minutes
Look over your freewrite, then brainstorm a list of self-care activities. Consider these questions:
- ☐ *What activities and experiences are restorative to me?*
- ☐ *Where do I find spiritual connection and serenity?*
- ☐ *What do I do (or did I do) for fun? (What did I do for fun when I was in elementary school?)*
- ☐ *Where do I find beauty, inspiration, and joy?*
- ☐ *Who are the people who bring me joy and calm?*
- ☐ *How do I like to connect to nature?*
- ☐ *If I had infinite time and money, what would self-care look like for me?*

You can return to this freewrite anytime, but for now, stop after seven minutes.

Step 3: Make your cheat sheet. 10 minutes
Reread your list and make a list of twenty self-care actions. Include a range of actions from teeny-tiny to grandiose.

Step 4: Schedule it! 5 minutes
Select three actions from your cheat sheet and schedule them for some time within the next two weeks.
Tip: Remember to consider the eight realms of self-care.

Step 5: Do it! 1 minute
Select one tiny action from your cheat sheet and do it right now.

Ready to go further?

Make a self-care menu.

 Download:
The Self-Care Menu Template

BEHIND THE SCENES: Shower Time

Throughout the process of making my documentary, I practiced self-care. This helped me manage the stress and renew my spirits. Each time we neared completion of a new cut (the equivalent of a manuscript draft), the pressure would intensify, and my self-care routines would fall away. Even though I noticed that foregoing self-care wasn't helping, as deadlines approached, I'd cut it out of the schedule. I figured that eventually, I would get back to practicing yoga, hiking, and being with friends.

It didn't seem like a big deal to skip my yoga practice for a week, but it was a slippery slope. I recall one particularly grueling week when things came to a head. We needed to deliver a new cut, but we had hit a wall. There was a transition that just wasn't coming together, and day after day we hammered away. The edit sessions grew longer, and we still couldn't wrap up the cut. After one especially long day, the computer crashed. As I headed home, the exhaustion hit me. I was hungry, tired, and hadn't showered in days.

After I grabbed a bite to eat, I jumped in the shower. As I worked the shampoo into my hair, I surrendered to the pleasure of the hot water, and my attention went to massaging the lather into my scalp. I let my mind wander, and the perfumed steam billowed around me. In a sudden flash, the solution to the story problem came to me. I wrapped myself in a towel and scrambled to find paper. Still dripping wet, I scrawled notes in my notebook. The next morning, my co-writer and I cleaned up the narration, and then I recorded the new voice-over. It worked!

Choosing self-care feels hard when there's an extreme deficit of energy, but I've learned that something as simple as taking a shower and making time to wash my hair can replenish my creative energy. Radical self-care is radical because it requires a major makeover. It's radical because when we need it the most, it can feel nearly impossible to make time to rest and restore.

Wonder

Winter: To calibrate we connect to curiosity and reclaim wonder.

The Calibrate Cycle can be activated by reclaiming a sense of wonder. We'll use the explorer mindset to calibrate your inner compass, and we'll designate a special journal for tracking your process and keeping "field notes." We'll introduce another fundamental of the Calibrate Cycle: "the bridge." This simple but powerful practice uses ritual to create a path back into the creative zone.

FIRST THINGS FIRST: Explorer Mindset

As you navigate the wilderness of your story, it's important to approach writing with a sense of adventure. The explorer has a destination, but the journey is one of discovery. Adopting the mindset of an explorer helps the writer stay curious. An attitude of curiosity helps us experiment so we can get our bearings when we lose our way. One of the best ways to calibrate is to infuse the process with a dose of wonder. Wonder re-energizes us when we hit a block and can free the writer from paralyzing perfectionism.

Writing should be fun. Struggle is part of the process, but the path of the tortured genius isn't the only way forward. Writing requires effort, but it can also be pleasurable. Tapping into wonder allows us to access the "beginner's mind." Feeling lost or frustrated is a sign we need to look at the work from a new perspective. When this happens, I like to shake up my routine by taking my laptop outside, migrating to the couch, or putting my coffee in an antique teacup. These minor adjustments wake up my senses and help me see with fresh eyes. Possibilities open up. Adding a little comfort, or a change of scenery, not only makes showing up more inviting, but it also reminds me to reclaim wonder.

Making mistakes is part of the process, so tapping into wonder is strategic. Wonder keeps the imagination alive, the mind flexible, and ingenuity activated. By savoring the process, we fortify our connection to the work, empowering us to enjoy the journey.

Claiming a sense of wonder is especially important when handling raw, messy, unpolished work. When I complete a draft, I print out the manuscript and have it bound. Holding the book in my hands makes the accomplishment undeniable. Instead of getting demoralized by the inevitable flaws of an early draft, the tangible artifact reminds me that my story is no longer just an idea. The concrete weight is evidence of my efforts, proof that I can do it.

A first draft, like a baby, is not fully formed and, similarly, it requires protection and care. When taking a newborn to their first checkup, no one frets about the fact that the baby can't walk or talk. When we look at a screeching, red-faced newborn, we see the miracle of life, brimming potential, and a beginning. Even as a baby becomes a toddler, we marvel at their imperfections and celebrate this work in progress. When the baby gurgles, or the new fawn stumbles and falls, the fumbles are endearing. So, when looking at an early draft, think about the newborn and the awkward fawn. Cherish your work.

Pick a Priority

The explorer mindset also reminds us we have a purpose and steers us away from mindless meandering. Be intentional about how you will spend your writing session. The principle of first things first will make your writing session more productive and enjoyable.

When you sit down to write, clearly define your focus. Sometimes you may want to narrowly concentrate on a specific element like a scene, chapter, or key moment. Other times, your attention might sprawl across the draft like when you are proofreading. As you become more familiar with the Story Cycles, you'll discover how best to sequence your actions.

ACTIVITY: Right Now   10 minutes

Pick a priority. What is the most important priority right now?

See the end of the chapter for step-by-step instructions.

FIELD NOTES: TRACK THE PROCESS

At the end of your writing session, reflect on how it's going. Like an explorer, record your observations and discoveries. These notes, or field notes, will help you find your way back to your project and serve as an invaluable guide to navigating the writing journey.

This practice is at the core of the Calibrate Cycle, so make a habit of setting aside time to track. In addition to having a journal for freewriting and doing exercises, designate a special place for writing about your process. At the end of your writing session, set aside a few minutes to jot down new ideas, questions, and insights. By focusing on the experience, you demystify the process and uncover the mindset and techniques needed to move forward.

Instead of simply tracking how much you've done, spend time looking at your experience. Assess the process, reconnect to motivations, and clarify intentions. Revisit expectations, so you can adjust and adapt accordingly.

When you don't feel productive, field notes provide invaluable information to help you can stay on track even when you hit challenges. In fact, tracking the process is as important as tracking progress. Documenting your experience will help you identify both internal and external obstacles. Field notes will expose the thought patterns that lead to self-doubt. By unearthing the recurring negative narratives, you can re-examine your thinking and free yourself from outdated beliefs. Staying connected to the process is one of the best techniques for reclaiming wonder.

ACTIVITY: The Field Notes Writing Tracker

Dedicate a specific notebook focused on your process. In addition to your Compass Notebook, where you're freewriting and doing exercises, you'll also want a Field Notes Writing Tracker entirely devoted to charting your writing journey.

☐ Designate a journal for tracking and observing your process. Any old notebooks will do, but consider using *The Field Notes Writing Tracker.*

 The Field Notes Writing Tracker: A Story Cycle Process Journal

Instructions
for living:
Pay attention.
Be astonished.
Tell about it.

—Mary Oliver

THE BRIDGE

Throughout the book, we will unpack a variety of techniques, but one of the easiest and most reliable is "the bridge." The bridge is a ritual to help you transition from the everyday into the creative mindset. Even a small act like lighting a candle can ignite creativity.

We've all heard the advice to put away distractions, but the blank page doesn't always feel inviting. It is difficult to climb out of the business of the day, so we need a transition into the writing routine. The bridge is like a gate, or a *torii*, found at the entrances to Shinto shrines throughout Japan. These traditional *torii* gates mark the transition from the mundane to the sacred.  Similarly, the bridge cues our subconscious that we are moving from the ordinary world into the extraordinary realm of creativity.

A great way to create a bridge is to activate the senses: light a candle, put a flower on your desk, uncap essential oils, or brew a cup of tea. Spark inspiration by writing in a new location, choosing a new pen, or inaugurating a new notebook. Making your writing space more inviting can wake up the writer within.

Another way to build the bridge is to make a habit of thoughtfully wrapping up your writing session. At the end of your writing session, take a few minutes and jot down notes in your journal. While the ideas are still fresh, review your work and make notes. If there was a section of writing that felt juicy, star it so you remember to come back to it. You might identify a particular emotion or moment to mine.

Your bridge notes then become the portal back to writing gold. So, when you sit down to write, rather than trying to figure out or remember what to write, your field notes help you find a path back to writing.

Once you cross into the world of your story, you will feel flow and inspiration, so before you end the session, make notes in your journal so you have a path back. You can always ignore your notes or discard the plan, but why not leave a breadcrumb trail back to the world of your story?

Consider writing by hand. The concrete action of putting pen to page is a different experience than using a computer. For tracking your process, write field notes by hand.

Bridge Journal Questions

Sometimes it is obvious what we want to do next, but when we sit down to face the blank page, it can be difficult to know where to turn. These questions will help you build your bridge.

What did I plan to do?
Take a moment to recall what you planned to do. It's not uncommon to have unfinished items on the to-do list. Take a moment to check in. Did you follow the plan?

What did I do?
Note what you did in your writing session. Perhaps you sat down to work on a scene, but maybe you ended up working on the backstory. Without judgment, jot down how you spent your session.

What do I need to do next?
Sketch out actions and insights so you have a plan in place when you sit down to write again. This is the breadcrumb trail back to your writing. Position yourself to hit the ground running. Whether it's twenty-four hours or two weeks later, you've got a plan. Even if you've lost the thread or inspiration faded, you've identified a path.

ACTIVITY: Build the Bridge   7 minutes

* See the end of the chapter for step-by-step instructions.

Each writer has a different approach. Find your own creative process and travel your own path.

A Quick Calibration

You don't need to confine taking field notes to just the beginning or end of a writing session. Consider making quick calibrations throughout your writing session. If you feel stuck and don't know what to do next, you likely need to reset. Return to your field notes journal and record your observations. Stepping back from productivity allows space for us to think more clearly, which can open up new solutions.

With a quick calibration, you can also separate feelings from facts. It's natural to experience doubt, disappointment, or confusion. With a quick calibration, you can acknowledge your emotions and then revisit the plan. Checking in with our emotions is an essential part of calibrating. When you compare what you planned to do with what you did do, often you will find discrepancies. To build the bridge, check in with how you're feeling.

Emotions are the lifeblood of story. Understanding our emotions—our psyche—helps us become better writers. Mini calibrations help writers grow emotional literacy and find the opportunity in the challenge. When you work through the bridge questions, ask yourself, *How do I feel about it?*

Are you happy and excited? Or are you disappointed and frustrated? Do you feel like you haven't done enough? Sometimes, even when we've done what we set out to do, we may not feel satisfied. If discontent motivates you to keep going, that's great. But if it makes you feel hopeless, it's time to pause and reset. Make micro-adjustments to continue moving forward on your creative journey.

No matter what story cycle you are moving through, a quick calibration can help you reset.

ACTIVITY: Quick Calibration   7 minutes

  * *See the end of the chapter for step-by-step instructions.*

RECAP: Calibrate and Continue

By adopting the explorer mindset, we renew a sense of wonder. The practice of keeping field notes will help you understand your process. When you pause to calibrate, you can continue forward with more clarity. The simple but powerful ritual of the bridge helps us transition from the everyday into a creative mindset.

Calibrate Your Compass

Ice Breaker: If you're feeling cabin fever, do something to change up the energy.
  ☐ Prepare yourself a special beverage, change your scenery, or light a candle.

Tools and Techniques
  ◎ Wonder
  ◎ Explorer mindset
  ◎ Field notes
  ◎ The bridge
  ◎ Quick calibration

Chapter Three Activities

Right Now

🕐 7 minutes

Pick a priority. What is the most important priority right now?

- ☐ Make an action list.
  - Brainstorm all the actions you want/need to take.
  - Consult your question list for ideas.
- ☐ Take a moment to calibrate.
  - Where are you in the Story Cycles?
  - What actions match this cycle?
  - What do you need to do before moving into the next cycle?
- ☐ Pick one priority and clearly identify a specific task that relates to that goal.

Build the Bridge

🕐 7 minutes

After your next writing session, use the bridge questions to create a path back to the world of your story.

- ☐ *What did I plan to do?*
- ☐ *What did I do?*
- ☐ *What do I need to do next?*
  - Is there an exercise or task you'd like to repeat?
  - Give yourself suggestions on what to do next.

Quick Calibration

🕐 7 minutes

In your Field Notes Writing Tracker, take a moment to calibrate. Check in and reflect. How do you feel about your writing today?

- ☐ Jot down observations about the activity.
  - Was the exercise useful?
  - If so, why?
  - If not, why not?

☐ What could make your writing session more pleasurable and joyful?
- Make a physical sensory change to your writing space. For example, pick a flower, brew a cup of tea, pull out that fancy notebook you've been saving, or light a candle.

BEHIND THE SCENES: Light It Up

New writers often imagine that once they achieve success (whatever that means to them) they will be liberated from self-doubt and words will simply flow effortlessly onto the page.

No one is immune to writer's block. Even my clients who've "made it" still knock up against challenges. I was reminded of this at one of my vision boarding workshops. One of my regular students brought along a friend, Nandi, a statuesque woman with dreadlocks, draped in a colorful tunic. She listened attentively as I guided the participants through a series of writing exercises. Then the students spread out so they would have space for the collage-making process.

As the participants leafed through magazines and cut out images for their vision boards, I circled the room, giving suggestions, and we talked about our projects. One person was making a vision board centered on his indie horror feature. Another was making one related to a documentary she was developing. Nandi's collage was an assemblage of butterflies, jewels, and flowers with a striking purple theme. Her aim was to spark inspiration. She said her mind felt dull and that she couldn't access her creativity. I explained the concept of the bridge as a tool to get into the right mindset. I suggested she might want to purchase one of my signature writing candles. She laughed and said she had forgotten that she used to make a habit of lighting a candle when she sat down to write.

Since Nandi was facing writer's block, I had assumed she was a novice, but after the workshop, I discovered that she had written multiple scripts for which she had won awards, and she was currently working in production for a premium channel. Once I knew her credentials, I was floored. She had so much experience and success. How could she have fallen into a rut? Ironically, it was her prestigious position that had thrown her off course. The job had stifled her creativity.

I felt embarrassed I had suggested to this accomplished industry pro that she try lighting a candle. It seemed so amateur and goofy, but as it turned out, reinstating this little ritual was a game changer. She had posted the collage she'd created above her writing desk to remind her to light the candle when she sat down to write. When Nandi and I last connected, she had not only completed her script, but she now had a project in development with impressive talent attached. Sometimes it's a simple practice that can rekindle the creative fire.

Why

Winter: Shift the focus from external to internal.

There are many reasons to write. We tell stories to entertain, heal, reveal, challenge, comfort, and inspire change. Perusing the aisles of a bookstore illuminates the diverse topics that inspire writers. Genres range from self-help to historical, from whimsy to world changing. When you reconnect with *why* you want to bring a story into the world, you can calibrate your creative compass and reset your intention. We'll wrap up this section with the ultimate calibration: The Story Cycle survey.

FIRST THINGS FIRST: Clarify Your *Why*

There are infinite ways to tell a story, so knowing your motivation will keep you on track. Your keyword is *why*. Each writer has their own destination and is driven by a purpose that is meaningful to them. If you lose sight of your intention, your *why* will help you calibrate so you can move forward on your writing journey.

The practice of clarifying your *why* will help you make decisions. For example, this book began as a collection of exercises I printed and bound into packets for my students. During the workshop, I verbally provided more detailed instructions and shared my thought process behind each activity. Sometimes, I used stories from my own experience to demonstrate a point. At my seaside retreat, one of my students told me how much she enjoyed hearing my stories. At that moment, I decided I would wrangle my teaching materials into a book. I had always thought of my experiences and explanations as superfluous, but she explained that this context brought the exercises to life. I realized there was value in these stories because they aligned with my *why*. I wanted to inspire writers and illuminate a path forward.

Take time to renew or revise your intentions. This tool is especially helpful when you feel confused, disconnected, or bored with your project. Tapping into your *why* activates curiosity and reconnects you to your sense of wonder.

Tapping into your why activates curiosity and reconnects you to your sense of wonder.

Reset

Regularly, recalibrate with *why*. Writing takes us into new territory, and our purpose may change across time and drafts. Often, a first draft is a way to make sense of your subject matter. As we move deeper into our material, it's not uncommon to refine our objective. We make discoveries during the process of drafting and new insights influence us, inform our perspective, and inspire us to reexamine our intentions at times.

When you return to your *why*, consider who you are writing for. Sometimes we write for an audience and other times just for ourselves.

Journaling is an invaluable tool for self-discovery. Creative writing helps us process experiences and heal old wounds. Sharing writing with friends and an inner circle is a beautiful way to connect. That said, it can be damaging to put work into the world that is meant for an intimate audience. Words are powerful and tuning into your *why* ensures you're moving your writing in a meaningful direction. Writing can make sink us or help us soar. As the author and scholar Bell Hooks writes, there is a distinction between writing that holds us back and writing "that truly rescues, that enables us to reach the shore, to recover."

Before evaluating your writing, reconnect to your purpose. Return to your *why*, to clarify and reset. Your Why is your North Star. It's your lighthouse. So, when the darkness descends or the fog rolls in, your reason for writing is the beacon that will carry you home. Each person has a different point where the pressure begins to build, so in your Field Notes Writing Tracker, chart your course by calibrating with *why*.

Calibrate with *Why*   6 minutes

Open the portal to your process with the magic key: Why?

In your Field Notes Tracker, use freewriting to explore the questions below. (2 minutes each)

- ☐ Why write? Why do you want to tell this story? Why do you care?
- ☐ Why you? Why are you the person to tell this story?
- ☐ Why now? Why does the world need this story now?
  Why do you need to write this now?

Why do you want to tell this story?

Why do you care?

Why are you the person to tell this story?

Why does the world need this story now?

BIRD'S-EYE VIEW

In addition to homing in on your *why*, pull back and take a bird's-eye view of your project. Look at the context and survey the landscape.

Just as each writer is driven by a unique purpose, each writer wrestles with their own challenges. While there isn't a one-size-fits-all approach, looking at the big picture will help you find a path forward. We identify the Story Cycle you're moving through so we can determine which tasks are best suited for the phase. For example, if the project is just a seedling, it's ill advised to focus on fine-tuning. (Revision comes later in the Craft Cycle.) In the early phases of a project, the activities of the Cultivate and Collaborate Cycles will probably be more helpful.

You will develop an intuitive sense of where you are in the process, but if you are new to Story Cycles, this multiple-choice survey provides a quick way to assess where you are, what you need to accomplish right now, and how best to move forward.

Like preparing the soil for planting, the Story Cycle survey helps illuminate areas of opportunity and reveals vulnerabilities. What makes sense right now? Every story has a season.

ACTIVITY: Bird's-eye View   ⏰ 30 minutes

Zoom out and look at the big picture. Look at your long-term goals. Where do you want to be in one, two, five, seven, ten years?

☐ How does your current project fit into your body of work?

☐ What's the most important step right now?

ACTIVITY: Story Cycle Survey   30 minutes

This quick assessment is really a questionnaire. Have fun.

  * *See the end of the chapter for step-by-step instructions.*

RECAP: The Big Picture

Along your writing journey, take time to calibrate your creative compass. Tapping into your *why* helps you stay on track. Consider where you are in the process, connect with your intentions, and zoom out to look at the big picture. As we spiral through the Story Cycles, we can also calibrate with The Story Cycle survey.

Calibrate Your Compass

Bird's-eye View: Look at the big picture. Where do you want to be in five years?
☐ Use freewriting to explore.

Tools and Techniques

- ◎ The why
- ◎ Bird's-eye view
- ◎ The Story Cycle survey

A distinction must be made between that writing which enables us to hold on to life even as we are clinging to old hurts and wounds and that writing which offers to us a space where we are able to confront reality in such a way that we live more fully. Such writing is not an anchor that we mistakenly cling to so as not to drown. It is writing that truly rescues, that enables us to reach the shore, to recover.

—Bell Hooks

Chapter Four Activities

Story Cycle Survey  30 minutes

The Story Cycle survey is a quick assessment to help you identify where you are in the Story Cycles so you can determine the best course of action. In Part I of the survey, you'll answer five multiple-choice questions. Next, in Part II, use the answer key to calibrate. Finally, in Part III, you'll wrap up with freewriting. Use your Field Notes Writing Tracker to write and reflect. Have fun. There are no wrong answers. Select all answers that apply.

Survey Part I: Reflect and Answer

1. What is your current project?

   A. Memoir
   B. Novel
   C. Script
   D. Essay
   E. No F*cking idea!

2. What is the status of the project?

   A. Seedling of an idea
   B. Sh*tty first draft
   C. Developing a concept
   D. Trying to get fired up
   E. Lost in the middle
   F. Almost Done

3. Talk about your process.

   A. I'm most comfortable dreaming and taking time to reflect.
   B. I'm most comfortable developing and brainstorming ideas.
   C. I'm most comfortable exploring, playing, and experimenting.
   D. I'm most comfortable finishing and sharing my ideas with others.
   E. The writing process is mostly uncomfortable.
   F. I have no f*cking idea.

4. Why do you want to write?

   A. I just like writing for the fun of it.
   B. I want to tell great stories that entertain and captivate audiences.
   C. I have a burning desire to tell a specific story.
   D. I want to understand and/or heal trauma.
   E. I want to make an impact and inspire social or political change.
   F. I want to inspire, uplift, and/or bring joy.

5. What are you hoping to gain by reading this book?

   A. I'd be happy if I were writing a few hours a week.
   B. I would love to feel more confident in my writing.
   C. I'm mostly focused on establishing my writing practice.
   D. I want to crank out a draft and need tools to find a path and build momentum.
   E. I want to take my draft to the next level and need help getting to the finish line.
   F. Something else.

Survey Part II: Calibrate

Here is an answer key with some thoughts to help you interpret your answers from Part I.

1. What is your curent project?

   If you already know what type of project you are writing, identify three titles similar to your project (or titles that you want your project to be like!)

   If you don't know what you want to write, pick out five books, movies, essays, or shows that you love. (These will come in handy in Chapter Eleven.)

2. What is the status of your project?

   Given where you are in the process, what is the next milestone?
   • Identify three small measurable markers on the way to that milestone.

   See Chapters Four and Sixteen to learn about milestones and markers.

3. Talk about your process

Given what you know about your process, what Story Cycle is most comfortable for you? Which is most challenging?

- If you selected A, then you like dreaming and taking time to reflect. You likely feel at home in the winter Story Cycle of calibration.

- If you selected B, you like developing and brainstorming ideas. You may find you are most at home in the lively activity of the cultivate phase.

- If you selected C, your sweet spot is goofing around and exploring. So, you likely feel at home in the summery, free-flowing Collaborate Cycle.

- If you selected D, you love finishing and fine-tuning, and you're a fan of the Craft Cycle. If you are desperate to finish, share your work and reap the rewards of the harvest. But if you feel stuck, then don't get too cozy in the Craft Cycle. Shake up your process with activities from the Cultivate or Collaborate Cycles. If you've lost your way, circle back to the Calibrate Cycle.

- If you selected E or F, then the writing process is mostly uncomfortable, or you have no f*cking idea what to do next. No problem! You are in the right place. This book will guide you to clarity and help you build the next steps. For now, focus on noticing which Story Cycles are comfortable and which are uncomfortable for you.

4. Why do you want to write?

- If you selected A, good news: you will find lots of new ways to have fun throughout the book.

- If you selected B, then take extra care to connect with your audience.
(Pay special attention to Chapter Thirteen.)

- If you selected C, that's great! The book is full of exercises that will help you move forward. To begin, clarify your why.

- If you selected D, then prioritize radical self-care and get to know your inner critic.

- If you selected E, awesome! The book will offer lots of ways to get your ideas onto the page. Be mindful not to get stuck in the Calibrate Cycle, but also don't rush to the Craft Cycle. Remember to clarify your why.

- If you selected F, you will find helpful exercises in the Collaborate Cycle. While you may think your audience is your anchor, to write with authenticity, you'll want to focus your why. Spend time calibrating and give space for discovery with activities related to cultivating.

5. What are you hoping to gain by reading this book?

After considering the preceding questions, is your goal realistic? If not, time to calibrate!

Survey Part III: Now write about it.

In your Field Notes Writing Tracker, use freewriting to review and reflect.

- Looking at your results, what do you notice?
- What cycle are you moving through?
- Do your goals match the cycle?
- Is your goal realistic?
- Calibrate.
- What's the next step?

BEHIND THE SCENES: The Big Tell

I looked out to the packed theater. The filmmakers were happy, nervous, proud, and all gussied up for the Big Tell showcase. We'd finished walking the red carpet, settled in with our popcorn, and waited excitedly for the premiere of their films.

As the lights went down, I couldn't believe this was the sixth year of the Big Tell.

I thought back to when I was asked to come on board as the mentor and consulting producer for the new initiative. The foundation that hired me had explained they would award a modest grant to ten filmmakers, and each grantee would be tasked with the same mission: to create a short documentary. Every year, the prompt is the same: tell the story of the Central Valley. In six years, no two films have been the same.

Being a part of the Big Tell crystalized my understanding of the power of *why*.

The concept of the Big Tell was to give the people of the Central Valley a platform to tell their own stories. I loved the idea, but I was more than a little bit skeptical that the program would work. As a fifth-generation Californian, I knew that the Golden State's inland corridor is a thriving agricultural hub that produces over half of the fruits, vegetables, and nuts grown in the United States. The foundation envisioned the Big Tell as an annual showcase. This seemed a little ambitious to me. Didn't the Central Valley consist mostly of rural countryside and farmland? I wondered, how many stories about agriculture could there be? How many filmmakers would even apply?

I remember the first year: just a few days before the deadline, we had received only eight applications. I prayed we'd get at least two more so we'd be able to award the ten grants.

The morning after the deadline closed, to my surprise, we had received over eighty applications. As we sifted through them, the program director explained that the foundation wanted to have stories from each of the six counties they serve: Merced, Mariposa, Madera, Fresno, Tulare, and Kings.

I worried the mandate was too narrow. While Fresno County is home to a bustling city of the same name, the smallest county, Mariposa, has a population of under three thousand. Would we even have an application from Mariposa?

We had one.

The Mariposa application hadn't initially caught my attention. The filmmaker proposed a story about a local library. She was a first-time filmmaker and, as much as I love libraries, the topic sounded like a snoozer, but we needed to represent the region.

She made it into the final ten.

We gathered the finalists together for an orientation. After introductions, I asked them each to write about why this story mattered to them. They had already written and won the grant, so they were a little annoyed by the assignment. I explained I could better support them if I understood their driving purpose and that their *why* would be their lighthouse.

The Mariposa filmmaker, Karen, missed the orientation because the roads were closed due to forest fires in her area. Given the circumstances, I couldn't be mad, but I was worried. At our first meeting, Karen explained on the call that she wanted to focus on the library's literacy program for adult learners. I challenged Karen to pinpoint why this story mattered to her. She was a bit frazzled, but I clarified that tapping into her *why* would also be helpful when she needed to make tough decisions about what to cut and what to keep. She got it. It turned out she was a retired journalist, so she understood she needed to refine her angle.

Over the next three months, Karen wrestled with the narrative structure and struggled to learn new technology. She also had to contend with the harsh realities of fire season. She had planned to do several interviews, but the area was devastated, and understandably, this derailed the shooting schedule. She was running out of time.

We revisited her *why*. I asked her to clarify her intention. Was it to educate, to heal, to reveal, to challenge, to inspire, to uplift, to bring joy, to make an impact, to celebrate? That last one struck a chord. She wanted to celebrate the profound experience of adult learners. With this in mind—and the deadline looming—she decided to highlight the journey of one student: an elderly man from a hardscrabble background who had dropped out of school at a young age because he needed to work to survive. She realized by focusing on his story, she could tell the larger story of perseverance.

Ultimately, she pulled together a sweet story. She was profoundly grateful for the opportunity and donated the equipment she'd purchased with the grant money to the library. But the most remarkable part of Karen's story was yet to unfold. The next year, she was again the lone applicant from Mariposa. This time she wanted to tell the unlikely story of a symphony orchestra, which plays an annual outdoor concert in Yosemite National Park.

She had already captured several hours of interviews, and the rough cut was way over the five-minute requirement. Between a few quick shots of the outdoor concert, she had crammed together interview clips from a wide range of subjects. The result was a rushed jumble of disjointed ideas: how the orchestra was formed, the accomplishments of the conductor, the struggles, the triumphs, the politics—but she had "buried the lead."

We discussed her *why*. Her core motivation was to reveal this little-known treasure in Mariposa County. I suggested she simplify and eighty-six the vast majority of interviews, so she could spotlight the impossible beauty of a symphony orchestra making classical music in the forest.

She reluctantly recalibrated and reworked the cut to highlight the ensemble of musicians, attired in black tie, playing against the stunning backdrop of Yosemite's natural beauty. Her ability to reconnect to her intention made the narrative come alive. Her exquisite film opened that year's program. The audience marveled at the delightful juxtaposition of the refined symphony in the wild, remote setting.

Every year, the Big Tell reminds me of the power of asking, *why?* While every participant tells the story of California's Central Valley, each storyteller brings their unique perspective and original voice to the challenge. It always takes a little time to distill their idea to its essence, but once they understand their *why*, the story comes together.

With the guiding light of *why*, we've produced a diverse collection of sixty unique stories that make up the rich tapestry of the Central Valley.

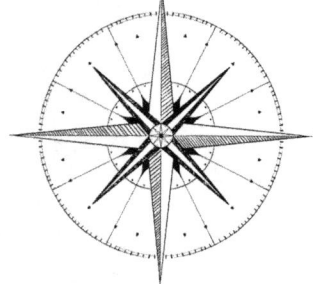

PART II

Cultivate

THE SPRING CYCLE

After the thaw, the work begins.

Roll up your sleeves and dig in.
Plan, plant, and prepare.
Below the surface, we ready the roots.

We toil, till, and tend,
but even after slogging
and sweating,
we've just begun.

Capacity

Spring: In the Cultivate Cycle, we toil, till, and tend.
Roll up your sleeves, dig in, and get dirty.

The creative process isn't linear, so the Cultivate Cycle may feel especially disorienting. The Spring Cycle is a time of possibility. Below the surface, we ready the roots. This requires the patience and attention of a gardener. We begin with this cycle's foundational concept: capacity. To endure the demanding development phase, the writer must respect one's limits and cultivate capacity.

FIRST THINGS FIRST: Instead of *If*, Ask *How?*

As you move through this Story Cycle, don't ask *if*, ask *how*. My mentor Caroline Donahue taught me this simple but powerful reframe. The moment she said it, it poked a hole in my self-doubt, and I felt the balloon of worry deflate and my creative energy expand. Instead of asking *if* I was capable, I simply needed to ask *how* . . .

This is my mantra during the Cultivate Cycle. Caroline's words were transformational because they interrupted my fear and shifted the focus back to what's possible. Assume it's possible and look for ways to calibrate.

Instead of asking if you can do it, ask how.

□ Ask how . . .
  How can I look at this differently?
  How can I change my approach?
□ Ask what . . .
  What time of day works?
  What's the next right action?
  What works for me? (Do I prefer analog, digital, or hybrid?)
□ Ask where/when . . .
  Where am I productive and inspired?
  When do I feel most alert and creative?
□ Ask who . . .
  Who can be an ally?

WARM-UP

One of the most difficult aspects of writing is getting going. So, start your session with a warm-up. This invaluable technique is appropriate for any Story Cycle. Begin your writing session with a short, no-stakes warm-up. This wakes up creativity and gets the energy flowing. Like an athlete stretching before a workout, the warm-up prepares you to transition from the mundane world to the sacred act of creating. Kicking off the session with an easy prompt cues your subconscious that it is time to express yourself in writing.

ACTIVITY: Twenty Shades of Gray   30 seconds

  * *See the end of the chapter for step-by-step instructions.*

CAPACITY

Many of my students struggle with the sense that there is "not enough time" or it's not the "right time." They believe that to be a writer, you need to have all the time in the world. In fact, the vast majority of writers work with a finite amount of time. Time is one of our most precious creative resources and one of the most important considerations when assessing capacity.

One of the main reasons writers give up is that they've set unrealistic expectations for themselves. Honor your capacity. Would you try to plant a seed in frozen ground or a parched desert? Would you try to pour a jug of water into a thimble? Would you ask a baby to climb a mountain? Would you try to drive across the country with only one gallon of gas? It is illogical and cruel to set unreasonable expectations. You may desperately want to dig in, but what is your actual capacity?

When a client hires me as a writing coach, we quickly bump up against the rest of their life. Our perception of time is always distorted. Some tend to worry there isn't enough time and others overestimate. When imagining what's possible, it's essential that we consider the context. Even if your day job is slow, those big swaths of time are not yours alone. If you're on and off calls all day, utilizing those pockets of time may be difficult. If you look after children, care for an aging parent, or have an illness, changing circumstances will impact your capacity. To achieve realistic expectations, respect the capacity of the people around you.

Each of us is part of an ecosystem. This network of connections impacts your capacity. Just as the creative process moves through cycles, we also move through different stages. Our bodies change and our relationships evolve. To honor the dynamic nature of capacity, look at the eight realms. This holistic view illuminates the opportunities and challenges, the resources and deficiencies, the allies and obstacles. Consider your mental and spiritual bandwidth. Even if you set aside a block of time to write, if your unconscious is tethered to another source, it can be challenging to access inspiration. It is hard to build momentum when you are going through a big life event like moving house, planning a wedding, a child's graduation, or coping with a loss. Your pace may slow, but by checking in with your capacity, you can uncover the next right step in your journey. The realities of life dictate how much time one can dedicate to creative work. Writing is a journey, so to go the distance, adjust expectations to match reality—in other words, your capacity.

ACTIVITY: What's my capacity?   ⏰ 10 minutes

In your Field Notes Writing Tracker, assess your capacity.

- ☐ How many hours per week can you dedicate to your writing practice?
    - Consider the eight realms.
    - Be conservative. It's better to under-promise and over-deliver.
    - A reasonable goal might start with writing for one to four hours per week.

- ☐ Look at the next two weeks and identify pockets of time.

- ☐ Add these writing sessions to your calendar.
    - Even if you only plan to write for ten or fifteen minutes, make an appointment and add that to your schedule.

* Be realistic. Consider work, family, health, and recreation.
* Give yourself buffer time and account for transition time.

WEATHER AND TERRAIN

Even when you make a thoughtful plan, there will be challenges, detours, and dead ends. The creative compass isn't a magic crystal ball. You're bound to encounter surprises. Organize an itinerary but be ready to calibrate: adapt to the weather and terrain.

The Ten-Minute Rule

Don't give in to the all-or-nothing mentality.
Start with the time you have. Even if you can't write
every day, it's worthwhile to write regularly.
Build your writing practice minute by minute.
Ten minutes of writing a day *will* yield results.

- ☐ Start with three minutes and build from there.

- ☐ Look at the next two weeks and identify pockets
  of time.

  - Warm up (3 minutes)

  - Free-write or write from a prompt (4 minutes)

  - Bridge (3 minutes)

- ☐ Make your writing space inviting.

  - Dash off a note to yourself with a few words of
    encouragement.

  - Set a flower on your desk.

  - Leave yourself a little treat: a candy, a beverage,
    or a piece of chocolate.

On the map, your journey may have looked like a short distance, but perhaps you discover that the route crosses a mountain range, or the road is closed for repairs, or a little creek has become a raging river. Respond to the prevailing conditions. If the heavens shower you with rain, bundle up, grab an umbrella, or consider taking shelter. It might be possible to stick to the plan, but you may veer off course or find yourself stuck in a storm.

If it feels like the creative process is zapping you with lightning, it might be time for extra self-care. Instead of forcing your way forward, why not pause to refuel and reassess? It's important to take breaks, slow down, and enjoy the journey.

Sometimes the delays present unexpected opportunities. I remember first learning about the necessity and value of detours when my daughter had just started kindergarten. I was plodding my way through a rewrite of a script. I had mapped out my writing schedule and was eager to get to work, but the universe had other plans for me.

That morning, I discovered that my daughter wasn't feeling well, so I kept her home from school. I got her situated with some juice and cued up one of her favorite shows. Then I went to work on my script. As soon as I sat down to write, she called for me. She wanted a glass of water. I got her the water and went back to my desk. Moments later, she called out again. She wanted me to open the window. I went back to writing, but—you guessed it—she called for me again. She just wanted me to be there, and I realized it was time to ditch my writing plan.

I turned off the TV and curled up on the couch with her. She asked me what I was doing in my office, and I explained I was writing. She wanted to know what the story was about. As I described the story, I realized she was my ideal demographic for this animated adventure. She begged me to read her "the story." I tried to explain that the script format would be confusing, and that it wasn't finished, but she insisted. I obliged.

We spent the rest of the day snuggled together, swimming through the story. She loved the world, fell in love with the characters, and laughed at all the right places. It turned out that her questions were more helpful than any reader's notes had been. What I thought was a delay turned out to be a special time with my daughter. I discovered she had a gift for storytelling, and it was the first of many writing consultations.

It's easy to feel discouraged when you veer off course, but the plan is just a starting point. Once you are on the journey, you'll encounter the unexpected and may need to adjust the plan. Making a course correction can be challenging, but even a quick calibration can illuminate a clear path forward.

RECAP: Assess the Landscape

To navigate the demanding process of development, assess the landscape of your reality. Consider the weather and terrain. What's happening inside and outside? Check in with your capacity. The plans will change and sometimes we'll go off track, so be ready to adjust expectations. Remember to ask *how*, not *if.*

Calibrate Your Compass

> When and where: Start your next writing session by looking at when and where you feel most productive and inspired.
> ☐ Freewrite about when and where you feel creative and alert.

Tools and Techniques

- Ask how, not if.
- Capacity
- Weather and terrain

Chapter Five Activities

Twenty Shades of Gray

⏱ 30 seconds

Warm up with list making. Give yourself a short window of time and a challenging target. The inner critic usually loves to quantify and compete, so this keeps the critic busy and gets the creative energy moving.

- ☐ Set a timer for thirty seconds and write.
- ☐ Make a list of things that are gray.
- ☐ Aim for at least twenty items on the list.
- ☐ Ready? GO!

> *For example, if the prompt was red, your list might include apple, fire truck, tongue, lipstick, red, red, red, red face, hand, tomato, shoes, red, red, red, anger, ball, balloon, etc.*
>
> ** In the spirit of freewriting, if you can't think of something, you may write the prompt until a new idea surfaces. Keep the pen moving!*

Ready to go further?

You can modify this warm-up by using other colors. You may also try it with specific senses. For example, make a list of sounds and focus it with specificity, like "soft" or "loud."

Every person's map of the world is as unique as their thumb print. There are no two people alike. No two people who understand the same sentence the same way . . . So in dealing with people, you try not to fit them to your concept of what they should be.

—Milton Erickson

BEHIND THE SCENES: Time Optimist

When Dan walked into the workshop, all heads turned his way. He had arrived a little late, but eyes lingered to take in the strikingly handsome man with an impressive afro. He was dripping with swagger. He had a mesmerizing combination of a superhero-like air of invincibility and an understated chill vibe. I soon learned that Dan's magnetic energy wasn't superficial style, but rather the natural cool of a musician. Behind his dark shades, he radiated kindness.

He came to the workshop brimming with creative energy. After years of working as a professional film editor, he knew story. He had won multiple Emmys, and his work had aired on networks like PBS, Disney, NFL, Discovery, and National Geographic. He was eager to put his talents toward his own work, and I was thrilled when he enlisted me as a creative coach.

I soon learned Dan was a classically trained musician. In his twenties, he'd taken up photography and established himself as a DJ. After some digging, I learned he'd also served as the bassist for a pioneering hip-hop group that performed with the likes of Run-DMC, A Tribe Called Quest, the Wu Tang Clan, and The Roots. I was curious how he had transitioned to editing. Dan explained that he had put music to the side when the band broke up and he became a single parent. He devoted himself to raising his daughter and parlayed his skills into editing.

His daughter was grown and now that he'd helped her through college, he was ready to invest in himself. At our first session, he was overflowing with ideas. I feverishly took notes as he ran through a dazzling array of potential projects. Each one had a compelling spark. He possessed an artist's vulnerable soul and a sophisticated intellect.

We sifted through possibilities. Each story had layers of nuance, deep resonance, and refined detail. It was difficult to know where to start, but I suggested we pick something manageable, and Dan decided to make a short film.

In the next session, we talked location and logistics. He wanted to get started right away and planned to shoot it in the following few weeks. He didn't have a script, but sometimes projects explode into reality. As a born artist and skilled film professional, Dan had both the talent and chops to make it happen. That said, I cautioned that the process might take longer than he imagined.

I proposed he try freewriting and suggested he start with a series of three-minute sprints. He scoffed. I could see he felt insulted. Why had I suggested such a tiny goal? Did I think he was an idiot? He was confident he could and would write for much longer stretches.

He tackled the writing, but he was dissatisfied with his results. We plugged on, but over the next few weeks, I discovered that he was working not one but two full-time jobs and moonlighting (for free) on a friend's documentary. He admitted it had been hard to find the time to focus on writing. I pointed out that these commitments made it impossible, not hard. He reluctantly acknowledged he was overstretched, but he was determined to push forward.

Over the next few sessions, he became increasingly disappointed in himself. He wasn't making the progress he had hoped. It became clear he was suffering from a serious condition. I recognized the disorder because I had suffered from the same malady. I broke the news gently; he was a "time optimist." When in the grips of this condition, one has overly optimistic expectations of what can be completed in a given time frame. As a fellow time optimist, I knew all too well the frustrating pattern.

I assured him his lack of traction wasn't a creative failing; rather, there simply were not enough hours in the day. I explained that the diagnosis was not fatal, but we needed to address it. The focus of our work together shifted to developing capacity. We switched gears, and he decided to turn our attention to what he called the foundations (a.k.a. radical self-care.) I agreed that before tackling any projects, we needed to build capacity. Gradually, he thinned his work schedule and strengthened his self-care habits. Instead of measuring time in weeks, we widened the lens and looked at setting quarterly targets. Instead of measuring creative output, we set markers and milestones around the foundations.

He optimized his morning routine, incorporated meditation, and began carving out swaths of uncommitted time. His life became more spacious and serene. This, in turn, revived his creative force. Now that he had opened up his schedule, he had capacity. He started shooting footage with his drone and returned to photography. Then he proposed a bold move. He opted to tackle something big and more important than any creative task. He decided to quit smoking cigarettes. It wasn't the first time he'd tried, but he was determined.

He kicked the habit, and he continued to build the foundations. While it hadn't been his goal, he also devoted time to creative exploration. He shot footage, made micro shorts, and began putting pen to page. He was flourishing and building momentum. Yet, on his one-year anniversary of being a nonsmoker, he confessed he was troubled. He felt badly he hadn't completed a writing project. I reminded him that we had ditched that goal and told him I couldn't be happier with his victories. Not only had he successfully given up cigarettes, but this herculean task was also reawakening his creativity and vitality. I reminded him of all the other milestones. Finally, he had created a human-sized work schedule and he'd even taken a vacation, traveling with friends all the way to Senegal. He also made a piece documenting the adventure. He had remodeled his loft and all while working a full-time job. Creating capacity was a significant success.

Not long after that, Dan revealed that he had a new goal. He realized more than anything, he wanted to start making music again. He began playing his bass regularly and remembered the joy making music brought him. Dan continues to teach me the importance of honoring one's capacity and the power of calibrating.

CHAPTER SIX

Discovery

*Spring: Honor the gestation phase.
Embrace this delicious time of possibilities.*

The lively Spring Cycle is when the writer plants and plots. Growing a story takes dedication, and making is messy. It's often in the muck where we discover the twists and turns of our character's journey. First, we'll reconsider what "writing" looks like. The Cultivate Cycle centers around developing ideas, so we focus on discovery writing. Like free-writing, this exploratory writing may end up on the cutting room floor, but it is an invaluable way to cultivate ideas. We'll fortify the process by charting the course with measurable markers and milestones. This cycle requires patience and persistence, so we'll celebrate along the way.

FIRST THINGS FIRST: Ebb And Flow

You will have shitty days, and it's okay. Even when you stick to the plan and work hard, sometimes it's just a crappy day. All writers have bad days. We experience both internal and external challenges. A creative project never goes one hundred percent as expected. Even a writing session rarely unfolds exactly according to plan. No two days are identical. Discovery is part of the fun of making art.

It's important to set intentions, and it's satisfying to hit our goals, but productivity ebbs and flows. The process moves through cycles of expansion and contraction, birth and death, waking and slumber, waxing and waning. Nothing blooms forever. It's natural to want answers, but finding a solution may take longer than expected. You may need wait out the storm or wade deeper into the muck. How do we know if it's time to pause or plow forward?

Before digging into our writing, we need to assess the internal landscape. Each artist is part of an ecosystem, and just as the temperature outside warms and cools, the writer's creativity energy inside ebbs and flows. The writer experiences sunny days and dark nights, clear skies and dry spells. We need to check the weather and study our individual rhythms and requirements. Check the forecast and take the pulse.

ACTIVITY: Take the Pulse   ⏰ 15 minutes

Look within. Use freewriting to consider where you are.

☐ Consider the eight realms.
- Do you feel full or empty? Energized or exhausted? Isolated or supported?
- Do you feel connected to your purpose? Curious or confused?
- How is your body? Do you feel strength and ease?
- Do you feel safe and secure? Do you feel order and calm?

☐ Read and review.
- Read through your writing. What do you notice?

☐ Tend the garden.
- Make an adjustment to support self-care.

DISCOVERY

Content creation is what most people think of as "writing." Typically, we think of writing as constructing or revising a scene, a chapter, pages, a section of dialogue, or a character description. It's satisfying to sculpt scenes, style snappy dialogue, and craft a lovely character description, but there are other ways to move your story forward. Before polishing, there are other critical steps.

Even if a day's work does not result in usable content, it may yield meaningful insights. Just like turning the soil in the garden, it's important to comb through the material in ways that may not yield instant results. This behind-the-scenes writing is essential but often undervalued. Each stage of the process requires a different type of writing, so let's reconsider what "writing" looks like.

The Cultivate Cycle is a good time to outline, develop characters, and plow through a first draft, but ideation is an essential part of the creative process. During the Cultivate Cycle, we brainstorm, explore possibilities, and investigate emotions. In the movie industry, this initial phase of turning a story into a viable idea is called "development."

Inevitably some material will end up on the "cutting room floor." This expression comes from the days when editors cut, spliced, and taped together real celluloid. Even brilliant filmmakers shoot scenes that don't "make the cut."

Be willing to take risks.
Stories rarely show up
erfectly formed, and
discovery happens when we
feel free to make mistakes.

Discovery Writing

By expanding the definition of "writing," we open up possibilities on how we can move forward. Each Story Cycle offers valuable categories of writing. Discovery writing includes developing backstory, world-building, plotting character arcs, mapping action, studying, and researching. This might include investigating the setting, a character's profession, a historical period, or details including customs, fashion, or important events. Be willing to explore and make a mess. Discovery writing might include freewriting, list making, or reviewing your work.

When we generate new material, it is especially important to take risks. Stories rarely show up perfectly formed, and discovery happens when we feel free to make mistakes. Before we can sculpt and refine, we need to pull the marble out of a mountain. Even after dedicated effort, you may be left with a rough hunk of stone. Sometimes we unearth a sparkling gem, but more often than not, the Cultivate Cycle is the arduous process of excavating rock from the quarry.

> Material first, jokes first, character first. Structure second.
>
> —Phoebe Waller-Bridge

Word by Word

All of my students ask questions like "How much time should I be writing?" "How many pages or words a day?" "How long will it take?" It's important to set goals, but each project has unique demands and our capacity ebbs and flows. Some days are an uphill climb. On other days, it's smooth sailing all the way. You must find your own pace.

So how much should you be writing per day? There isn't a universal rule or formula. Each writer has their own rhythm and must set goals that feel right to them and that match the project. A poet will likely have a different word count goal than a novelist, and even authors working in the same genre may have different goals. Looking at daily word count goals for a handful of successful writers shows the range:

Anne Rice:	3,000 words per day
Mark Twain:	1,400-1,800 words per day
Margaret Atwood:	1,000-2,000 words per day
Stephen King:	1,000-2,000 words per day
Ernest Hemingway:	500 words per day
Graham Greene:	500 words per day
Amanda Gorman:	300 words per day
James Joyce:	90 words per day

Find the pace that works for you. No two writers have identical methods, so set goals that honor your natural tendency and current capacity. While the writer must adapt, setting goals keeps us on track, and making progress bolsters confidence.

First, consider how you will measure your progress. You may count pages written, words generated, or time spent. If you choose to measure your progress by quantity, remember that even one writer's word count goals will vary.

Goals will change based on what type of piece you're working on and where you are in the draft. When you revise a challenging scene, you might need to focus several writing sessions on this one finite area. On the other hand, when you conduct a final proofread, you might gallop through entire chapters or swaths of your script. When writing a first draft, you may only be able to eke out a few lines a day, but if your goal is to churn out a messy first draft, you may be best served to set a higher word count goal. Again, find the pace that works for you and for each specific project. We cannot rush the story-making process. Consider what actions are best suited to the moment.

- Is it more productive to make decisions or ask questions?
- Should you dive into discovery, or does a deadline demand you finish?
- Are you ready to focus and refine, or is it time to dream and reflect?
- Do you feel the expansive energy of the Collaborate Cycle or the cooling energy of a wintry pause?

Somedays the climb is steep, and your pace slows. Enjoy the journey. Savor the small victories. Sometimes you can only find the right path after taking a few wrong turns. A day when you throw out everything you've written but learn something new about your story in the process is a good day.

MARKERS AND MILESTONES

When road-mapping your writing process, chart your course with tangible markers. Keeping track of your progress will help you reach your destination. Just as the mile markers on a highway keep you apprised of where you are on your journey, recording your progress will help you navigate challenges and seize opportunities. If you know there won't be a gas station for another hundred miles, then seize the opportunity to refuel.

It is difficult to measure creative progress, and if you haven't set a clear goal, how will you know when you are done? No amount of hard work will be enough, and no course correction will be effective.

Sometimes the signs of progress can be subtle, so consider making SMART goals. The popular acronym stands for Specific, Measurable, Achievable, Relevant, and Time-Bound. Taking time to quantify and set clear parameters will illuminate the path. These reference points help you get oriented if you go off-course.

To identify specific goals, set concrete and measurable markers. For example, instead of making your goal to "start writing," a specific goal might be "Generate three hundred words" or "Write three times a week for one hour."

Traditional markers—like setting a target number of words and page count—work well, but until you find your natural rhythm, measuring time spent is often a more reliable way to track the journey. During the craft phase, measuring progress in pages or words might work well, but in the Cultivate Cycle, consider measuring time spent. Development requires space for discovery.

In addition to setting goals, identify milestones. A goal is the ultimate destination, while milestones are indicators that you are on the right path. If your goal is to publish a book, milestones might include the following: make an outline, finish a first draft, write a character description, do research, proofread, give a draft to beta reader for notes, send a script to an agent, or submit an essay to a contest.

In other words, assign meaning to the key steps along the way. New writers often set nearly impossible goals. It may motivate you to set an aspirational target, but more often than not, I see writers throw in the towel because they've placed unrealistic demands on themselves. To avoid this trap, identify key milestones that help you measure progress.

ACTIVITY: Markers and Milestones   10-40 minutes

The road to a finished project can be long. Let's make the process more tangible by identifying manageable and meaningful milestones.

* See the end of the chapter for step-by-step instructions.

If you haven't set a clear goal, no amount of hard work will be enough, and no course correction will be effective.

CELEBRATE

Even though the writer toils and tills, seeds don't instantly sprout. Naturally, most writers are eager to get to the finish line, and it can be uncomfortable to slosh around in emotions. But the creative process can't be rushed, and it's not uncommon to return to the spring season again and again. Celebration and ceremony help the writer move through the Story Cycles.

It's especially important to celebrate during the Cultivate Cycle because often you won't see the immediate results of your efforts. Celebrate milestones: savor success, highlight new beginnings, create closure, weigh the sorrow of loss, embrace gratitude, award achievement, witness a union, and honor transitions.

Something as simple as tuning into the moon cycles can connect the writer with nature's rhythms and renew intentions. For example, I like to mark the new and full moon by writing affirmations in my Field Notes Writing Tracker. I shift my focus from to-do lists to dreaming and visioning. Syncing this exercise with the phases of the moon helps me make this a regular practice. The waxing and waning moon also reminds me of the natural ebb and flow. The beautiful night sky with its dazzling, distant stars and the luminous moon helps me embrace life's mystery.

CELEBRATION FOR ANY SEASON

No matter what the season, make time to celebrate. Throughout the ages and across all cultures, humans have used rituals to give life meaning. If you don't already have a set of meaningful traditions, there are plenty of inspiring examples. A perfect starting point is to mark the turning of the seasons. By celebrating the change in seasons, we deepen our understanding of cycles and fortify our ability to make transitions.

Winter: Give Thanks.

In Winter, we give thanks. In fact, Christmas evolved from pagan traditions celebrations of the solstice and festivals of gratitude, like the wild Roman festival Saturnalia to honor the god Saturn. Romans marked the winter festivities with raucous parties, turning social norms upside down.

Spring: Set Intentions.

Spring is a time of renewal. This is a great opportunity to set intentions, to re-dedicate to a goal, or to reclaim your territory. Long before the Easter bunny hopped onto the scene, ancient mythologies from all corners of the globe celebrated this season of rebirth. The custom of spring cleaning has its roots in the purification ceremonies in anticipation of the new life that the season brings.

Summer: Gather Together.

Summer can feel like one long party. The long days lead to later bedtimes and shake up the routine. It's an opportunity to gather together and give gratitude. The summer solstice has long been a moment to celebrate. This turning point heralds a period of ripening and abundance. In ancient days, farmers sought the blessings of the gods and marked the occasion with a feast.

Fall: Honor The Ancestors.

In Fall, we give thanks for the harvest, and as days become darker, as the plants begin to die, many make offerings to the dead. The veil between the worlds is thought to be thinner, and spirits are said to travel more freely between their realm and ours. For some, it's an opportunity to honor and connect with ancestors through a candlelit altar featuring photographs, beverages, and treats that help the ancestors find their way back. Treats include favorite foods and items that were important to the dead, such as a cherished book, musical instrument, or favorite object like a bowl, cup, or scarf. Holidays like Halloween date back to the Celtic celebration of Samhain, which marked the end of the harvest and welcomed the new year.

Look for ways to add celebration and ceremony to your creative practice. Start by tuning into the seasons. Connect with nature's rhythms, renew intentions, and celebrate successes.

> Nature does not ask permission. Blossom and birth whenever you feel like it.
>
> —Dr. Clarissa Pinkola Estés

ACTIVITY: Track And Treat   20+ minutes

Even if you didn't hit your original goal, it's important to celebrate the work you have done.

* See the end of the chapter for step-by-step instructions.

RECAP: Word by Word

A story is built word by word, sentence by sentence, and scene by scene. The Cultivate Cycle is a fertile time ripe with possibilities, so to move through the spring cycle, set markers and milestones. Discovery writing turns daydreaming into action. Plot the course forward and celebrate along the way.

Calibrate Your Compass

Spring cleaning: Dedicate your next writing sessions to getting organized.

☐ Clear away the clutter and clean up your action list.

Tools and Techniques

- Ebb and flow
- Discovery writing
- Measurable markers and milestones
- Celebrate: track and treat

Chapter Six Activities

Markers and Milestones  10-40 minutes

The road to a finished project can be long. Make the process more tangible by identifying manageable and meaningful milestones.
Use your Field Notes Writing Tracker or a journal of your choice.

1. Use freewriting to calibrate: clarify where you are starting and where you want to land.

   Set a timer for two minutes and consider these questions:

   Where are you in your process?
   What is the ultimate goal?
   What do you know for sure about your project?

2. Next, use list making to find the concrete steps to move forward on your path.

   Set a timer for four minutes and make a list of all the pieces of the puzzle.

For example, identify the various elements you want to develop:

- key events
- characters
- important details about setting
- topics to research
- books/movies to watch for inspiration
- outline

3. Pick ONE action to start your next session with.

Reminder: Calibrate after each exercise with a mini bridge.
Jot down observations about the activity.

Was the exercise useful?
If so, why?
If not, why not?

Track And Treat   ⏱ 20+ minutes

Take your process to the next level and plan how you will celebrate the milestone once you've reached that goal.

Step 1: What upcoming transition or milestone might you mark?

☐ In your Field Notes Writing Tracker, use freewriting to identify possible milestones on your writing journey and important transitions.

Step 2: How do you like to celebrate? What fuels your muse?

☐ Use freewriting to reflect on how you like to celebrate wins. Here are examples of ways to celebrate:
- Gathering with others
- Treats and rewards
- Scenic view
- Historical marker

- Rest stop
- Refueling

Step 3: What type of treats do you prefer?

☐ Use freewriting to get specific.
- Do you enjoy consumables like food, drinks, or experiences?
- Do you prefer gathering treasures from nature?
- Do you like adding art objects to your writing space?
- Do you like buying yourself jewelry or other wearables like clothing, shoes, or accessories?
- Do you like buying statuettes or icons of spiritual deities to set on your desk?

Tip: Look at your self-care cheat sheet for ideas.

Step 4: Pick a milestone to mark and match with a celebration.

☐ Review your freewrite and plan a celebration.

Step 5: Celebrate!

☐ Do it!

Download
The Treat Tracker

BEHIND THE SCENES: Mother's Day

I was driving across town to celebrate Mother's Day with my mom when I got the call. She had taken a fall. I headed to the hospital, where I found her sitting in a wheelchair with both legs elevated and wrapped in ice. Her typical sunny disposition was clouded by pain. We soon found out she had broken her right ankle and her left foot. Ever the optimist, she pointed out that she had gotten over fourteen thousand steps in already.

She wilted as the doctor explained she wasn't allowed to put any weight on either foot. Thirty stitches and a dozen staples later, she still needed round-the-clock help. I jumped into action. For the next several weeks, I played nurse, shuttled her to doctors, and strategized with my siblings on how best to care for her. The time I had cleared for writing evaporated.

It could have been a derailing interruption, but instead, the detour was full of discoveries, and the time with my mother was priceless. We laughed and shared tender moments. I got to go behind the scenes of her life. She could have easily canceled everything, but instead little by little she adjusted to her new reality. I observed how she adjusted her routine but kept her spirits up by sticking to her daily rituals. She had to slow way down, but she plotted her course bit by bit. Taking a page from her book, I made a point of "touching" the work each day.

It would have been easy to abandon the rewrite of my script, but instead, I revisited my field notes and reevaluated my plan. I no longer had the same space and time to dedicate to writing, so I modified my expectations and adjusted my goals accordingly.

My capacity to be creative was severely diminished, but I gave myself tiny assignments and deployed discovery writing. The script centered on family relationships, so being thrust into the center of my family of origin was an opportunity to uncover new gems. I mined my emotions and uncovered important insights. I didn't get as much done as I had planned, but the time with my mother was precious. The writing journey is sure to have surprises, and the seasons of life can turn on a dime. Sometimes doing less yields more.

Expect the unexpected. Knowing how to honor capacity is especially helpful when unforeseen responsibilities hit.

Explore and Heighten

Spring: The Cultivate Cycle is a time of daring. Embrace the mystery.

At its core, the spring cycle is about possibility. This cycle isn't so much about moving forward as it is about fostering fertility. Cultivating requires a willingness to take risks and travel into uncharted territory. We'll deploy the improv theater principle of "Yes, and . . ." Writers can use this mindset to fuel ideation and move into the unknown. We'll wake up the senses with another improvisation technique: explore and heighten. Finally, we'll corral our unanswered questions and set them aside with the "question list."

FIRST THINGS FIRST: When In Doubt, Agree

"Yes, and . . ." activates the Cultivate Cycle because it trains the writer to accept what materializes in a writing session. Our mission during development is to unearth new information about our story, its world and characters, and what they want and feel.

In the world of improvisational theater, the "Yes, and" technique works to fuel momentum in a scene. Once a player establishes a detail in a scene, the other player begins their response with the words, "Yes, and . . ." This naturally builds on what's been established and anchors the players into the same reality. When actors affirm and add, the action continues, and the scene comes alive. Likewise, this principle helps the writer generate material. The commitment to agreement fuels authentic innovation.

The "Yes, and . . ." technique is like the childhood game "I packed my bag for grandmother's house, and in it I brought . . ." The challenge is to remember everything that comes before. But, as a child, what I enjoyed most was the humor that came from the unexpected collection of items. It was also liberating to be free from rules about what you could pack in the suitcase. Similarly, the "Yes, and . . ." mindset untethers the writer from logic, inspires imagination, and makes the generative process easy and fun.

In the early phases of a project, the "Yes, and . . ." practice is especially valuable. For example, I often deploy this tactic when generating the first draft of a scene. Once, when building an action sequence in a script, I got bogged down in the demands of the form. The screenplay format requires tight descriptive paragraphs, and after hours of tinkering, my progress stalled, and my creative energy fizzled.

I reminded myself that during the development process, the priority is to foster fertility. I realized it wasn't time for pruning and weeding. Instead, the story needed watering. I decided to use the "Yes, and . . ." technique to brainstorm. I started with "She topples over a cart full of apples." Then I continued: "Yes, and she breaks the lock on a cage of chickens. Yes, and she grabs a bottle of water. Yes, and she keeps running," and so on. By using "Yes, and . . ." to link each action, I filled the page with possibilities. Then I sifted through the brainstorm, cherry-picked ideas from the pile, and strung together a high-energy action sequence.

THE QUESTION LIST

One of the trickiest aspects of the development phase is sitting with unanswered questions.

When the writer is not able to set aside a question, the process stalls, and self-doubt often creeps in. It's frustrating when we can't find solutions, but not knowing is part of the process. Spring is a time of gestation. Don't get caught in a whirlpool of indecision. Embrace the mystery.

Writers can keep moving forward by employing the question list. The question list is the practice of wrangling any and all questions into a dedicated section in your journal. Note points of confusion and nagging questions. One of my students calls this "the parking lot." My mentor Caroline calls this the "decision list" and describes indecision as trying to drive with the emergency brake on. Indecision leads to inaction and distraction. Instead of puzzling and perseverating, allow the answers to percolate in their own time.

Once you write it down, you can continue to cultivate what's below the surface. The question list can include anything that is slowing down your writing session. Questions can be as basic as deciding a character's name or determining details like a character's job, the story location, or the number of characters. Some of the common areas of the unknown might include the following:

- Determining if X character is in or out of the story
- Sorting out the particulars of a character's backstory
- Identifying where we start or end a scene, conversation, or event
- Deciding the sequence of events
- Estabishing details that rely on research or special knowledge

One of the Rules of "Yes, and . . ." is don't reply with a question because posing a question is a challenge and rejects what's naturally surfacing. Similarly, questions can cut off brainstorming, which is an essential task of the Cultivate Cycle. Knowing you've logged your question, you can continue building with "Yes, and . . ."

Writing down questions is a way to stay connected to the story even when we feel disconnected. If you can't find the answer to a question, maybe you're asking the wrong question. Maybe you're trying to answer too many questions at once. Or maybe the answer is just around the corner. Instead of daydreaming and contemplating, commit the question to paper so your unconscious can chew on the problem. Sometimes the next right step will only be clear once we've identified the right question to ask.

The urge to find an answer is correct, but the quest for the right answer can be an unconscious way to slow the process. Sometimes circling around a problem is a way to avoid going deeper into the emotional material. Often these questions resolve themselves. If an unknown is holding you back, keep in mind that at a certain point, the impact of not deciding is more damaging than picking the wrong way forward.

ACTIVITY: Question List   ⏲ 5 minutes

There are no dumb questions, but there are distracting ones. Free up your mental bandwidth and make a question list. Rather than wondering or worrying about how, who, what, when, why, and where, write the question down. Use freewriting and list making to generate questions.

- ☐ First, identify the focus of the question list.
  - It may center around a specific project you are working on, an idea that you are exploring, or it might relate to process.
- ☐ Next, write all the questions floating around in your head. (Include anything that you are pondering.)
  - For example, consider decisions that you need to make, events that you are contemplating, characters who are unformed, outcome options, possibilities, etc.
  - Challenge yourself to identify twenty questions.

Tip: Keep your question list in a place that's easy to find. I recommend dedicating a special page in your Field Notes Writing Tracker.

There are
three rules
to writing
a novel . . .
unfortunately,
no one knows
what they are.

—Somerset Maugham

EXPLORE AND HEIGHTEN

A great way to develop material is with another improvisation technique: explore and heighten. This directive invites actors to respond rather than to perform. Similarly, this mandate prompts writers to tap into the senses, surrender to spontaneity, and trust their instincts. Rather than trying to think up a scene, the players set their focus on solving a common problem.

The "explore and heighten" technique was pioneered by Viola Spolin, who is recognized as the creator of theater games. Her seminal book *Improvisation for the Theater* and her groundbreaking work has inspired countless creatives. Her son, Paul Sills, is credited with popularizing Spolin's philosophy of play and was the founding director of the legendary Second City Theater (where many SNL cast members got their start.)

The rules of each game vary, but all Spolin games have a focal point that unites the players around solving a problem together. Thus, the emphasis is placed on cooperation, listening, and empathic connection. The noncompetitive atmosphere of the games gets actors out of their heads. Similarly, writers can use play to liberate themselves from overly intellectualizing the creative process. In fact, Aretha Sills, daughter of Paul Sills and granddaughter of Viola Spolin, teaches improvisation for writers to encourage intuitive play and discovery. Play frees the writer from the fear of being wrong and the trappings of trying to be right.

During an improvisation, the teacher or director often coaches the players by reminding them to "explore and heighten" something specific that is emerging in the scene. For example, the side coaching might direct the player to explore that object or the temperature or that facial expression. So, instead of forcing material with thinking, the players construct by exploring. Organically, the scene builds from what's been established because the players connect and draw upon the environment.

When the rational mind is shut off, we have the possibility of intuition.

—Viola Spolin

The act of exploring naturally builds energy. This technique invites writers to go bigger, brighter, deeper, and louder. For example, writers might investigate taste: Is it salty? Is it sweet? Is it sharp? When we consider the sensation of touch, we might explore the texture and temperature. Is it hotter or cooler? Is the sensation painful or pleasurable? We unearth detail by investigating and intensifying the emotions, details, and senses. Consider all the dimensions of the senses.

sight – *color, shape, light, close, far*

taste – *salty, sweet, bitter, spicy, sour, savory, umami*

touch – *texture, temperature, pain, pleasure*

smell – *sweet, sour, pleasant, revolting, nostalgic*

sound – *silence, language, music, noise, loud, soft, pitch, rhythm*

The Spolin games are experiential lessons in the skills needed to spontaneously cocreate. The focus on play gives writers access to a state of intuitive flow. Spolin recognized that noncompetitive play engenders self-expression, imagination, and collaboration. The Spolin games reinvigorate the creative process, and the cooperative spirit revitalizes the task of getting words on the page.

ACTIVITY: Explore and Heighten   10 minutes

Write about a mundane event with intense detail.

   * *See the end of the chapter for step-by-step instructions.*

THE MUCK

Writers often abandon projects because they feel stuck, but getting stuck is a part of the process. The development phase is the time before the seed sprouts. Later, when we reach the Craft Cycle, we'll refine and revise, but in order to develop an idea, the writer must wade into the muck. Embrace the mystery. Just as we nourish the soil with water, we nurture the garden of our story with emotions.

Emotions reveal important information, but to find the answers you must settle into the muck. Accept it. Explore it. Emotions are anything but easy to understand, but they can be separated into two basic categories. The first are feelings when needs are met: happy, loving, or content. The second are feelings when needs are unmet: sad, angry, or fearful.

Working with these simple categories helps us navigate the complex experience of being human. While there are countless feeling states, most can be distilled down to one of these five core emotional states. By identifying the pure emotions that create that experience, the writer can tap into desire. Emotional truth drives the narrative and pulls the audience into the story. By distilling complex emotional experiences, writers gain insight into the character's experience and our feelings as the author.

- By simplifying the character's emotional truth, we can illuminate motivation, stakes, and secrets.
- When we identify the base emotion, we unlock subtle nuances and open up more ways to express with clarity.
- Naming the emotional essence of an experience can be a tool for ferreting out the character's way of thinking and perspective.

Faux Feelings

By breaking down a feeling state to its root, we avoid the trappings of faux feelings. Watch out for false feelings like "feeling" betrayed or manipulated. These words describe real experiences, but they are not emotions. Underneath these descriptive words, you'll find a cluster of feelings and an entire story.

When someone says, "I feel abandoned," this phrasing hints at a past event. It indicates that the current experience is a result of someone else's actions and can even imply (and often wrongly assume) intention. The most important reason a writer shouldn't settle for a faux feeling is that it robs your character of agency. A faux feeling often casts blame and skips over feelings of vulnerability.

Often, faux feelings frame the experience from a place of powerlessness and victimization by someone else's actions. Ironically, deploying a faux feeling is a way to identify blame, but this perspective does not protect your character. In fact, relying on a faux feeling can calcify a painful experience and unintentionally give power away. Rather than settling for a faux feeling, be more specific about what the character is feeling. What are the emotions tangled up inside this reaction?

Examples:

When Jane felt betrayed, she felt sad, lonely, and angry.

When Mary felt manipulated, she felt angry and embarrassed.

When Bob felt bullied, he felt scared and helpless.

Cultivating a deeper understanding of emotions will also help you better navigate your process. Staying attuned to your inner landscape helps you treat your story and your experience with tenderness.

FAUX FEELINGS

Abandoned	Ignored	Neglected
Abused	Intimidated	Put Upon
Attacked	Invisible	Rejected
Betrayed	Let Down	Rushed
Bullied	Manipulated	Unappreciated

FEELINGS CHEATSHEET
Feelings When Needs Are Met

HAPPY		CONTENT	LOVING
Adventurous	Inspired	Alive	Affectionate
Amazed	Intrigued	Confident	Friendly
Amused	Invigorated	Glad	Moved
Astonished	Joyful	Grateful	Proud
Curious	Overjoyed	Peaceful	Thankful
Delighted	Refreshed	Pleased	
Determined	Relieved	Relaxed	
Eager	Stimulated	Satisfied	
Ecstatic	Surprised	Tranquil	
Encouraged	Thrilled		
Excited	Touched		
Fascinated	Trusting		
Giddy	Upbeat		
Hopeful			

FEELINGS CHEATSHEET
Feelings When Needs Are Not Met

FEARFUL		ANGRY	SAD
Afraid	Jittery	Aggravated	Bored
Alarmed	Nervous	Agitated	Depressed
Anxious	Overwhelmed	Annoyed	Disappointed
Apprehensive	Panicky	Apart	Discouraged
Bewildered	Perplexed	Cranky	Disheartened
Cautious	Puzzled	Disgusted	Dismayed
Concerned	Reluctant	Exasperated	Grieving
Confused	Restless	Frustrated	Helpless
Disconcerted	Scared	Furious	Hopeless
Disturbed	Shocked	Impatient	Hurt
Dubious	Stressed	Indignant	Lonely
Embarrassed	Terrified	Infuriated	Melancholic
Impatient	Worried	Irritated	Tired
		Resentful	Troubled
		Upset	

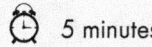

Tap into your inner world. Notice your emotions.

- ☐ Settle into a comfortable seated position, then set a timer for two minutes.
- ☐ Close your eyes and observe your breath.
- ☐ Turn your attention inward.
- ☐ Notice the sensations in your body, the chatter in the mind, and come back to your breath.
- ☐ When the timer goes off, open your eyes, pull out your journal, and set the timer for one minute. Use freewriting to explore your emotions.
- ☐ Prompt: I feel . . .
- ☐ Read and review.
- ☐ Look over your freewrite. What feelings are most present?
- ☐ Consider a calibration.
- ☐ Do you need a little self-care?
- ☐ Consider the eight realms.

Sometimes to find the answers you may need to dig deeper into the muck.

⊘ Calibrate Your Compass

Spring in Your Step: It's easy to get stuck in the development process. To move through the muck, move your body.

☐ Get your heart pumping, stretch, or simply go barefoot.

Tools and Techniques

- ◎ Yes, and . . .
- ◎ Explore and heighten
- ◎ Emotions and senses (the muck)
- ◎ The question list

RECAP: Move into the Mystery

The development process is all about moving into the mystery. The writer can liberate themselves from the comfort and safety of the known by employing the "Yes, and" technique. Spring is a time to explore and heighten. The writer nourishes their story by digging into the muck: in other words, emotions and senses. It's easy to get distracted during the Cultivate Cycle, so instead of getting stuck in whirlpools of wonder, set questions aside on your question list.

Chapter Seven Activities

Explore and Heighten   ⏰ 10 minutes

Write about a mundane event with intense detail. Transport your reader by bringing the senses alive. Consider your vantage point. You may choose to:

- Write from the point of view of one of your characters.

- Write from your point of view and state of mind today.

- Explore the emotions of an ordinary moment in your story (especially for memoir writers).

Step 1. Put your character in a no or low-stakes situation.   1 minute
   The more boring the better.

   ☐ Here are examples of no/low-stakes events:

      • eating breakfast
      • brushing teeth
      • tying shoes
      • making the bed
      • walking into the kitchen
      • opening a door
      • flushing a toilet

Step 2. Pick an emotion to explore and heighten.   1 minute

   ☐ Select the core emotion you want to explore.

      • Happy, loving, sad, angry, or fearful

   Refer to the Feelings Cheatsheets on page 107

Step 3. Next, select an even more specific version of that emotion.   1 minute

   • Look at the feelings list for ideas.

Step 4. Use freewriting to describe the minutiae of the scene.   5 minutes

   • Explore and heighten the emotions.

Step 5. Review your writing and record your observations.   2 minutes

   • Jot down your observations in your journal.
   • What did you discover about your character?
   • Add questions to the question list.
   • Make notes about your process in your Field Notes Writing Tracker.

Ready to go further?

Try out one of these options:

- Continue to explore that emotion with freewriting.
- Explore the same emotion from a different character's point of view.
- For nonfiction writers, use freewriting to write about a key moment when this emotion is in play.

 Download
The Feelings Cheat Sheet

BEHIND THE SCENES: Pillow Fight

Andy threw the pillow. I caught it and said, "Yes, and she was always on the phone." I tossed the pillow back.

She pulled it into her belly, and shouted, "Yes, and she was always sick!"

Andy and I were writing a play about a mother and her two teen-age daughters. The idea was to draw on our experiences to create a fictional story that explored the mother-daughter relationship. The result would be a stage play, and our intention was to write a comedy. At first, the process had been smooth, but we had hit a wall. In the last few writing sessions, Andy had begun slipping into a depression. Her mother had died from cancer just two years earlier, and she had been ill for much of Andy's childhood.

Andy had dark eyes and a wicked sense of humor. She was an accomplished poet and new to scriptwriting, but the collaboration had been going well. The story centered around a larger-than-life mother who was the star of a popular cooking show. We had created the mother character by merging characteristics from each of our mothers, and we created two sisters who were always at odds. We had outlined the story and written some great monologues, but each time it came to writing dialogue, Andy clammed up.

The tension between us had been building. As we shared details about growing up, it was clear she had buried her trauma, and she felt the wounds were too painful to access. In addition to her mother's illness, Andy was an only child and grew up in poverty. She knew I had lived a privileged life, and while we both experienced loneliness when we were kids, I at least had siblings to turn to. I could feel her resentment building. Understandably, Andy was sinking to a low place, but I knew we needed to find a way into those painful emotions. I suggested we try something different.

I told Andy to meet me at a dance studio the following week. She looked at me skeptically when I said she should wear comfortable clothes.

When she showed up, she was surprised to see me sitting on the floor surrounded by pillows. She snorted and rolled her eyes.

Andy took off her shoes, picked up a pillow, and paced while I explained to her the "Yes, and . . ." concept. I proposed we start by each doing a freewrite. Next, we'd play a game using the "Yes, and . . ." technique, then do another round of freewriting. The goal was to generate material. So, the only rule of the game was that as soon as you got the pillow, you had to say, "Yes, and . . ." then something about your mother, the fictional character we had created, or anything that came to mind. It didn't have to be true.

It started tense, but as we volleyed the pillow back and forth, we both relaxed, and it became more lighthearted. As the game continued, we moved around the studio and picked up the pace. Andy beamed the pillow at me, and I said, "Yes, and she was never home."

I lobbed the pillow back, and she whispered, "I miss my grandmother."

Something had cracked open her heart. Without speaking, we opened our journals and started writing. The game was silly, but by rooting it in agreement, we were able to access deeper emotional layers. We read our freewrites to one another. I was captivated by the monologue she'd written. It was from the point of view of her grandmother, and Andy came to life as she spoke in the thick Irish brogue.

I knew that Andy's grandmother had lived with them, but I hadn't known how close they'd been. Her grandmother had been the one who had listened to Andy, the one who was wise, and she shared Andy's wry sense of humor. Remembering the tender moments with her grandmother gave Andy space to tap into those tougher memories. This then gave birth to a grandmother character who became the emotional heart of the story. I often think back to the watershed moment of the pillow fight. The "Yes, and . . ." approach helped us break through a major block. Not long after, we completed the script and mounted a local production of the play. Yes, and the play was a success.

Roots of Desire

Spring: It's time to cultivate. When we plant, we must fortify the soil.

Plotting is an important part of the spring cycle, but to outline the narrative, we must nourish the roots of desire. Take time to cultivate and develop the emotional core of your story. We'll dig deeper into the character's inner world, and we'll make their journey more difficult by adding obstacles. We will expose secrets and fears.

FIRST THINGS FIRST: All or Nothing

There are times when it's best to do nothing. Just like the farmer rotates crops and deliberately lets the land rest, sometimes the writer needs to set aside a project. In agriculture, the fallow period allows the soil to recover. Rest nourishes and revives production potential and reduces the population of pests. Similarly, there are times when the writer is best served by taking a break from a project. Not every waking moment must be devoted to pushing material through the productivity pipeline. There is value in rest.

Sometimes it's appropriate to put a project on the back burner. We may need an extended break to refill the well or to reassess priorities. That said, before putting on the brakes, it's worth taking time to evaluate. One peril of the development phase is the all-or-nothing mindset.

This usually looks like tossing a project to the side and moving on to a new idea.

One of the most common reasons writers give up is that they don't feel as though they've made progress. In fact, more often than not, it's because the writer has decided that their progress isn't worthy of acknowledging, or they're not even sure if they did what they set out to do.

Not every project will bear fruit, but you're more likely to see the bloom with patient tending to the garden of your story. Small actions may not feel worthwhile, but as the saying goes, the journey of one thousand miles begins with one step. Practice patience. After you've toiled away on rewrites, it's natural to feel tired and to tire of your story, but don't jump ship because you're tired or you've entered an uncomfortable phase. Before you turn your attention to a different project, make a quick calibration.

RESET: Five Quick Calibrations to Get Back on Track

 These five quick calibrations will get you back into the writing groove.
1. Match the approach with the Story Cycle.
2. Focus on the next right action.
3. Do less.
4. Do one thing at a time.
5. Take a mini break.

TENSION

The Cultivate Cycle is an opportunity for the author to create tension. Regardless of medium or genre, the character's desire gives the narrative

ACTIVITY: Calibrate Your Compass   ⏰ 7 minutes

In your Field Notes Writing Tracker, take a moment to calibrate your creative compass.

🧭 Check in and reflect on your current progress and the process.

☐ Use freewriting to explore these questions:
- *How do I feel about the process?*
- *What are the obstacles in my way?*
- *Am I trying to tackle too much at once?*
- *Does my approach match the story cycle I am moving through?*
- *Am I clinging to an idea that's no longer relevant?*

☐ Read and reflect.
- *What's the next action?*
- *Are there small actions I can take?*
- *Do I need rest?*
- *Can I make the writing process more pleasurable and joyful?*

☐ Calibrate.
- *Make a physical sensory change to your writing space. For example, pick a flower, brew a cup of tea, pull out that fancy notebook you've been saving, or light a candle.*

---

momentum. Emotional truth is the power source of your story. Desire creates drama. Trying to outline before you know what's driving your character is like putting the cart before the horse. It's logical to crave order, but structure grows out of character.

Stories captivate audiences when we care. We feel connected when we understand what the character wants and why they need it. Once the writer knows what's driving the character, they will have the seeds of structure. In the Craft Cycle, we look more closely at shaping the dramatic arc, but as author Lisa Kron writes, "Outlining the plot before you develop your protagonist traps you on the surface in the external events that happen."

Let's look at how a character's desire unlocks structure:

The character wants something.

Then an obstacle gets in the way of what they want.

Finally, either they get what they want, or they don't get what they want.

Of course, all stories have more nuance than this, but focusing on a character's desire is an essential exercise. Cultivating desire nourishes the soil so you are ready to plant the seeds of structure.

A Note to Nonfiction Writers

Looking at desire is just as necessary in memoirs and nonfiction as it is in fiction. You can apply the techniques of this chapter to all genres. Look at your own emotions and consider the desires and fears of your reader. In fact, the main character of "how-to" and self-help books is the reader.

For example, when putting together this book, I tapped into my students' worries and wants. I considered the reader's goals (desires) and the problems they face. Underneath the obstacles, I found the writer's fears. For instance, even though a lot of students come to me because they think they are struggling with structure, often the real stumbling block is a fear of failure. Before we start tinkering with the structure of their story, I work with students to acknowledge their emotions. We identify fears and clarify desires. This builds emotional literacy and helps the writer separate feelings from facts. Usually, this liberates the writer, and an organic solution to their story problem materializes.

Focusing on your reader is invaluable during all Story Cycles. Tapping into my students' fears helped me identify the most important concepts and tools. This, in turn, helped me plot the structure of the book.

Outlining the plot before you develop your protagonist traps you on the surface in the external events that happen.

–Lisa Kron

MOTIVATION

There is something your character desperately wants or wants to hold on to—or maybe it was something they once had but lost. Whether the character knows it or not, they are trying to get what they want at every moment. Usually, there's both an external and an internal goal. Without motivation, the story will lack emotional tension. So even if your story has a lot of exciting action, if the audience doesn't understand the character's internal motivation, no amount of spectacle will keep the audience engaged.

To uncover the internal and external motivations, look at their desire from different angles. Ask the following questions:

- What does your character want?
- What internal desire drives your character?
- Is there an event or person who inspired this desire?
- What is the character's external motivation?
- What's the payoff your character seeks?
- What do the other characters think their motivation is?
- What does the character think their motivation is?
- What is your motivation? (Yes—you, the writer)

SECRETS AND FEARS

Another way to dig into the fertile ground of desire is to go deeper into the secrets and fears underlying motivation. Fear can make a character more compelling because fear reveals a character's vulnerabilities and insecurities. A weakness makes the character relatable. The reader will care about the protagonist when they can connect to their fears. When you let the audience in on a character's fear, the audience will understand their motivations, they will be more likely to root for them, and, in turn, they will be more interested to find out what happens next. Uncovering what's motivating your character to keep a secret will illuminate what is at stake.

What have you got to hide?

Consider what the character is trying to hide and why:

FEAR of exploitation, judgment, pain, shame, ruin, exposure. Fear is at the heart of many secrets. The character may fear judgment, pain, and exposure. In turn, if this fear is discovered, it will cause conflict or an unwanted consequence.

- Perhaps the character has crossed a moral line.
- Fear is often connected to a character's formative emotional wound.

PROTECT one's reputation or cover up for someone else. Maybe your character wants to protect their own or someone else's reputation, status, or inclusion in a group. The human need to belong is often the source of a secret. Here are some examples of secrets:

- Infidelity (cheating on a spouse or lover)
- Theft or destruction of another's property
- Bullying or "throwing someone under the bus"
- Taboo: something that crosses moral lines or customs
- Having a special power or ability

GAIN advantage or avoid consequences. A secret can also grow out of a character's desire to gain an advantage. For example, perhaps your character has made an important scientific discovery or has a superpower. There are many different reasons the character might want to keep that a secret.

Conceal Before You Reveal

One of the reasons secrets are so powerful is that withholding information creates tension and pulls your reader into the drama. Consider the classic literary device: the arrival of a letter. We want to know what's inside. What does the letter say? Who is it from? The audience will stick around to find out. The writer can set up an expectation that something will be revealed with the ring of a telephone, a knock at the door, or by hinting that a potent question is about to be answered. Even if we cut to a commercial, end an episode, or wrap up a chapter, a secret will compel the reader to turn the page or tune back in.

When we conceal before the reveal, the audience will ultimately be more satisfied. Then when you give the audience the inside scoop, they feel included and connected. The power of secrets applies to all genres and formats because secrets help us cultivate tension and pique the audience's curiosity. Who doesn't want to know juicy secrets?

ACTIVITY: Motivate Me   15 minutes

* See the end of the chapter for step-by-step instructions.

MAKE TROUBLE

The Cultivate Cycle is the perfect time to unearth drama. As writers, we look for trouble: accidents, mistakes, and mishaps. Conflict doesn't need to be a fistfight or a high-speed car chase. I love a good thriller or superhero movie, but tension can be created in a mundane situation.

In fact, the more intimate the drama, the more tension we can create. A more personal clash might be infidelity, a betrayal, a missed opportunity, a failure on the job, or a family feud.

When the narrative isn't grounded in character, you will find yourself powerless to access solutions. Prematurely assigning story beats locks the writer in a sterile, superficial matrix. On the other hand, tapping into the nuances of character can reveal themes, build tension, and make for a satisfying journey for the writer and the audience. The reader is pulled forward when a character wrestles with a problem that is relatable.

To find a compelling obstacle, tap into your character's fears. Your protagonist might be afraid of public speaking or terrified of wearing a bikini. If your character has a fear of heights, then make them ride a crazy rollercoaster or send them up a ladder. Put your character in a situation where they must confront their deepest fear.

Earlier, we talked about how a story will grab our attention when a character needs something. Now let's make it difficult for them to get what they want. This pumps up the tension and will make the audience want to know: *What's next?*

ACTIVITY: Day of Drama   15 minutes

Let's make trouble for our characters. It's time to throw obstacles in their way.

* See the end of the chapter for step-by-step instructions.

> It all boils down to intention and obstacles. Somebody wants something. Somebody's standing in their way of getting it. They want the girl, they want the money, they want to get to Philadelphia. It doesn't matter, but they have to want it bad. And if they need it, even better.
>
> —Aaron Sorkin

RECAP: Raise the Stakes

When your writing feels flat or dull, it's time to cultivate. If your character is sailing along without a care in the world, it's time to excavate obstacles using the tools and techniques of the spring cycle. By developing desires, secrets, and fears, we discover how to complicate the character's journey. Knowing a character's fears gives new ways to create consequences that amp up the tension and raise the stakes. What are they willing to do to protect a secret? When you want to pour Miracle-Gro on your story, dive into drama and make trouble.

Calibrate Your Compass

Spring Break: The Cultivate Cycle requires both footwork and faith, so if you are losing faith, it might be time for a mini staycation.

☐ Book a few hours to goof off.

Go to a museum, schedule a friend date, or make your own spa day at home. (Think radical self-care.)

Tools and Techniques

◎ Make trouble
◎ Desire and motivation
◎ Secrets and fears

Chapter Eight Activities

Motivate Me

 15 minutes

Find what's motivating your character. By digging into desire, fear, and secrets, we'll nourish the roots of your story.

Step 1. Warm-Up: I want, I fear

Before we dive into your character's desires, take a moment to personally connect to the energy of desire and fear.

☐ Use freewriting to explore.

   Give yourself three minutes for each prompt.
   - *I want . . .*
   - *I fear . . .*

☐ Jot down insights, observations, questions, or discoveries in your Field Notes Writing Tracker.

   - What did you learn about your process?

Step 2. What's at Stake?

Explore motivation.

☐ Write about what's at stake. Consider these questions:

- What is motivating your character to keep this secret?
- Why is this character determined to keep this secret?
- How does this secret create complications for our character?
- How might the discovery of this secret make the journey to their goal more difficult?
- How does this secret raise the stakes?
- How does the secret align with the character's beliefs and morals?
- Is this secret relatable?

Step 3. Synthesize

Read over your writing and make note of any insights, takeaways, or questions.

- ☐ Distill your character's desire using this template.

  - The character wants _____
  - The main obstacles in the way are_____
  - The character's biggest fears are_____
  - If the character gets what they want, the payoff will be_____

Day of Drama

⏰ 12-40 minutes

Let's make trouble for our character.

Step 1: Make a quick sketch of your body. (2 minutes)

- ☐ Draw a simple stick figure or crude outline of your body.

Step 2: Label aches and pains. (5 minutes)

- ☐ Mark up the figure to identify injuries or pains.

  - Like list making, the goal is to just jot down a few words. It doesn't need to make sense to anyone but you.
  - Identify scars, injuries, deformities, illnesses, bumps, bruises, bites, or breaks.

Step 3: Write about it. Set a timer for five minutes.

- ☐ Using freewriting, select option A or B and describe in detail a day of drama!

OPTION A: Pick one of your pains and write about that.

OPTION B: Using your pain for inspiration, give your character an injury and write about it.

If you get stuck or want more guidance, consider these questions:

- What happened?
- Where were you (or your character)? Why were you there?
- What time of day was it? What time of year was it? Your age?
- Who was with you? What was the weather like?
- What happened? What happened next?
- Whom did you tell?
- What did people say? What did your partner/parents/boss say?
- What did you feel?
- If your pain were a color, what color would it be?
- Did you ask for help? What were you thinking?!?!
- What hurt the most? What was the scariest part?

TIP: Use the senses.

Ready to go further?

Pick a pain and describe how that created fear or a secret.

 Download
13 Ways to Make Trouble

BEHIND THE SCENES: Need Makes the Lead

I learned how desire shapes narrative when I made my first feature film, an offbeat comedy, *Mango Kiss*. The lesbian rom-com was based on the stage play *Bermuda Triangles*, written by Sarah Brown (no relation). I wrote the script with the playwright, and we took great pains to make a faithful adaptation.

I had tremendous respect for Sarah's work. The play was a perfectly crafted work of genius. The stage production had been wildly successful, and I wanted to honor her voice as the original author. So, during the writing process, our intention was to stay true to the play. That said, when we adapted the play, we wanted to take advantage of the medium.

While plays come alive with words, film relies more heavily on visuals. The nature of live performance impacts the audience experience. In the theater, the viewers are submerged in the experience and swept away into the immersive live-action spectacle. Plays often include long monologues and scenes with tons of dialogue, whereas films can frame and focus the viewer's experience with close-ups and editing. The original play's poetry was hypnotic, and it worked as a sprawling ensemble, but in the screenplay, we broke up the play's long scenes of dialogue into a series of several shorter ones. In the process, we created the momentum we needed for the screen, but something else happened during the adaptation.

On the first day of the shoot, the writer joined me on set, and we watched the scene unfold on the monitor. After the first take, our eyes met. She went back to the hotel to start cutting. Seeing the actors in close-up, she realized the words were superfluous. Sarah worked quickly to make revisions, but the jump from stage to page had changed the story.

After we completed shooting, I worked with an editor to cut the film. Something wasn't working. I realized we had centered the story on the wrong character. Sassafras was loveable and charming, but the real lead was her love interest, Lou. Lou had a clear desire and took action. Sassafras had been the center of the play, but in the film adaptation, she seemed reactive and her desires vague. It was a wild idea, but I went ahead and restructured the film with Lou as the lead.

I wrote new scenes and churned out voice-overs to fill gaps. We did some reshoots and wove the story back together. The film finally came alive.

Why did it work to have Sassafras as the lead in the play but not in the film?

I realized it wasn't just about the changes on the page. Something had shifted when we went from stage to screen. In both the theater production and the movie, Sassafras expressed her desires and fears in words, but in the film what stood out was how Lou actively showed her desire. The audience knew what Lou wanted because they could see her pursue Sassafras. We hadn't anticipated that simple gestures like Lou giving Sassafras a gift would put her in the driver's seat. The character with the strongest need is your lead character.

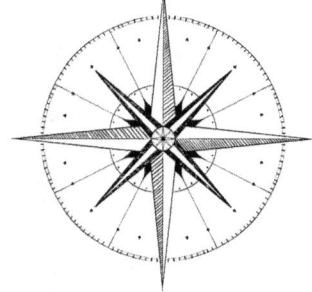

PART III

Collaborate

THE SUMMER CYCLE

Long days shake up the routine.

The noisy garden invites celebration.
Summer is the time to play and improvise.

The season brims with festive, free energy and possibility.
Soon, summer may feel like one long party, making the sun
our fierce, fiery host.

There is a risk of exhaustion, so rest up and find a shady retreat.

The summer solstice marks a turning point, stirs up questions,
and makes spring's knobby bulbs bloom.
No more hiding, no more secrets.

Amidst the frenzy of fruit ripening and flowers blooming,
remember the fall harvest is coming.
Take time to water and weed.

The Power of Play

Summer: Shake up the routine, improvise, and play.
It's time to collaborate. Let go of control.

As the Collaborate Cycle's name suggests, the core feature of this phase is connection. Even a solo writer who hides out in a remote cabin must learn to collaborate with the unconscious. Just as improvisation helps us during development, the mercurial summer cycle demands a willingness to let go of control. Play helps us move into the mystery. Inspiration inevitably waxes and wanes, and productivity ebbs and flows. We can rekindle creative connection by injecting whimsy into the process. We'll take inspiration from the surrealists and stir up some serendipity with a little foray into tarot.

FIRST THINGS FIRST: Leap into the Unknown

One of the challenges of the writing process is it demands that writers leap into the unknown. You may be reluctant to dive into the void, but it's not possible to map out every step. In fact, making mistakes is part of the process and getting lost can lead to delightful discoveries.

It's natural to have expectations about pace and productivity, but the Collaborate Cycle teaches us the value of going off track, falling behind, and losing our way. Sometimes there needs to be a breakdown before there is a breakthrough. The Collaborate Cycle is about exploration and adventure, so to harness the summer season's vitality, make time to wander.

Buried deep within each human being is a potent mix of thoughts, memories, desires, and instincts. Often, the answers are found in the unconscious because the conscious mind is tiny compared to the vast unconscious. As Sigmund Freud once said, "The mind is like an iceberg; it floats with one-seventh of its bulk above water."

Even though we may not be aware of our unconscious urges and tendencies, it is the unconscious that drives our behavior, and it is a vast resource of imagination. Psychoanalyst Carl Jung proposed that the unconscious mind is the result of past collective experience of humanity, rather than being shaped by singular, personal experience. He believed every person is born with ancestral experiences responsible for deep-seated spiritual beliefs, sexual behaviors, phobias, and instincts. He called this the collective unconscious.

While Jung and Freud made these concepts popular at the turn of the twentieth century, expansive concepts of consciousness existed long before the Western tradition. For centuries, Buddhists believed in a cycle of rebirth or samsara. Australian Aboriginals describe time as a cycle of consciousness and believe reality takes place on a continuum of past, present, and future. Their concept of Dreamtime reflects the idea that one can access the memory of the Earth's origins and ancestral figures. The Aboriginals eloquently refer to this as the "time before time" or the "Everywhen."

Touchstone

Stories allow us to bridge time and transcend the ordinary. This instinctual tradition weaves in and out of the human experience across the ages. While written narratives have only been in circulation for about 3,500 years, visual storytelling has existed for over 36,000 years, and the oral tradition has been around for over 50,000 years.

Stories are more than words. Stories are fundamental touchstones for humans. The enduring power of story is evidenced by the pictures etched inside French caves, the hieroglyphics in Egyptian pyramids, the symbolic designs on Mayan treasures, the epic tales embroidered in Asian tapestries, and the dramas captured in Greek frescos. Storytelling is instinctual. So, rather than looking for answers outside ourselves, we must search inside. This summer cycle is an invitation to be intuitive.

ACTIVITY: The Refuge of Storytelling  7 minutes

In your Field Notes Writing Tracker, use freewriting to explore why you love stories.

☐ Consider these questions:
- What's the first memory you have of writing?
- What's the first story that you remember writing?
- What's the most fun you've had with writing?
- How does it feel to share your writing with others?

 Download:
Ignite Inspiration: Five Ways to Get Fired Up

WORD CLOUDS

In the spirit of the Collaborate Cycle's impulse to wander, consider making word clouds. This brainstorming process is also known as clustering, bubble mapping, and mind mapping. The idea is to use free association to develop or discover an aspect of your story. If you are more linear, this technique may be uncomfortable, but this nonlinear mode of generating is a great way to access the unconscious.

Start by placing a word at the center: a character, a key event, an emotion, or an activity. Then, explode outwards. Each branch begins with the word at the center, but anything is fair game. As long as the word you add relates in some way to the adjacent word, you are good to go. (If the association only makes sense to you, that's good! It means you're tapping into the unconscious.) This approach frees the writer from logic and reveals new material by allowing unexpected discoveries.

Word clouds can be a back door into the world of your story. Let's look at the word cloud example from my notebook. At the center is "photography." I chose this word because I was writing a story in which my main character was a photographer. I was feeling disconnected from the material and having trouble focusing, so I decided to goof around with a word cloud. Without trying to find answers, I followed each spoke using free association.

I let go of control and let my mind meander. Once I finished, I studied the word cloud. I noticed that the branch starting with *chemicals* led to the word *alone*. A lightbulb went on. I hadn't understood what was driving the character's obsession with photography. When I landed on *alone*, I realized her pursuit of photography was rooted in her desire for belonging and connection. This insight energized the process, and I felt ready to dive back in.

The Word cloud's nonlinear approach can also be more focused. For example, you might seed each branch with a directive word like a particular emotion or sense. This technique can also facilitate the investigation into a story element including relationships, backstory, theme, conflict, fears, and secrets. Anchoring the exploration with a specific word guides the process while still allowing for play and improvisation.

ACTIVITY: Explore with Word Clouds   10 minutes

* See the end of the chapter for step-by-step instructions.

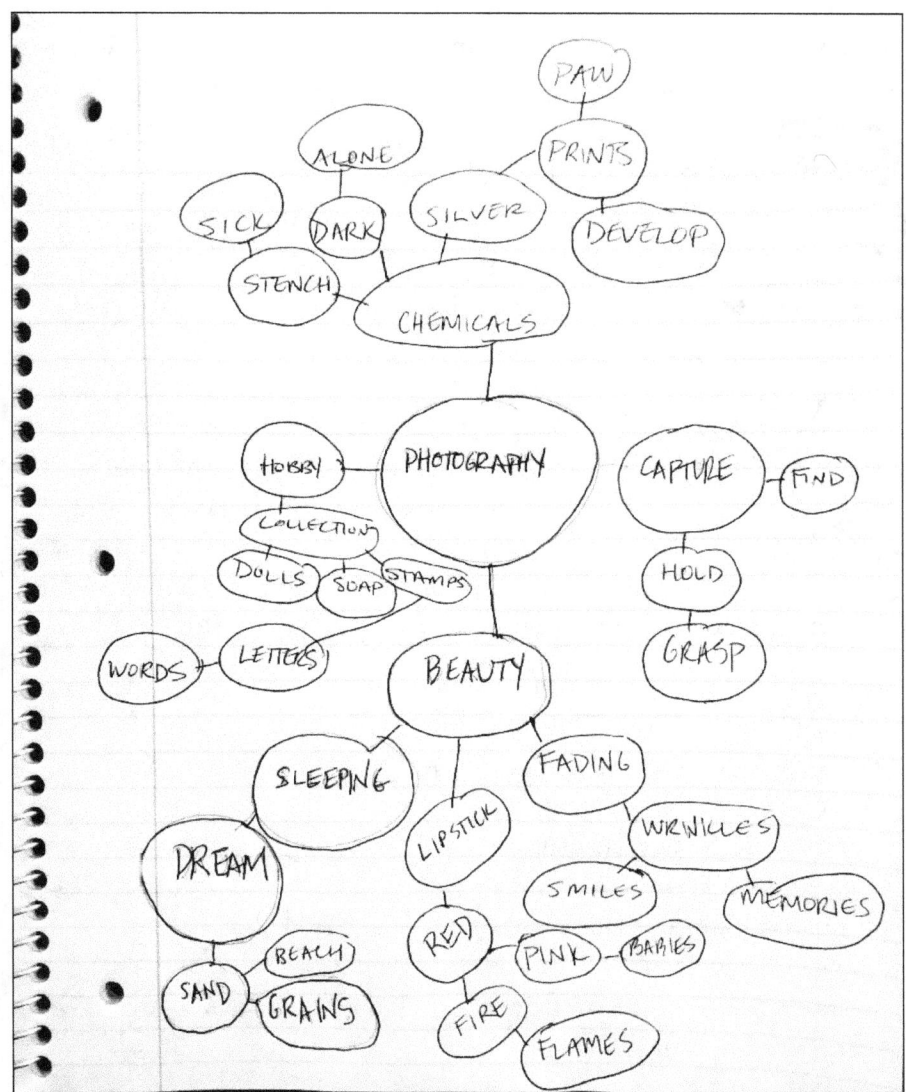

PLAY

To activate the Collaborate Cycle we can also turn to the cheeky surrealists for inspiration. They loved to play games with words and pictures. Surrealists understood the power of play in art and literature. They found mystery in the ordinary and made the bizarre normal. In search of new ways of seeing, they tapped into the unconscious and dreams. They believed we find truth when we let go of logic, lose control, and embrace improvisation.

If there were a patron saint of play, it would be Salvador Domingo Felipe Jacinto Dalí i Domènech, Marquess of Dalí of Púbol, or—as he's popularly known—Salvador Dalí. In addition to his ridiculous name and his crazy mustache, he fashioned an absurd persona and was devoted to disrupting the ordinary. His famous sculpture, the lobster telephone, is emblematic of the surrealist philosophy. By playfully modifying an ordinary object like the telephone, he grabs the viewer's attention and sparks the imagination. The surrealist approach embodies the mindset of the Collaborate Cycle.

Another group that valued play was the Dadaists. They rejected the logic and aesthetics of modern society. Like the surrealists, they used nonsense and surprise to collaborate with the muse. The literary Dadaists rejected traditional conceptions of poetry and broke from the tradition of formal structure. They believed that a more authentic expression was achieved when the writer partnered with the world and welcomed whimsy.

Collage

The Dadaists used collage to collaborate with the chaos of the world. They developed a technique called "chance collage," which involved dropping torn scraps of paper onto a larger sheet and then pasting the pieces wherever they landed. They also cut words from newspapers, or randomly selected from a book, and used these fragments to write poetry. Like the surrealists, Dadaists embraced serendipity.

Inspired by the Dadaists, the author William S. Burroughs famously employed what he called the Cut-Up Method in which he assembled "a collage of words read heard overheard." Similarly, many songwriters rely on play to come up with lyrics. In an interview, David Bowie described how he used the cut-up technique as "a kind of Western tarot." He explained, "You write down a paragraph or two describing different subjects, creating a kind of 'story ingredients' list . . . and then cut the sentences into four or five-word sections, mix 'em up, and reconnect them." Similarly, television writer Phoebe Waller-Bridge encourages a playful approach of generating material and then piecing the story together. She once confessed she gets a kick out of discarding material.

ACTIVITY: Dada Daring   5 minutes
Pull words at random from the Dada Daring Word Bank.

  * See the end of the chapter for step-by-step instructions.

 Purchase:
Vision Boarding: Find Focus With Writing And Collage

WHEN IN DOUBT, TAROT IT OUT

Another way to fire up inspiration is to spark ideas with serendipity. Use tarot, astrology, anagrams, or any kind of oracle deck. Pulling a tarot or oracle card is a great dip into the unconscious and a playful way to uncover what's driving your character. The random aspect of drawing cards relieves you of needing to know so you can sneak past the critic. The human mind reflexively makes meaning and connections because we are wired for story. Find clues by listening to the inner rumblings.

There are times when all you need to do is just write. Get everything you love onto the page and figure out how it all fits together later. Do the fun stuff.

—Phoebe Waller-Bridge

When I hit a wall or find myself unable to make a decision, I like to pull a tarot card at random. As my mentor Caroline wisely says, "The mind abhors a vacuum." Our subconscious rushes in to assign meaning. The traditional meaning of cards is less significant than your reaction. I used to look to tarot for answers or predictions, but after taking Caroline's course Story Arcana, I began relying more on my intuition.

Before you draw a card, focus your mind on a story question.

- What is this scene about?
- What's really going on for my character?
- What is my character afraid of?
- What is the character hiding?

You don't need a fancy deck, and it doesn't even need to be a tarot deck; you can use oracle cards, animal cards, or a visually rich source of your choice. Select a deck with images that you find compelling. You do not need to become a tarot expert, nor do you even need to buy a deck. There are plenty of free resources online.

Archetypes

Tarot employs ancient symbols and powerful archetypes, but most of all the tarot is a portal. I like the tarot because it draws on universal themes, but rather than trying to decode a message, consider it a mirror, an affirmation, or a doorway. Rather than being predictive, the cards spark reactions because the mind naturally fills in the blanks. Give it a try.

Once, as I was drafting a pilot, I needed to kill one of my characters. I was toying with several ways to knock them off. In a writing session, a gruesome scene came flowing out. My beloved character was killed by a swarm of bees. His hobby was beekeeping, so this made sense, but I wasn't sure. Wouldn't he know how to expertly handle the hive?

As my colleague likes to say, "When in doubt, tarot it out." I grabbed my Mother Peace Deck and posed the question: What do I need to know about this character's death? I pulled the five of swords that, in this deck, happens to feature bees as the dominant image.

The card didn't give me all the answers, but it allowed me to set aside my doubts and keep moving forward. Over the next few writing sessions, the answers came to me, and I was able to sketch not just how the character died, but I also unearthed important information about the killer. Working with tarot builds mental flexibility and allows you to open up to messages from unexpected places.

ACTIVITY: Tarot or Tea   20 minutes

* See the end of the chapter for detailed prompt.

RECAP: Collaborate with Chaos

In this chapter, we use play to tap into our instinctive ability to create stories. The summer cycle is an invitation to wander. It's time to collaborate with the chaos of the world. Nonlinear techniques, like making word clouds and working with tarot, give us access to our unconscious. There's value in going off track. Sometimes there is a breakdown before there is a breakthrough. Sometimes the only way to move forward is to let go of control. With whimsy and serendipity, surrender to the adventure of the summer cycle.

 Calibrate Your Compass

Summer Daze: When the Collaborate Cycle melts your brain, it's time for some summer fun. A doodle a day keeps the doctor away.
☐ Pick a word and start doodling.

Tools and Techniques
- ◉ Play
- ◉ Collage
- ◉ Word cloud
- ◉ Tarot and tea
- ◉ Wander

Chapter Nine Activities

Explore with Word Clouds

 10 minutes

Create branches to link ideas and build clusters of connections. You may find an unusual discovery that illuminates something you hadn't been able to articulate.

Step 1: Pick a topic.   2 minutes

Step 2: Explore the topic using the word cloud technique.   5 minutes

Step 3: Use the word cloud to freewrite on a topic of your choice.   3 minutes

Examples of topics:

- Fear, Secret
- Lessons, Advice
- amily, Me
- Yesterday, Today, Tomorrow
- Maybe, Yes, No

- All You Need Is Love
- Likes, Dislikes
- I'm Tired Of . . .
- In My Wildest Dreams, I . . .

Ready to go further?

Consider using a guiding theme for branches of the word cloud. For example, you might use the senses to spark sensory detail.

 Download
3 Word Cloud Templates

Dada Daring

 5–30 minutes

Drawing on the Dadaist sensibility, pull words at random from the Dada Daring Word Bank and let your unconscious guide your writing.

Step 1: Pick three words from the Dada Daring Word Bank on the next page.

Step 2: Write the words in your journal.

Step 3: Freewrite using those words.

 Download
Dada Daring Word Bank

Dada Daring Word Bank

BAREFOOT GLOOM LOST AND FOUND HEAT ACCIDENT MEMORY
LETTER TROUBLED WATERS CONFIDENTIAL PARANORMAL CHASE
HIDE PURSUE ROADBLOCK LOVE COMPLAINT UNPLUGGED
EXPECTATION LOVABLE MONSTER BRAVE WISE BEAUTIFUL
STRONG COLD CRUEL OBEDIENT GIFT BOSSY SCARY GROUCHY
BITTER SELFISH VAIN WARRIOR WARDROBE RAGS BIKINI ARMOR
GOWN WINGS ERUPTION AVALANCHE TSUNAMI BLIZZARD FLOOD
FIRE TORNADO FAMINE LIGHTNING STORM FOREST WATER
UNDERGROUND DESERT SWAMP FARM COUNTRYSIDE OUTERSPACE
CLOUD CITY FLAG MAP PARALLEL UNIVERSE FOREIGNERS TRAP
DOOR HIDDEN STAIRCASES IMPOSSIBLE ALIBI PROOF MOTIVE
CLUE POSTCARD WILL VOICES GRAVITY SUNRISE SUNSET DUSK
DAWN GROWL HOWL BARK HISS REPAIR RUPTURE VEGETABLE
ABSORB FLOAT FLY FREEZE GLIDE TRASH TREASURE GRACE
METAL WOOD FIREWATER AIR EARTHNOW PRESENT PAST PUBLIC
FUTURE JOKERKING QUEEN JACK CROOK POLITICIAN
ENGINEER CRASH SMASH KISS BIG RAIN LAVA ROCK STAR
SIDEKICK TAROT MONDAY TEEN TODDLER BABY ADULT TWEEN
BROTHER SISTER MOTHER FATHER GRANDPARENT ELDER
BABYSITTER HERO JOURNEYELIXIR CAVE CLIFF MESSAGE SHOW
HIDE LOSER MOON STARS DICTATOR SON CAPTAIN DROPOUT
SHERIFF HAT GLOVE SOCK SHOE PIANO DESSERT DINNER
BREAKFAST LUNCH ILLUSION REALITY BODY HOT COLD TIGHT
FACT BURGER FAN DETECTIVE HISTORICAL FIGURE SEASONS
WOLF OWLCAT HOME SUMMER SPRING FALL WINTER HOLIDAY

Tarot or Tea

Option A: Tarot

☐ Pull a tarot card for each question, then pay attention to your gut reaction.

☐ What do the images on the card make you feel? What thoughts pop into your mind?

☐ Jot down your observations.

Note: Most tarot decks come with a "little white book" that explains the traditional meaning of each card, so these details can add another dimension. But, most importantly, tune into what the image sparks inside you.

 Download
3 Easy Tarot Story Spreads

Option B: Teatime

Allergic to tarot? It's okay—tarot isn't for everyone. Instead, invite your character over for a chat.

☐ Have a dialogue with your character while you enjoy a cup of tea or a snack.

☐ Write each question in your journal.

☐ Then switch pens and answer.

Questions:

- What do you believe you need to be happy (or loved or fulfilled or accepted or successful)?

- What's your view of the world and your place in it?

- What rules (or restrictions) are pressing on you?

- Are there cultural norms, taboos, or expectations that impact you?

☐ Now read over your writing. What do you notice?

- Record your observations in your Field Notes Writing Tracker.

☐ When you are done, do a little pampering. It's time for a little radical self-care.

- Remember to consider the eight realms.

Tips:

- Characters don't always answer truthfully and may go off on tangents.

- Allow them to rant.

- Listen for false beliefs.

  - Are they uninformed or misinformed about how the world works?

  - Do they have an incorrect belief about themselves or the world?

BEHIND THE SCENES: Confession

I was a child when I first experienced the power of storytelling and the joy of letting the unconscious guide my writing. I had just moved from California to New York. I was in fourth grade, and my parents had just divorced. I missed the sunshine, my freedom, and most of all my friends. My new school couldn't have been more different from the rowdy coed public school I had attended since kindergarten. The prim and proper all-girl Catholic school, located in an eighty-room Italian-Renaissance-palazzo-style mansion, was in Manhattan's posh Upper East Side.

We were required to wear gray jumpers and brown shoes. Worse than the uniforms were the mandatory weekly prayers in the school chapel. I awkwardly followed the intimidating choreography, terrified my teachers and peers would find out I hadn't been baptized. I was pretty certain I was a sinner. To avoid confession, I hid in the bathroom.

To make matters worse, I was floundering academically, and I was especially behind in English. One Friday, the teacher tasked us with a writing project. We were to write a paragraph in our composition books about anything we wanted. Being that I hadn't made any friends, I spent the weekend pouring my heart into the assignment. I dropped into my unconscious and let the pen lead the way. I took refuge in the world I created.

The next week, I was surprised when I was asked to read my story aloud. I thought maybe I was in trouble because it was an irreverent retelling of "Jack and the Beanstalk." (Jackie and Jack wore leather, drove motorcycles, and broke rules.) When all the students turned to look at me, I felt my face flush. Now everyone would know I wasn't a good Catholic. As I read, I felt the energy in the room change. The students were on the edge of their seats and laughed in all the right places. When I finished with a cliffhanger, the class roared for more.

In the following weeks, I penned new installments, and my classmates begged the teacher to let me read each new adventure aloud. It hadn't been my intention to impress my peers, but it was thrilling to entertain. More importantly, I felt a sense of belonging, and I found solace in the act of creating. I was hooked. There's nothing like the thrill of sharing stories, and ever since then, I've chased the intoxicating high.

CHAPTER TEN

Muse and Critic

Summer: The Collaborate Cycle stirs up fiery energy.
Ignite inspiration: Call in your muse and make friends with your critic.

The summer cycle reminds us that the writer doesn't go it alone. We must connect with the audience, call in the muse, and communicate with the critic. It's natural to want to give the critic the slip, but let's make time to get to know them instead. Sometimes writing leads us into vulnerable territory, so we'll scaffold the process with radical self-care.

FIRST THINGS FIRST: Turbulence

Writers are sensitive creatures, so it's natural to experience emotions about our work. Putting pen to page can spark chaos and turbulence. Disruption can trigger doubt, and fear grows in uncertainty. The critic feeds on darkness. Writers need the darkness, and we need the critic.

To create, we need to be able to move through the full spectrum of emotions. The critic's go-to emotion is fear, so the idea of destroying the critic is appealing. Feeling fear is uncomfortable, but a flare-up of feelings is a sign you care about the work. When we experience intense emotions, it means we have a lot invested in the work and that the impact of our writing matters to us. Experiencing fear is part of the process.

Often, the desire to share a story is rooted in the human need to be seen and heard, but just the thought of being truly witnessed can expose insecurities. Rest assured; you don't need everyone to love your work. People find flaws in even the most wildly successful books and movies. It's important to find ways to handle criticism. If we want to put our work into the world, criticism is part of the deal. When you share your work, people will respond, and they will have opinions. Feedback is part of the process. Prepare accordingly. Getting to know your inner critic helps you be ready to face feedback. If you can't bear the voices in your head, how will you handle real-world critiques?

> When you put work into the world, people will respond, and they will have opinions. Getting to know your inner critic helps you be ready to face feedback.

THE CRITIC

The critic suffers from serious FOMO, so don't be surprised when they crash the party. Some teachers tell students to crush the critic by writing down the critic's complaints, then ceremoniously burning or tearing up the paper. I wanted to believe in the magic of this ritual, but I never could break up with my critic. Even though the critic wasn't treating me right, I couldn't give them up. I couldn't resist calling them. It felt like a lusty obsession with a bad boyfriend. It was my mentor Caroline who made me realize why I was stuck on the critic. She offered a new perspective. She proposed a revolutionary idea. *What if the critic was trying to protect me?*

The horrible cacophony of negativity in my head wasn't the screeches of a ferocious beast on the prowl but the growls of a fiercely protective mama bear. While the critic can be cruel and pessimistic, usually below their harsh exterior, they are sensitive creatures, and they want to help. We need the critic because it's their job to keep us safe.

Before acting, pause. Before you start attacking a story problem, do a body check-in and make sure your tank is full.

ACTIVITY: The Body Check-In   ⏰ 3 minutes

Do a quick scan. How do I feel in my body?

- ☐ Settle into a comfortable seated position, then set a timer for two minutes.
- ☐ Close your eyes and observe your breath.
- ☐ Turn your attention inward.
- ☐ Notice the sensations in your body, the chatter in the mind, and come back to your breath.
- ☐ When the timer goes off, open your eyes, pull out your journal, and set the timer for one minute.
- ☐ Jot down your observations.
- ☐ *Am I hungry, thirsty, physically off balance?*
- ☐ *Am I feeling lonely or in pain?*
- ☐ *Am I feeling tired or rested?*
- ☐ *Calibrate with self-care.*
- ☐ *Is there something I can do to feel better?*

Cozy Up to The Critic

The critic can help us make the work better because the critic helps us consider the audience. Being concerned about what others will think is good. We need to care about and connect with our audience. It's normal to want our work to be liked and natural to wonder how others will respond to our writing. Being visible is being vulnerable. This duality makes it especially important to cozy up to the critic, but what do we do when the critic sounds the siren?

It's human to be concerned about what others will think. This is good. We need to care about and connect with our audience.

A Convincing Case

The critic presents a convincing case. Their words feel believable because they know all our fears and secrets, but the critic sees the world through a lens of fear. When they swim in the subconscious, they selectively gather evidence. When we go to new depths, they twist half-truths, unleash old stories, and make false conclusions. It's their job to hold back the unwieldy flood of information churning below the surface. The critic stands guard like a watchman at the gate, and when we go into uncharted terrain, the watchman charges forward and sounds the alarm.

The critic's alarm activates worry, and this triggers fear. Once our body chemistry changes, it's difficult to shift the emotional energy. Even if intellectually we know the critic's complaints are untrue or irrelevant, when the critic presses the panic button, it disrupts our equilibrium. The noise the critic makes is unpleasant because they need us to pay attention. Like the piercing alarm of a smoke detector, the critic's complaints communicate important information. Just as a baby's cries tell the parent they need something, when the critic gets loud, it's time to check in with our needs. If we can't stop their chirping, it's time to change the batteries. The critic's cries mean it's time to refill the well. A dose of Story RX calms the nervous system and restores our creative energy.

When your critic sounds the alarm, it may be an indication that the subject matter is triggering old trauma or revealing painful discoveries. Often it has nothing to do with your project. Maybe the current Story Cycle is simply unfamiliar or uncomfortable. The critic's cry might mean you are having some kind of physical or mental 911 unrelated to your story. Maybe you recently suffered a loss or are just coming down with a cold.

There will be shitty days. If you're like me, the critic is always close by. Lurking, watching, waiting. Whether I'm dreaming up a new idea, revising a draft, or preparing to share my writing, the critic is bound to crash the party. Some days it feels like the board game "Operation." One wrong move and the critic sounds the alarm and stops me in my tracks with a loud electric zap.

Spot the Critic

If we want to collaborate with the critic, first we need to be able to spot them. Instead of waiting until the critic shows up uninvited, we'll get to know them. Our mission is to find out what the critic fears and what they need. First, we'll learn to recognize the critic's voice. Here are some signs that the critic is running the show:

- The critic is a wet blanket.
  - They'll tell you you're falling behind and it's too late.
- The critic likes to find flaws, knock down ideas, and reject plans.
  - When you feel stuck or overwhelmed, the critic has hijacked your writing session.
- The critic demands attention and likes to prove why they're right.
- The critic is rarely satisfied and prone to pondering.
  - The critic is content to endlessly ricochet from one idea to another.

Meet the Critic

It was during one of Caroline's courses that I finally got to meet my critic. My critic is a prim and proper lady. Meet Doctor Konstantina Parfait. (Konstantina like constant and Parfait like perfect.) Dr. Parfait is always immaculately dressed, not a hair out of place. She'll have you know she's a higher-up and holds a position of great importance. She is a senior employee of the Fear Factory, a large bureaucratic organization dedicated to manufacturing worry and doubt.

Unlike me, she went to grad school and has multiple degrees. Her job is to look for danger and point out mistakes. She speaks seven different languages and is an expert at translating feelings into destructive judgments. Dr. Konstantina, like most critics, loves to spotlight mistakes and drag up the past with barbs like *if only you had more schooling, if only you had a writing partner, if only you had talent . . .*

On the flip side, I've discovered that Konstantina's highly organized and an excellent notetaker. While she's prone to panic, she has a tender heart, and I've found she has a highly developed emotional intelligence. She's a skilled researcher, and her attention to detail makes her a thoughtful project manager.

Three Ways to Cozy up to the Critic

1. Calm your critic.
   - Let the critic know you are just putting words on the page.
   - Remind them that you can always decide later to change something to protect the innocent (or the guilty).
2. Reassure your critic.
   - Promise that you will revise and polish before you show it to your [fill in the blank (father, sister, daughter, husband)].
3. Include the critic.
   - Schedule a date with the critic before you release it into the world.

Old Stories

The critic can be sneaky, but often their complaints are new renditions of old stories. In real life, most of my family members are highly accomplished. I'm surrounded by high-ranking individuals with graduate degrees, C-suite positions, and official honorable government titles. So, it makes perfect sense that my critic would have loads of credentials. I thought I had moved beyond that tired narrative that I'm inferior, but the critic loves to replay outdated stories. (Upon closer examination, I've discovered Konstanina has a B.S. degree.)

When you find yourself swirling in negative thoughts, ask, *Says who?* Whose voice is it? Maybe that familiar voice in your head is somebody from your past. The critic's voice may remind you of a terrible teacher, a nosy neighbor, or a shaming boss, but it might just be the critic.

One of my students discovered that her critic wasn't operating alone—instead they were a nasty gang of mean girls like the ones who'd taunted her in middle school. Another client's critic, Rehtom, was a Viking-like marauder from another planet. The student revealed that the origin of this brutal voice could be found in the critic's name spelled backward (mother). Another found that his critic sounded just like his angry uncle.

The critic loves to ambush the writer, so instead of hoping the critic doesn't strike, let's capture the critic. Let's get the critic out of your head and onto the page.

ACTIVITY: Capture the Critic   50 minutes

Let's cozy up to the critic.

  * *See the end of the chapter for step-by-step instructions.*

You do not even
have to believe in
yourself or your
work. You have
to keep open and
aware directly
to the urges that
motivate you. Keep
the channel open.

–Martha Graham

THE MUSE

Just like learning to work with the critic, learning to collaborate with the muse will help you navigate your writing journey. Don't wait until you're stuck to reach out to your muse. When you fall into an abyss of doubt and confusion, you want the muse on speed dial.

How do we find the muse?

To find your muse, you may look to myths and ancient traditions. The most well-known muses are the nine sister-goddesses in Greek mythology, but countless deities are celebrated around the globe. Perhaps you feel a connection with a religious saint or icon. You can find your muse in all kinds of places. You may feel inspired by animals or nature. One of my students believed her muse took the form of a butterfly and takes great pleasure in unexpected visitations. Another client took solace in the moon and regularly checked the night sky for inspiration.

You can even cast an actual person as your muse. Choose someone from the present or a figure from history: Audre Lorde, Frida Kahlo, Lucille Ball, or Thich Nhat Han, the Buddhist teacher. We can also find inspiration from our ancestors. For example, I call upon my grandmothers, not because they were writers, but because their energy buoys me. Grandma Jeanne was a teacher with a great sense of humor; Grandma Bernice was a gardener with a tenacious will.

You don't have to be monogamous with your muse; you can flirt with other muses or even have a string of one-night stands. You might pick a card from a tarot deck to be your muse for the day. Even a word, phrase, or mantra can be your guiding light. Rather than looking to the muse for answers or predictions, consider this a relationship. The relationship is a collaboration, a give and take, and it requires nurturing and attention.

ACTIVITY: Help Wanted   20 minutes

Enlist your muse in the project of preparing to put our work into the world.

* See the end of the chapter for step-by-step instructions.

One of my muses is my grandmother, Bernice Brown.

Creative Fire

The summer cycle can be especially exhilarating, so temper the creative fire by making time to reflect and rejuvenate. Just as there are overwriters and underwriters, some overindulge, while others are prone to restriction. Left to your own devices, how often do you refill the well? Are you a spa junkie or a deprivation addict? Are you a write-a-holic or a procrastinator? Are you a serial monogamist or a compulsive collaborator?

Writers are especially susceptible to ideation addiction during the summer cycle. When ideas spark, the fire of collaboration can be mesmerizing. It can be difficult to move into the next Story Cycle. Instead of searching for the perfect, best, or right idea, just for today, pick an idea. Don't censor yourself before you've gotten material on the page.

The summer cycle demands freedom and play, but one hazard of the summer cycle is the temptation to overindulge in celebrating. Beware of the endless summer. The seductive summer cycle can pull writers into a fever dream of passion. Many brilliant writers and artists have burned out or self-imploded, like journalist Hunter S. Thompson and the hard-drinking Ernest Hemingway. After decades of debauchery, both men took their own lives despite (or perhaps because of) their success. Substances are no substitute for the muse.

When the creative fire burns bright, remember radical self-care. Enlist your muse so they can guide you back to the light.

RECAP: Muse and Critic

Sometimes summer's fiery energy sparks chaos and wakes up the critic. Instead of trying to silence or ignore the critic, make friends and collaborate. Invite your muse to join you on the writing journey. Temper the creative fire by making time to reflect and rejuvenate.

Calibrate Your Compass

Chill out: Dip back into the cool Calibrate Cycle with a quiet pause. It's time to go solo.
☐ Read a book, meditate, or take a nap.

Tools and Techniques

- ◎ The critic
- ◎ The muse
- ◎ Letter writing
- ◎ Your ideal reader

Chapter Ten Activities

Capture the Critic

🕐 50 minutes

Let's cozy up to the critic. Let's see their warts and fangs, and we'll listen to their complaints. Next, we'll name them, then finally, we'll write them a love letter.

Step 1: Prepare

5 minutes

☐ Pick your poison.

- You might be wondering how the heck to corral the critic. The simplest approach to tracking your imaginary frenemy is to write in your journal in a question-and-answer format OR you may choose to simply write the critic a letter. (Another option is to do a voice recording and then transcribe it.)

Tip: Use a special color for the critic, so you know these are the critic's words. (Does your critic have a signature color?)

☐ Gather your supplies.

- Your Field Notes Writing Tracker is the perfect place to write down your observations.
- Time and place.
- Assess your state of mind. Is now the right time?
- You will need to be well rested, nourished, and have a clear head.
- Going toe to toe with your critic requires strength. Consider your ability to process information.
- If you are in crisis or exhausted, it is not the right time.
- Schedule it and give them fair warning.

Tip: Avoid spontaneity. Usually, the critic hates surprises.

☐ Set the Mood.

- Create a pleasant experience with candles, soothing music, or a yummy beverage. Be someplace where you feel free to experience emotions.

☐ Begin with a body check-in.

Step 2: Describe your critic in detail.   10 minutes

Consider these questions.

☐ What are your critic's concerns?

- What is worrying them?
- What are they afraid might happen?
- What do they value? What do they fear?
- Write down any messages they have for you.
- What emotions are most alive in this creature?

☐ What do they look and sound like?

- Are they all human or part creature?
- Do they have defining characteristics? Such as fangs, talons, horns, or a tail?
- What do they wear?
- What does their voice sound like? What's their catchphrase?

☐ What's their routine?

- How and where do they spend their days and nights?
- What is their habitat?
- When do they show up?
- Are they a night owl or an early bird?
  Tip: Usually, they are the opposite of what you are.
- What gives them energy? What do they hunt?
- How can they be satisfied? Distracted? Appeased?

☐ What are their special skills? Magical qualities? Graduate degrees?

☐ Does your critic remind you of anyone?

☐ What's your critic's tell?

- Like even the best poker player, your critic has something that will tip you off when they're bluffing. What's their tell?

Step 3: Review and reflect.   7 minutes
☐ Read what you've written.

- What patterns and themes do you notice?

- What topics interest them?
- What insecurities or fears have they tapped?
- Is there a rant running on repeat?
- Have they recycled a story from your past?

Step 4: Give the critic a name.   3 minutes

☐ If a name doesn't spring to mind, give them a nickname.

- The name can be silly or serious.
- We are building a relationship, so be kind.
- Examples: cutie pie, silly goose, tiger

Step 5: Write a love letter to the critic. Consider these topics.   7 minutes

☐ Thank them for looking out for you.

☐ Let them know you will set aside time to listen to their concerns.

☐ Affirm what you love about them. It's important to acknowledge their special talents.

☐ Create a boundary. Request they zip it until their presence is requested.

☐ Thank them again for their ideas and let them know you do not accept unsolicited complaints, critiques, and suggestions.

☐ Reassure them you will be available later.

Step 6: Share your observations with a trusted friend or mentor.   13 minutes

While the exercise outlined is a one-on-one operation, ideally this shouldn't be a solo expedition.

☐ Dream Team

- Who has your back? Involve your muse in this process and assemble a dream team. Build in some extra support with a friend or mentor. Human connection helps you get out of your head.
- Check in with your original intention.

- Even with careful planning, you may not achieve the outcome you desire.

Step 7: Bookend with radical self-care. 10 minutes

☐ Order up a refill of Story RX or take yourself on an artist date.

- Consider the eight realms.

Tip: Give the critic an assignment. Help them focus their discerning eyes. Enlist their expertise. Put them to work.

Help Wanted 🕐 25 minutes

Prompt: Create a job description for your muse.

Enlist your muse in the project of preparing to put your work into the world.

Step 1: Explore with word clouds. 5 minutes

☐ Identify the qualities you're looking for in your muse.

Step 2: Synthesize your ideas and create a want ad. 5 minutes

☐ Include

- Job title
- Describe position
- Elaborate on job requirements
- Highlight preferred qualities

Step 3: Read and reflect. 5 minutes

Review your writing.

☐ Record observations in your Field Notes Writing Tracker.

Step: 4: Find an image to represent your muse.   5 minutes

☐ Post a picture of your muse where you write.

Step 5: Dedicate a page to your muse.   5 minutes

Onboard your muse.

☐ Welcome the muse to the team.

☐ Reiterate their duties.

☐ Find a picture of your muse to add to your writing desk or paste it into your journal.

BEHIND THE SCENES: Mean Girls

Like many of my students, Kaili came to me with an idea she'd been kicking around for years. Her dream was to make a short film. She could feel the emotional beats, hear the character's dialogue, and even see flashes of the story, but she hadn't been able to write a first draft. At the outset of the course, all she had was a stack of random images and scraps of paper with snippets of dialogue. I was curious why she was blocked.

Normally, I'd suggest she read scripts to familiarize herself with the medium, but as a working actress she was fluent in the conventions of screenwriting. As an actor, she had also developed an ear for dialogue and an intuitive understanding of story. She had built a career around bringing the words on the page to life, but the responsibility of writing was daunting. Since she'd been reading scripts for years, she knew a good one when she saw it. She confessed the Craft Cycle was intimidating. I warned her not to compare her messy first draft to the polished shoot scripts she'd read over the years. Not only was she holding herself to an unrealistic standard, but she also wasn't allowing space for discovery.

Kaili was wrestling with finding her voice. I assured her a writer's signature style doesn't happen overnight. It requires experimentation, space to make mistakes, and—most importantly—a willingness to play. The first order of business was to infuse the process with collaborate energy. Instead of working on the script, I asked Kaili to personify the critic. I could see she was reluctant, and she later admitted that the exercise had seemed ridiculous, but to her surprise, this activity uncovered important insights. She discovered her critic was a clique of middle-school mean girls.

The exercise revealed that the critic's voice was an echo of the old wound. Kaili remembered how she had been an outsider in middle school and was bullied for being different. She had moved past this experience long ago. She realized she was an artist and didn't even want to fit in. She had matured into a confident adult who embraced her uniqueness, but the writing process had kicked up old insecurities. The noisy jumble of negative voices in her head didn't go away, but now she could discern the different voices and was no longer oppressed by the chorus of snotty jabs.

This epiphany took the critic's power away. Getting to know her critic freed up Kaili to get the words down on the page. She enlisted the mean girls' help. Debbie Downer was a drag, but her eye for problems guided Kaili to areas that needed strengthening. When it came to proofreading, Penny Persnickety was an ace. Finally, Kaili was able to build momentum.

Not long after Kaili completed the course, I came home one day to find a package on my doorstep. I opened the beautifully wrapped bundle to find Kaili's script. After years of dreaming, she'd finally completed the script. As I read it, I was stunned. Each scene moved, the story flowed, and the dialogue felt natural. I had worried that as an actress she might add line readings, but instead she cued the reader with evocative descriptions.

Kaili had spent years getting tripped up on technique, but it was when she broke free of the critic's spell that Kaili finally tapped into her voice. Just weeks later, she found an executive producer to come on board with funding, shot the film that summer, and is now editing the cut.

Facing Feedback

*Summer: When the sun burns bright, it's natural to look
for a shady retreat, but when it's time to collaborate,
there's no more hiding, no more secrets.*

Facing feedback is part of the process, but even criticism from a trusted
guide can chill inspiration and knock the writer off balance. The tools
of the Collaborate Cycle help us connect with our audience. We'll
consider when and how to present work for notes. Harsh words have
prompted many writers to abandon projects or give up entirely, so it
might be tempting to dismiss feedback altogether. Constructive criticism can be destabilizing, so instead of slipping into an abyss of despair,
we'll practice the art of listening and we'll rekindle the creative fire with
"the kind critic" and "the love list."

FIRST THINGS FIRST: Rejection

The first draft is for the writer, but the final draft is for the audience.
So, if you are making work to share with an audience, getting feedback
is essential. A new perspective helps us see our story in a different light
and reveals meaningful insights. Still, even thoughtful comments and
simple questions can derail the writer. It can be enraging to be misunderstood and demoralizing to discover we've missed the mark.

Many brilliant writers have struggled to brush off criticism. The novelist Octavia Butler aptly characterized the pain of rejection as "like being told your child was ugly." Poet and novelist Sylvia Plath fell into debilitating depression when her work was rejected. She once wrote in her journal, "I want to kill myself, to escape from responsibility, to crawl back abjectly into the womb." Tragically, on the cusp of fame, she took her own life.

Author John Steinbeck stated in a journal entry, "I am not a writer. I've been fooling myself and other people." While penning his Pulitzer Prize-winning novel *The Grapes of Wrath*, he wrote in his diary, "I am assailed by my own ignorance and inability . . . Sometimes, I seem to do a little good piece of work, but when it is done it slides into mediocrity." Apparently, even talent doesn't make you immune to 'imposture syndrome.' Ray Bradbury also recognized the perils of facing "the snowstorm of rejections," and he wisely counseled, "The blizzard doesn't last forever; it just seems so."

ACTIVITY: Call in your muse.   ⏰ 25 minutes

☐ Write a note to your muse and invite them to join your next
   writing session.
☐ Make an offering: Light a candle or give them a token of your
   appreciation: a flower, a piece of fruit, a feather, or a prayer.

FACING FEEDBACK

Notes can be a shock to the system. It is no coincidence that the term "feedback" describes the brutally piercing screech of a microphone when it accidentally amplifies itself. The word "feedback" simply means *responses, signals*. It's important to know how to listen to the signals, and it takes practice.

Timing

When is the right time to share your work? Often the closer one gets to completion, the more difficult it is to experience the story with fresh eyes. The words lose meaning. Like saying or writing a word over and over again, what once made sense starts to look strange. Repeatedly rereading a manuscript or watching a cut can dull the senses. When we can no longer see the forest through the trees, it's time for feedback.

Sometimes, when we need an outside perspective the most, the writer and the work may both be in vulnerable states. It is important to be thoughtful when you open yourself up to feedback, but often it's less about when and more about knowing what kind of feedback will be helpful. Understanding which Story Cycle you are moving through will inform what feedback will be most valuable.

If the project is in an early stage, you may be open to a critique of the overall concept, but if you are further along, you may want to focus comments on a specific element, such as dialogue, a scene, or an action sequence. Are you looking for feedback on the content, or do you simply need proofreading? If you don't have capacity, it's time for Story RX.

- If you are in the Craft Cycle, it's time to dot your i's and cross your t's. It might be the right time for expert feedback.
- If you are in the Collaborate Cycle, it may be time to enlist beta readers or it may be better to call in your muse.
- If you are in the Calibrate Cycle, instead of feedback, look to a therapy session or a night out with a friend.

THE ART OF LISTENING

When receiving feedback, your job is to listen. It's the reader's job to respond. The impulse to protect one's writing is good, but during a critique, the goal is to open space for the reader to share their authentic response. Receiving criticism can be highly uncomfortable, but practicing the art of listening will help you sift through feedback to find gems.

Calibrate with Why?

There are infinite ways to approach a subject, so before soliciting feedback, get clear on your motivation. Calibrate your compass and reconnect to why you want an outside opinion. Also revisit your *why*. When you clarify your intention, you know where you are headed, so you'll recognize notes that will take you off course. Your destination may change, but the change needs to be consistent with your purpose.

- Why does this story matter to you?
- What's driving you to tell this story?

Yes, And . . .

It can feel counterintuitive to listen to criticism without defending your choices, but this helps you really hear what someone is saying. Energize the process with the cultivate technique "Yes, and . . ." Just as this reliable rule of improv keeps a scene going, the "Yes, and . . ." framework builds the energy and opens the space for the reader to share candidly but constructively. Ask your reader:

- What pulled you in?
- What did you want more of?
- What else did you notice?
- Can you say more?

Remember: Don't explain or defend. Always thank them for their time and feedback.

It may feel counterintuitive to listen to criticism without explaining or defending your choices, but adopting an open stance helps you hear what someone is saying. Listen.

Diagnose

The heart of the art of listening is discernment. Sometimes beta readers offer brilliant insights, but other times their notes wildly miss the mark. When a reader doesn't accurately diagnose the problem, they will offer a misguided solution. Before disregarding a note, take time to unpack their observations, so *you* can properly diagnose the problem. Remember, just because something isn't working doesn't mean it can't work.

Before you assess the value of a note, ferret out more information.

- Tell me more . . .
- Yes, and what else did you notice?
- That's interesting. Can you say more?
- I hear that, and I'm taking note. What else?

The Note Below the Note

Most people are not trained on how to critique, so the writer needs to decode the reader's response. Sometimes teachers articulate notes clearly, but not always. Even experienced executives may not be skilled at giving notes. Stories come alive when the reader feels something, so look for where the reader experiences emotion. Sometimes a reader might be angry with a character or feel sad about something that happens. This isn't necessarily a bad thing. It might mean you haven't brought the story to a satisfying conclusion, but it's a good sign when readers respond emotionally.

The most reliable barometer is the emotional experience of a reader. Notice where the reader feels a connection to the story and when they feel something, be it love or hate.

- Listen for emotion.
- Listen for themes in notes.
  - Notice the hot spots where multiple readers respond.
- Listen to what's said and also what isn't said.
  - If a reader doesn't like a scene, dig deeper.
  - What's missing?
- Find out what the reader expected.
  - Did they want more action, romance, or mystery?
  - Does this align with the story you want to tell?

When you understand what's motivating their notes, you can decide if that's something you want your story to deliver. We want the reader to feel a connection to the story, but your story isn't for everyone, and that's okay. Does the reader even like the genre you've written? Even a well-intentioned reader might offer a derailing opinion born out of their disinterest in a subject.

I remember when one reader suggested I turn a script into a musical. This seemed like a ridiculous note. I had no interest in making a musical and didn't understand what he was getting at. Looking back, I can now see he had picked up on the story's raucous, bawdy humor. His note was about pushing the comedy even more over the top. If I had been writing a novel rather than a script, I would have wanted to listen more closely to this feedback. Since I was both the writer and the director, I was able to pump up the camp in the story by using bold colors in the production design, cheeky cinematography, and dramatic editing. It's the author's job to sift through the notes.

This manuscript of yours that has just come back from another editor is a precious package. Don't consider it rejected. Consider that you've addressed it 'to the editor who can appreciate my work,' and it has simply come back stamped 'Not at this address.' Just keep looking for the right address.

—Barbara Kingsolver

What's Working?

Only focusing on what we need to change can be overwhelming, so also solicit positive feedback. Not only is it easier to listen when we feel loved and appreciated, but also we're more able to discern valuable information to know what works. Help redirect the reader and find out what aspects of the story they connect to.

When something is working, it may feel so natural that it is unremarkable to the reader. The reader may not bother to acknowledge that you've captured the theme, created the tone, or set the mood. Use these questions to guide the conversation.

- What draws you in?
    - What do you want more of?
    - What themes are interesting?
    - Which story elements pull you in?
- Where do you feel emotion?
    - Where do you connect to the material?
    - When do you care about these characters?
- What's confusing?
- Tell me more . . .
    - *Yes, and* what else did you notice?

Note: Don't force answers to every question; instead, open space for observations.

Pick Wisely

Be thoughtful about who you share your work with. Before jumping into bed with any old beta reader, consider your objective. By understanding your goals, you can guide the reader and set parameters. Just as motivation helps the writer cultivate character, it's useful for the writer to examine their motivations. This can guide us toward the right reader.

A word of caution: Even the people who love us may not be the best beta readers—including friends and partners. The opinions of our loved ones are powerful, so proceed with caution.

Ménage à Trois

If possible, get notes from three readers at a time. This way, you can see themes and patterns. For example, one scene or element might draw vastly different reactions. I recall one round of notes on a feature script. One reader said the first act was great, but he thought the story fell apart in the second act. Another reader said they found the first act confusing, but as soon as we got to the second act, the script was fantastic. Similarly, when I gave this book to beta readers, one thought there should be more "behind the scenes" stories and fewer exercises. Another reader recommended I include fewer "behind the scenes" stories and more exercises. By getting multiple points of view, I was better able to evaluate notes and find the right balance.

Cat-titude

Sometimes a reader has an important observation but delivers the feedback in an unhelpful way. Beware of cat-vomit-caliber comments. This is the technical term for notes that are reactive, unmanageable, and delivered with cat-titude. Cat-vomit comments are never sugar-coated and are usually rude. Feline feedback may begin playfully (while perhaps overly energetic), but without warning, the session turns wild and destructive. Your mild-mannered friend is now possessed with cat-titude.

The hallmark of a cat-vomit comment is a wholesale rejection of the material. Sometimes a reader will fail to digest and process your writing. Often their response has nothing to do with your writing, and they may harp on something insignificant or even nonexistent. This overpowering assessment has a stinky, sour smell.

Trust your senses. If you smell cat-vomit-caliber comments, you don't need to let your work be torn apart. This is not the time to collaborate on solutions. If you query for clarification, it's more likely that they'll sink in their claws or ceremoniously gift you with purr-fect ideas (usually in the form of a dead rodent or mauled bird). When you're dealing with a solitary hunter, your best hope is the pussy will get bored and take a nap.

When you get a whiff of a shitstorm brewing, and you suddenly find everything about your material nauseating, it's time to call in the kind critic.

MEET THE KIND CRITIC

During the revision process, it's natural to focus on the problems, but if you only look at what needs to be fixed, you may become overwhelmed. After receiving feedback, call in the kind critic. It is especially important to bring that sense of awe to early drafts. When your work is messy and imperfect, take time to recognize the fruits of your labor. Invite the kind critic to join the conversation.

Wonder

It may be difficult to have a sense of wonder after rereading and rewriting. In fact, a common phenomenon is that the closer we get to being

FEEDBACK SURVIVAL GUIDE

Here are the five essentials to surviving whatever criticism comes your way.

1. Practice the art of listening.

2. Enlist the kind critic.

3. Calibrate with the love list.

4. When it's time for readers, go for a ménage à trois.

5. Tune into the Story Cycle you are moving through.

done, the less awe the material inspires. It's a bit like parenting a teenager on the cusp of adulthood. Most parents will tell you when it's time for their young adult to leave the nest—even your darling daughter may start getting on your nerves. There's even a scientific name for this struggle: it's called "parent-offspring conflict." Repulsion or clinging are both natural responses to the important rite of passage of letting go. When it's time to send your creation into the world, you might feel fed up with its flaws or protective of its imperfections.

ACTIVITY: Fan Club   ⏰ 10 minutes

Before seeking feedback, reclaim your sense of wonder.

- ☐ Use freewriting to explore.

    Prompt: Wow, you created that!

- ☐ Consider these questions:

    What would the president of your fan club say?

    What hurdles have you overcome?

    Detail your discoveries and victories.

    What do you love about your story?

- ☐ Review and reflect.

    Review your writing and pick out five affirming compliments.

- ☐ Write those affirmations in your Field Notes Writing Tracker.

THE LOVE LIST

Call in your muse and challenge her to find reasons to love your project. The love list isn't simply an emotional pick-me-up; it helps you reconnect to your story. Just like a tuning fork helps you find a perfect

Only one attitude enabled me to move ahead. That attitude said, 'Rejection can simply mean redirection.'

—Maya Angelou

note, the love list shows you when you've hit the mark. Acknowledge the elements you care about. Rediscover what matters.

I recall a tough critique of a pilot I wrote. The reader's comments were solely focused on faults. The reader was a former studio executive and a working television writer. I had wanted her to compliment the work and encourage me, but she exclusively highlighted what wasn't working and delivered the critique in excruciating detail. I knew there was value in her feedback, but my confidence was upended. My inner critic went into overdrive, and I wanted to burn it all to the ground. I tried to calibrate, but I couldn't even get in touch with my *why*. The criticism felt insurmountable. I wanted to abandon the project and crawl under a rock.

Luckily, I crossed paths with the reader a few days later. She greeted me with a warm smile and after the niceties of small talk, she asked how the rewrite was going. I dodged the question and she unexpectedly added, "I hope you keep going. You had a lot of good ideas."

This tiny drop of positivity satiated my intense longing for praise and momentarily broke the hold of the debilitating impostor syndrome. I realized she had never said to give up—*I* had. It was time to make a love list.

Kill Your Darlings

Inevitably, cuts must be made. It's often said that a draft is never finished, only abandoned. Some writers describe the editing process as the time when we must kill our darlings. If you find yourself unable to edit, it's time to enlist your muse. Take a moment to honor that brilliant scene, fabulous character, or hilarious dialogue. Celebrate and appreciate before you exterminate. Maybe a scene isn't working yet, but perhaps you've nailed the setting description. Screenwriters need to adhere to strict formatting rules, so it is worth celebrating when you've managed to distill the action into a lean passage.

In addition to evaluating the words on the page, notice progress. Perhaps you've sorted out a timeline issue or uncovered a character's secret. Transitions and effective corner turns are examples of creative choices that are easily overlooked. Perhaps you had started the scene much too early in a previous draft and, in this draft, you chose to start the scene later. While it may not be evident to a new reader, finding the point of entry in a scene is a victory. Notice the problems you've resolved.

Notice what you love about your idea and intention. Even when something hasn't fully come together, you may have unearthed a valuable discovery. Slow down and savor the tiny morsels of good. This will help you understand the flavors that you want to amplify. It's even worth loving the bits that aren't working. Sometimes just taking a moment to appreciate what you like will help you let go and make space for something new.

If you find yourself slipping into a slump, remember that your emotional reactions are often rooted in your affection for the project.

WAYS TO LOVE

Here are different aspects of your work to appreciate. No detail is too small.

- Character
    A description, trait, or name; a character's entrance or exit
- Dialogue
    A line that's authentic or funny; banter that flows
- Action
    A specific moment like an interaction, a meeting, or a juicy conflict
- Prose
    A vivid description, a turn of phrase, language
- Setting
    A discovery about the world of the story, a promising location, a little detail that brings forward the period
- Intention
    The project concept, a kernel of an idea, theme

ACTIVITY: Write a Love List

30+ minutes

Find at least twenty ways you love your project.

See the end of the chapter for step-by-step instructions.

RECAP: Facing Feedback

Sharing your writing is an important part of the process, but putting work into the world can be scary. Criticism is valuable, but it can be hard to decipher notes. So, fire up the Collaborate Cycle with the love list and the kind critic. Practicing the art of listening will help you unearth authentic responses during critiques. Calibrating with *why* helps you face feedback by reconnecting to your intention.

Calibrate Your Compass

Time is on your side: Imagine you have all the time in the world. What would your day look like?

☐ Put something fun on your action list.

Tools and Techniques

◎ Facing feedback
◎ The art of listening
◎ The love list
◎ The kind critic

Chapter Eleven Activities

Write a Love List   ⏰ 30+ minutes

Find at least twenty ways you love your project. Remember, for this exercise, no detail is too small. Search for the aspects to appreciate.

Step 1. Take time to notice what you love and identify specific details.

For example, consider the following:

- ☐ The process
- ☐ The characters
- ☐ Character detail or trait
- ☐ Authentic dialogue
- ☐ A particular line of dialogue
- ☐ A specific moment
- ☐ The period of the story
- ☐ The world of the story
- ☐ Emotional moment [sad, scary, funny]
- ☐ The tone or mood

- ☐ Theme
- ☐ Character name
- ☐ Tension
- ☐ Vivid description
- ☐ Smooth transition
- ☐ The entry point of a scene
- ☐ A resolution
- ☐ Intriguing secret or mystery
- ☐ The intention behind the project
- ☐ Compelling element

Challenge yourself to find at least one thing you love on every page of your piece.

Step 2. Review and reflect.

Read over your love list and record observations in your journal.

Step 3. Highlight.

Select three highlights about your process and add those to your journal.

BEHIND THE SCENES: Darling Husband

Jane is one of the most gifted writers I know. She had nearly completed the rough draft of her novel, a hilarious and soulful romantic comedy. It was Jane's first novel, and while it wasn't quite complete, I was sure she would make it to the finish line. She had graduated summa cum laude from an Ivy League school with a degree in creative writing. She'd been published in anthologies, she'd performed her work to sellout crowds, and she was regularly invited to perform her monologues around town.

Jane, being a performer and a writer, was used to workshopping material, and she was a pro at taking feedback. She had mapped out what would happen and was ready to bring all the threads together. She always read the work aloud so she could get fired up to write the final climactic scene.

Before we had the opportunity to meet up, Jane jumped at the chance to share the opening chapter with her new husband, Dick. Jane and Dick were very much in love. She adored him and valued his opinion. Dick wasn't a writer, but what he lacked in experience he made up for with confidence. Even though he never put pen to page, Dick fancied himself a wordsmith.

Jane read the first few pages, then Dick interrupted with a friendly suggestion. Jane asked what he thought. His response was "Meh." Jane bravely encouraged him to say more. He couldn't articulate his thoughts, but she pressed him to share honestly. He proceeded to pick apart the first paragraph word by word. In jest, she suggested he try to rewrite it.

To her surprise, Dick took the challenge seriously. That evening he dug into a rewrite. He edited the manuscript document (without bothering to track changes.) For the next few days, Dick tinkered, and Jane listened to him tapping away at the keyboard. Finally, Dick showed her his handiwork. As she read through the changes, Jane marveled at Dick's beautiful descriptions and eloquent language.

I was baffled. There hadn't been anything wrong with her prose, and the opening chapter had been riveting. Her draft barely needed a copy edit. Even if she wanted to adopt his changes, I encouraged her to work through the ending rather than circling back to do a page-one line edit. She was convinced he was a much better writer than she was. To be charitable, I conceded that the small section Dick had rewritten contained some beautiful sentences, but I also noted that now the story dragged. His flowery descriptions sucked the energy out of the scene.

On a mission to make it more beautiful, Jane attacked the draft. It wasn't long before she was utterly dejected. The skilled writer that she is, Jane had been able to mimic Dick's literary style, but it didn't feel right. I suggested that she stick with her own voice and stressed that the opening hadn't needed a rewrite. I explained, even if his prose were lovely, his style wasn't her voice and didn't work for the playful comedy of errors.

I didn't want to speak ill of her husband, but I delicately suggested that he had overstepped. It wasn't his story after all. In her eyes, Dick could do no wrong. They were still in the honeymoon phase of the relationship, and she simply could not see fault in what he had done, even if this meant she was rejecting her own voice. Slowly, her confidence had eroded, and she questioned the validity of the concept.

Jane abandoned the project and moved on to a new idea. Dick was a decent writer, but a nightmare beta reader. While he may not have meant to crush her spirit, he did. Looking back, I wish I had suggested the love list.

Story RX

Summer: It's time to stop and smell the flowers. Behold the bloom.

Play ignites the imagination and sparks possibilities, but sometimes too many possibilities. Even the most carefully nurtured seeds may not sprout. Setting a project aside can feel like failure, but it's impossible to bring every idea to fruition. Honor the expansive Collaborate Cycle by learning when to let go and when to refill your cup. To handle the heat of the summer, make time for self-care.

FIRST THINGS FIRST: The Ebb

You will have projects that ebb more than they flow. You will have great ideas that fall by the wayside. You will have projects that die and come back to life. Even if we logically know it's impossible to bring every idea to life, it can be emotional to abandon an idea. You might even experience grief when you put a project to the side.

STORY RX

When you feel depleted, lost, or stuck, it is time to refill your cup. There are so many ways to rejuvenate. Simply ask, *What sparks joy?* Julia Cameron, in her seminal book, *The Artist's Way*, invites writers to go on "Artist Dates."

Story RX is a prescription for a dose of art: watch a movie, visit a museum, or read a book. You might decide to dabble in another creative practice like painting, gardening, cooking, or knitting. It can relate to your story but doesn't need to. Choose something that feels easy and/or fun. How will you refill your cup?

ACTIVITY: Story RX   ⏰ 30+ minutes

It's time to refill your prescription. Make time for a little Story RX.

Step 1. Consult the Story RX and select a treatment.   20 minutes

☐ Review the doctor's note and consider which therapy is needed.
- Media meditation
- Sound bath
- Terra therapy
- Art therapy
- Lotions and potions

☐ Book a fifteen-minute therapy session.

☐ Time to dose!

Step 2. Review and reflect.   5 minutes

☐ After a dose of Story RX, write about the experience in your Field Notes Writing Tracker.
- Any new story discoveries or ideas?
- Any insights into the process?
- How did it feel?

Step 3. Book a follow-up.

☐ Review your writing and schedule your next Story RX session.
Repeat as necessary.

Download
Story RX

Sascha Brown Rice, S.D.
Story Doctor
Muse & Moon
911 Inspiration Road, Writingtown, CA

Story RX

Date: _____

Take at least one:

- ☐ Media Meditation
- ☐ Sound Bath
- ☐ Terra Therapy
- ☐ Art Therapy
- ☐ Lotions & Potions

DOSE: Take daily or as needed. For best results, combine.
If unable to tolerate the recommended dose, try micro-dosing.

If condition worsens, supplement treatment with:

- ☐ Good Cry
- ☐ Healing Touch
- ☐ Chill Pill
- ☐ Day Off
- ☐ Retail Therapy
- ☐ Field Trip

Doctor's Note

1. MEDIA MEDITATION
   - ○ IMMERSION: SOAK IN MEDIA STREAM (DECADENT, DELIGHTFUL, AND FUN)
   - ○ HOMEOPATHIC: CONSUME A SHORT FILM, POEM, OR PIN ON PINTEREST.
2. SOUND BATH
   - ○ LISTEN TO MUSIC, MAKE MUSIC, OR ATTEND A SOUND BATH.
   - ○ CREATE YOUR OWN "WALK-UP MUSIC." PLAY THE HYPE MUSIC BEFORE YOU WRITE.
3. TERRA THERAPY
   - ○ SPEND TIME LOOKING AT CLOUDS, STAR GAZING, OR WATCH THE SUNSET.
   - ○ TRY FOREST BATHING, HIKING, OR VISIT A BEACH, GARDEN, OR NATURE PRESERVE.
4. ART THERAPY
   - ○ GOOF AROUND WITH A DIFFERENT ART MEDIUM: PAINTING, CRAFTING, CALLIGRAPHY.
   - ○ GATHER A BANK OF IMAGES THAT INSPIRE AND COLLAGE.
5. LOTIONS AND POTIONS
   - ○ INDULGE IN A BUBBLE BATH, FACE MASK, A MANI-PEDI, MASSAGE, OR HOT TUB SOAK.

Side effects may include: joy, serenity, inspiration, laughter, inner bliss, creative flow.

Uses: writer's block, premise envy, plot allergies, congestive art failure, creative constipation, story dysmorphia, protective author syndrome, character detachment disorder, general funk, malaise, art-thritis dialogue diarrhea, completion phobia, itchy cliché, bacterial backstory, cracked motive, superlative fever, analogy ulcers, chronic indecision, goal stones, obsessive confusion disorder, bloated scene, style decay, conflict sores, loss of senses, thematic anemia, inflammation of the inner Critic, mild-to-moderate procrastination, resolution aphasia, hema-tone, hypo-POV, bacterial mansplaining, gastro-trite-ice, doubt, chronic idea overwhelm, muse-on-pause.

If condition persists, seek a story professional.

Sach Brn Ri

_____
Signature

SHOOTING RATIO

There are underwriters and overwriters. Both approaches work and knowing your tendency can help you navigate the process. Overwriters generate loads of material, while underwriters have a lean approach. Do you tend towards brevity, or do you love to ramble?

Similarly, each filmmaker has a different "shooting ratio." The shooting ratio describes the proportion of film shot versus the amount included in the final product. Some directors follow a "less is more" approach and give actors only one or two "takes." Other filmmakers like to play and explore, and they may run through over sixty takes. Stanley Kubrick was known for the grueling number of takes he required. Documentarians often shoot tens or even hundreds of hours of content, even when making only a ninety-minute film.

Under and Over

I'm an overwriter. I love to tinker, experiment, and write my way to clarity. I always generate way more material than I use. The revision process for the overwriter requires cutting the excess, while the underwriter needs to embellish and expand. When I wrote the first draft of this book, I gleefully crammed in every idea I ever had about the creative process. The draft was stuffed with exercises and activities. The end result was deliciously abundant but unwieldy. Even though this approach sometimes feels ridiculously inefficient, this method helps me build momentum. Trying to be tidy shuts down my creativity.

Knowing your "shooting ratio" will help you make peace with your process. If overwriting sounds stressful or insane, you are probably an underwriter. Both styles are valid, and no matter where you fall on the spectrum, relax into your natural tendency. Especially during the early phases of drafting, stick with a process that resonates. There's no perfect path.

If you chronically make unreasonable demands, you will burn out or give up. Sometimes it's better to do less.

Holding On and Letting Go

The writer needs to water and weed the garden. When we cultivate, we plant lots of seeds. But overcrowding will inhibit growth, so in addition to pruning, we need to thin the seedlings to create ample spacing for your project to thrive. You will have great ideas that fall by the wayside. You will have projects that die and come back to life. Which project will you nurture?

How do we know when to hold on and when to let go? Is it time to push through or move on? Expand or contract? Where should you put your attention? Is it time to jump ship or seek a safe harbor to wait out the storm? Is it the ebb or the end? A dose of Story RX helps you recharge and also gives you perspective. When you are rested, you are better able to assess the best course of action.

Tackling too much at once is a common mistake during the Craft Cycle. I love multitasking, but sometimes by trying to do too much at once, I end up doing nothing at all. It's not uncommon to tinker with different story elements at one time, but toggling between objectives can be unproductive. Once I'm rested, I can better assess what's realistic.

When we pause, we neutralize the critic. When the writer is nourished, they are less likely to fall for the critic's "blood, sweat, and tears" sob story. Clinging to an element that no longer works is a common stumbling block during the Craft Cycle. The critic praises your hard work and insists the only way forward requires blood, sweat, and tears. The critic loves to cheer you on as you try to push a square peg into a round hole. Then the critic uses the failure as evidence that the idea is junk— or worse, the critic trashes the idea and demands we begin again.

If the critic says, "Try harder!" it's time to pause and calibrate. Maybe you need a different tool for the job, so don't wear yourself down by applying a technique that isn't appropriate. Pause and evaluate. Consider your capacity. Maybe your eyes were bigger than your stomach. If you chronically make unreasonable demands, you will burn out or give up. Sometimes it's better to do less.

We won't bring every idea to life, and even the most carefully nurtured seeds may not sprout. Do you need a break, or is it time to buckle down? Sometimes it's just a matter of letting go of an expectation about the timing, the end goal, or even a feeling.

Let it Go   55+ minutes

What can you let go of?

  * See the end of the chapter for step-by-step instructions.

RECAP: Make Peace with the Process

Stop to smell the flowers and enjoy the expansive collaborate cycle. When the summer cycle gets too hot, take time to refill your cup. Even the most carefully nurtured seeds may not sprout. Learn when to hold on and when to let go.

 Calibrate Your Compass

> Summer fling: Put the writing to the side and dabble in another medium.
>   ☐ Pick up a paintbrush, bake a cake, or doodle all day.

Tools and Techniques

  ◎ Story RX
  ◎ Holding on and letting Go
  ◎ Overwriters and underwriters

Chapter Twelve Activities

Let it Go

⏰ 55+ minutes

It's hard to know when to hold on and when to let go. Do you need a break, or is it time to buckle down? Where should you put your attention? What can you let go of?

Step 1. Put your cards on the table.   15 minutes

Use list making to identify your options, obstacles, and opportunities.

☐ If you're trying to decide which project to prioritize, list the options.
   • List the various projects.
   • List the possible permutations and next steps.

☐ List the obstacles and opportunities.
   • What are your expectations?
   • What's tripping you up?
   • What are you afraid of?
   • What are you hoping for?
   • What does your critic have to say?

Tip: If the critic has a nagging question, just jot it down on your question list. This way, your critic will feel confident it won't be forgotten, and you can focus on the big picture.

Step 2. Wander and walk away.   24-72 hours

Calibrate with a dose of Story RX. The Collaborate Cycle is all about connection. Bask in the sunshine of love and leisure. Reset with connection.

☐ Walk away.
   Even if for one day, put the project to the side. If possible, take a few days off.

☐ Wander.
   • Take yourself on an artist date.
   • Spend time in nature and with friends.

Step 3. Review and reflect. 20 minutes

Revisit the cards on the table. Now that you've taken time to recharge, reconsider the options, opportunities, and obstacles.

- ☐ Ask, *What am I making it mean?*
  - Sometimes the issue isn't the issue.
  - Lean into the emotion and ask, What am I making it mean?

- ☐ Is the noise the critic's making even related to your project?
  - Is the material triggering an old trauma?
  - Look at the context. Is the critic responding to something in real life?
    Ask, Is something happening with my health, the weather, the world, or a family member?

- ☐ Ask, *Do I agree?*
  - Is that a valid concern? Is it something to consider later?
  - What if everything you're doing is fine?
    - What if your pace is perfect? What if you are exactly right on schedule? What if you aren't doing anything wrong? What if you aren't lacking? What if you have what you need?

Step 4. Discard. 10 minutes

- ☐ What can you let go of?
  Shed and release options, opportunities, or obstacles.
  - Let go of an idea.
  - Let go of the timeline.
  - Let go of the relationship.
  - Let go of the reward.
  - Let go of the feeling.
  - Let go of an outcome.

Step 5. Ask *how*, not *if* . . . 10 minutes

- [ ] Ask, *How can I resolve this?*
  If it's time to suit up, then don't get mad at the rain; grab some gear.
  - What do you need?
  - Do you need support? Call in a mentor or the muse.

- [ ] Assess your capacity.
  - Look at your calendar and see what's possible now.
  - How many hours per week can you dedicate to your writing practice?
  - Be conservative. It's better to under-promise and over-deliver.

- [ ] Look at the next two weeks and identify pockets of time.
- [ ] Add these writing sessions to your calendar.
  Even if you only plan to write for ten or fifteen minutes, make an appointment and add that to your schedule.

* *Be realistic. Consider work, family, health, and recreation.*

The artist date is a "festive, solo expedition to explore something that interests you. The artist date need not be overtly 'artistic'—think mischief more than mastery. Artist dates fire up the imagination. They spark whimsy. They encourage play. Since art is about the play of ideas, they feed our creative work by replenishing."

—Julia Cameron

BEHIND THE SCENES: The Bachelorette Party

As the spectacular New Mexico sky stretched endlessly across the horizon, my stomach ached. I tried to forget about the email I'd just read. For the first time in three years, I had left my documentary project behind. It was the first day of my vacation, and the plan had been to be gloriously away from it all, unplugged and out of range. I had traveled to New Mexico for the wedding of one of my best friends. Even though I now lived in Los Angeles, I had volunteered to cohost Kate's bachelorette party and was looking forward to being back in New Mexico.

I had planned the trip almost a year ago, and I needed the break more than I expected. I had just completed what I thought was a solid cut of my film. This was my second feature but my first documentary. Piecing together my grandfather's story began as a wonderful adventure, but it had turned into an epic trek. It felt like I would never finish.

The stakes felt high. I always knew the film would be political. It was a story about a politician, but when I set out to make the movie, the Brown family was out of the public eye, which is where I wanted to be. However, while I was making the film, Uncle Jerry increasingly showed up in the headlines, unexpectedly, pulling the documentary into the limelight. It was becoming relevant in a way that most filmmakers hope their work will be, but I had felt more comfortable off the radar. I wasn't ready for this deeply personal project to be so visible. The magnitude of the responsibility had set in.

I desperately wanted to reach the finish line. The stink of the notes lingered. The latest round of feedback revealed that I had miles to go, but I was determined to enjoy the vacation. I didn't have a roadmap, but I knew I needed to set the project aside and have a little fun. Here's the first rule of finishing:

Wander and walk away.

I just needed to give myself time to process the feedback. I needed a reset.

I was disoriented and demoralized, but I told myself this Taos adventure would be training to face the rugged terrain on the road to finishing. I couldn't see the solution, and I didn't know how I would weave the story together, but that was okay. For now, it was time to walk away and wander. I would return to work renewed and refreshed.

I thought I was ready for feedback, but it felt like I had been helicoptered into a jungle and left naked and alone. All I had was a grain of rice and half a map . . . and, of course, the map was to some other faraway place.

Feedback has weight when it's from someone you love, and it's especially hard to metabolize when you think you're nearing the home stretch, but instead, you find there's another steep climb ahead. This wasn't going to be a quick fix. I had known I would need to rewrite the narration, but the structure wasn't working. We'd need to shoot more interviews and spend more time in the edit room. This meant we had to raise more money. It was painful to accept, but the finish line was much further than I had expected.

I tried to force myself to forget about the notes, but the toughest feedback wasn't from any random person; it was from the film's executive producer who was also my older sister. I thought back to when I'd asked Hilary to come on board the film. There were so many reasons, but most of all, I wanted her on the team because I trusted her. I hadn't considered how deeply I wanted my sister's approval. Here's the next rule on the road to completion:

Spend time in nature and with friends. When you hit a milestone like completing a draft, wrap yourself in love and get out of town or at least manifest a change of scenery.

Finally, it was the day of the bachelorette party. I barreled down the rural Taos highway with Pamela, my other bestie. Since I had moved back to California, it had been far too long since we had spent time together in person. Just being with her was a serotonin boost. Throughout the filmmaking process, Pamela had been my faithful champion and stalwart defender. No matter what the drama, she was always one hundred percent on my side. I had pushed the notes out of my mind. We gabbed, sighed, squealed, laughed, and I was blissfully transported into the present.

As we passed the Taos Gorge, I fell under the spell of the vast, intoxicating New Mexico landscape, the Land of Enchantment. Having the party in the middle of nowhere suddenly seemed like a great idea. This was going to be fun. We twisted along the mountain pass, and I surrendered to the rustic rural vibes. The exquisite palate of colors soothed me. The dramatic rise of the mountains on the horizon reminded me that the world is big and beautiful, and my film was but a grain of sand in the cosmic order of it all. I relaxed into a forgotten space: the world outside the narrative of my film.

As we turned off the main road, the journey to reach destination-bachelorette-party became a metaphor for completing my documentary. Just like the bumpy road to the party, the creative process could be rugged. I didn't need to worry about the film. I just needed to stay the course.

I turned the map upside down and sideways. We tried to decipher the chicken scratching. Was it before or after the cow pasture? Was *that* the right field, or was it one of the dozen fields before? The Taos Bachelorette Cohost had assured us the yurt cabin would be easy to find, but the road seemed to be taking us nowhere.

Storm clouds gathered, and an epic shadow crawled across the road. The veil of serenity lifted. I caught myself thinking about the film, worrying and trolling for answers. A dark feeling spread throughout my body. If this was a metaphor for finishing the film, what would it mean if we couldn't find the destination? Would this mean my instincts were completely wrong? What if I never finished my film? What if I was incapable of finding the story? What if I did finish, and it was terrible? To release a project into the world, I couldn't let that stop me. Rule Three:

Let it go.

The creative journey has twists and turns. Sometimes the best way to move forward is to let go.

I turned my attention to the dusty road and searched the horizon for our addressless destination. Suddenly, Pamela stopped the car in the middle of the narrow road. She was sure we were lost and certain we had missed the turn. I thought we should forge ahead, but she wanted to turn around. She looked at me skeptically.

I closed my eyes, and I heard a tiny voice inside say, *You've got this.* I said aloud, "Trust me." We turned down an obscure, unmarked road, then ambled over the cattle guard, and drove in silence down the rutted road. I held my breath. It was no longer about arriving on time to the party. The symbolism of the journey had raised the stakes for me. In the context of my self-imposed metaphor, everything felt outsized. My greatest ally was doubting me. It felt like a "kick in the teeth," as my grandfather liked to say. I needed to let go. Let go of her approval, let go of certainty, let go of being on time. Let go of having it my way.

Planning the bachelorette party had been a lesson in letting go. I wasn't prepared for the off-the-grid pioneer spirit of my cohost. I had assumed the cohost and I would agree on the basic features of a bachelorette party. I wanted to nail down the date ASAP, but Taos Bachelorette wanted to go with the flow.

Whenever I reached out, she was off the grid. She was snowshoeing, hiking, or maybe off chasing buffalo. Once we finally connected, I proposed we hold the gathering at a restaurant. She informed me it would be at a friend's place. That sounded cool, but then I found out it was under construction and wasn't quite furnished yet. Taos Bachelorette assured me it would be fine. We'd be outside. I had lived in New Mexico before, so I knew August brings monsoon rains. I suggested we make a contingency plan in case there was a downpour. Taos Bachelorette was annoyed and assured me it wouldn't be a problem. Instead of trying to control the situation, I decided I needed to let it go.

I suggested catering, but she insisted on a potluck. I countered that would be tricky for all of us out-of-towners. I could tell she thought I was being fussy, so I relented. I asked for the address to include in the invitation, but she explained that "everybody" knew where it was, and there wasn't exactly an address anyway because it was "just outside of town." I proposed we put together signage to help guide the out-of-towners. She shot down the idea. The subtext was "You're a total LA wuss." There was no use fighting with Taos Bachelorette. Kate had deputized her, and after all, she was now a mountain woman too. I needed to get on board. It was time to adapt. I needed to employ Rule Four:

Don't get mad at the rain; grab some gear.

It was time to suit up. I needed to be ready to adapt.

If it was going to rain, so be it. I made a mental note to pack a rain jacket.

We rounded a thicket of piñon trees, then passed a string of worn Tibetan flags, and voila: we were there. At that moment, I promised myself no matter who doubted me, no matter what slimy self-doubt surfaced, I would finish my film. To move past obstacles, I would stop asking *if* and focus on *how.* I remembered the most important rule of all:

Ask how, not if.

The creative process inevitably includes obstacles. To navigate those beastly hurdles, we need to believe that we can reach our destination.

Not long after the festivities began, the clouds predictably burst, and a torrent of rain drenched the bachelorette party. We piled into the tiny yurt cabin. After a few rounds of margaritas, the divide between the city dwellers and the pioneer women dissolved. We dove into a raucous bout of crafting, and we bonded around our common purpose: a celebration of the bride-to-be.

The party wasn't perfect, but it *was* perfect. It was hilarious, memorable, and the ideal way for me to refill the creative well.

After the bachelorette party, it would be almost twenty more months before I completed the film. I had other dark moments, but taking time to wander and be with friends renewed my faith in the process. Now, whenever I find myself staring bleakly at the ever-receding horizon, I think of the bachelorette party and remind myself of these five rules of the road.

FIVE RULES OF FINISHING

Rule One: Wander and walk away.

Rule Two: Spend time in nature and with friends.

Rule Three: Let it go.

Rule Four: Don't get mad at the rain; grab some gear.

Rule Five: Ask how, not if.

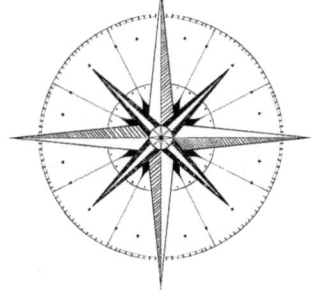

PART IV

Craft

THE FALL CYCLE

The days become shorter.
The world erupts in a bewildering array of colors.
The changes signal a time of transformation.

Days grow darker, death descends, trees lose their leaves.

The veil between the worlds thins, and spirits travel
more freely. Pay tribute to those who came before.
Call upon the ancestors for guidance.

Clear away the debris, gather, inventory, and stock up
on supplies.

Last stop before winter.

The alarm bells should be sounding. Get it done.
The harvest is here.

Revision

Fall: Before the rewards of the harvest, we review, revise, and refine.
The Craft Cycle is a time of turning and returning.

The fall cycle is grounded in pragmatics and offers a cornucopia of tools and techniques. So, when it's time to craft, the writer tinkers with structure, syntax, style, stakes, character, dialogue, point of view, voice, mood, theme, tone, tension, transitions, endings, beginnings . . . oh, my! The sheer number of literary devices makes this cycle demanding. For this reason, we'll begin with strategy. We'll learn how to navigate the mists of maybe, we'll look at the drafting process, and we'll rethink the fundamentals of structure by finding your story's beating heart and spine.

FIRST THINGS FIRST: Decision Fatigue

Making decisions is probably the single most important task of crafting a story. During the generative phase, it's important to stay open to possibilities, but decisions must be made to make it to the finish line. Indecision is a classic critic trick. When you find yourself in a never-ending loop of reworking, the critic has taken over. Jot the question down on your question list and carry on.

Sometimes you have questions that don't need to be answered or can be answered later. A decision may feel important but may be inconsequential. Sometimes we fret over option A versus option B, but it might be a choice between six or half a dozen. If you are unable to move forward, it's time to calibrate. To find clarity reconnect with your *why*. You may be experiencing decision fatigue. You can recharge with self-care or simply by taking a short break.

Even if you're not sure exactly where the story will go, in order to finish, it's critical to keep moving forward. Revision requires making decisions and sometimes, in order to move forward, the writer just needs to make their best guess. Don't get lost in the paralyzing mists of maybe.

MISTS OF MAYBE

If you find you are spinning your wheels, you've fallen victim to the mists of maybe. Revision is an essential step but investigate why you are tinkering. Like most writers, I love to tinker. Part of why we write is the act of writing itself. When I find myself endlessly playing with words, I need to examine the motivation behind why I am tinkering. My writing mentor Caroline likes to ask, *Am I making it better or different?*

If you're just making it different, you might be avoiding completion. The act of making a choice is a daring act, and it will reveal new information.

> Another trap is the belief that everything has to be perfect before you can take the next step. You won't move onto that second chapter until the first is written, rewritten, honed, tweaked, examined under a microscope, and buffed to a bright mahogany sheen . . . it's important to be prepared but at the start of the process, this type of perfectionism is more like procrastination. You've got to get in there and do.
>
> —Twyla Tharp

Walk Through the Door.

We don't always know what's around the corner. Sometimes we need to walk through the door to find out what's next. Before we can evaluate the work, we need to write the end of the story. That said, wrapping up a story isn't always simple. One of the best ways to find your ending is to write it. This may seem obvious, but if you have not written an ending, give it a try.

- It's okay for it to be messy. Let go of pretty and slap together your best effort.
- Instead of wrapping up every detail, write a broad summary of what happens.
- It's even okay if it's a crash landing or even not the "right" ending.

You don't need to be one hundred percent sure it is the right ending. The process of writing will lead to discovery. Stop wondering and start writing. Daydreaming is not writing. Thinking is not writing. Writing requires writing, so write it. You don't need to get it right. It doesn't need to feel good. Just get something on the page.

ACTIVITY: The End   20 minutes

Write an ending to the story.

   * See the end of the chapter for step-by-step instructions.

Pick a Priority.

It's especially important to coordinate and sequence your efforts during the Craft Cycle. Before you begin fine-tuning a scene, you want to be confident that the scene matters. How does it connect to the whole, and will it even make the cut? While discovery writing is an essential part of the process, it may end up on the cutting room floor.

Crafting isn't a science, but the revision process accommodates less improvisation. It's a bit like baking. When you bring all the elements together, there's a little chemistry. Unlike making a stew or blending up a smoothie, baking demands the use of particular ingredients, exact proportions, and a specific step-by-step sequence. Similarly, the exacting nature of craft brings us back to the principle of first things first.

It's nearly impossible to generate material and revise at the same time. When you're still pulling the marble out of the mountain, it doesn't make sense to start sculpting. Writing and rewriting require different techniques and opposite mindsets. That said, some writers find tinkering to be a turn-on, so it might work well to massage as you amass the marble. Even so, to complete a draft, stay focused on the task at hand. When you stray from your objective, pause, calibrate, and return to the priority. If your priority shifts and changes, it's time to consider which type of editing is most appropriate.

TYPES OF EDITING

The three main stages of revision are developmental editing, copy editing, and proofreading. The developmental edit is when we look at the big picture. The writer assesses the overall structure and the completeness and coherence of the content. The developmental edit is the first pass after the messy first draft. Often the story changes as you get to know your characters, but the developmental edit provides scaffolding so you can continue building.

After completing the development edit, the writer shifts their focus to copy editing (sometimes called line editing.) Copy editing is when the writer goes sentence by sentence, smoothing the flow, cleaning up, polishing, and eliminating redundancy. It is natural to tinker with sentences along the way, but it's important to evaluate the project as a whole before getting too caught up in refining. The final stage is proofreading. To proof, the writer goes line by line, word by word. Proofreading is like copy editing, but when we proof, we're laser-focused on SPAG (Spelling, Punctuation, And Grammar).

In addition to these three main editorial phases, the writer will cycle through the draft many times. On occasion, the manuscript needs a housekeeping pass to clean up continuity or a clarity pass to make sure the piece is holding together. An author might also do one lap around the track to make sure historical or technical details are accurate. Sometimes you may want to narrowly concentrate on a specific element like a scene, chapter, or key moment. Other times, your attention might sprawl across the draft to track a specific character.

As the narrative evolves, you will return to the beginning again and again. Knowing where you are in the process will make the revision more efficient and enjoyable.

Pantsers and Plotters

Before exploring structure, take a moment to consider your natural approach to the creative process. Some writers see the plot before they begin, but many writers need to write their way to clarity. In the world of novel writing, these two types are known as pantsers and plotters. A pantser is someone who writes "by the seat of their pants." A plotter takes a more methodical approach and prefers to follow an outline as they draft. Both methods are viable, and it's helpful to know which camp you're in.

Plotting has the advantage of being a more efficient process, and plotter tactics are especially helpful when crafting epic sagas, complex mysteries, and sci-fi fantasies. That said, for many, this linear approach shuts down creativity. Plotters run the risk of never truly starting for fear of getting it wrong. And sometimes, plotters cling to ideas even when the story leads them into new territory.

While plotters might miss out on innovating, a pantser might meander forever, get lost, or lose steam. The pros of pantsing include the joy of making unexpected discoveries, the thrill of tapping into the unconscious, and the freedom of being able to create without a roadmap. Both approaches work. Honor your nature.

If you're like me, you may not identify as one type or the other. I'm a practitioner of what I've dubbed "the mosaic method." I start with a rough sketch. It's not an exact outline but more like a shape. Once I've amassed a quantity of scenes, characters, events, and themes, I inspect all the pieces, revisit the shape, then sort, sift, and assemble. I like to dumpster dive and pick through my freewrites for gems.

ACTIVITY: Pick a process.   ⏰ 15 minutes

What's your natural tendency? Are you a pantser, a plotter, or something in between?

- ☐ Use freewriting to reflect on your process.

  - Do you need to see the plot before you begin, or do you prefer to write your way to clarity?
  - Do you like ideation or prefer getting down to brass tacks?
  - Do you delight in unexpected discoveries or avoid improvisation?
  - Do you prefer following a roadmap or wandering?

- ☐ Review and reflect.

  - Reread your writing. Are you a pantser or a plotter?
  - You don't have to fit in a box. Consider coming up with your own moniker.

THE STORY SPINE

Before sculpting the dramatic arc and fine-tuning the narrative, look for the spine of your story. I first encountered this concept in Linda Seger's book *Making A Good Script Great*. The spine concept makes structure feel alive and malleable. The spine is vital, but we're only skeletons without muscles, ligaments, tendons, and blood. The Story Spine metaphor is flexible yet sturdy. It isn't abstract. It's familiar and tangible.

A story comes alive when it sends a chill down the spine. Instantly, emotion is conjured when we say someone is spineless or has backbone. If we are locked and blocked, the tension can be massaged away and, in dire situations, surgery is an option.

Before sculpting the dramatic arc and fine-tuning the narrative, look for the spine of your story.

X-Ray

Like a spine, when the structure is out of whack, you feel it! It hurts. Desperate to get back in alignment, writers turn to templates, but it can be counterproductive to plot dramatic twists and turns according to a template. This keeps the writer on the surface and is often as futile as rearranging deck chairs on the Titanic. Instead, dive deep. Sort out structure by turning your attention back to character.

Sometimes the inner world of the character can get complicated, making structure feel elusive. So, it might be time for an X-ray. Look at the bones of your story. Make a timeline of key moments in your character's journey. This liberates you from the conventional constraints of outlining but gives you a snapshot of the big picture. This activity shows if there is a break by illuminating a missing setup or a payoff. The physical act of making a timeline is tactile, so it also gets you out of your head.

ACTIVITY: Timeline   30+ minutes

Find your way to (or way back to) structure by making a timeline.

 * See the end of the chapter for step-by-step instructions.

Seven Roads to Revision

Streamline the writing process by clarifying what type of editing you are doing.

1. Developmental edit:
   - ☐ This is a deep dive into the structure and the themes of your narrative. Before you fine-tune, it's typical to evaluate the drafts with an eye on the overall concepts and content. We look at the logical flow and sync up the setups and payoffs.
   - ☐ When evaluating a book manuscript, a developmental edit ensures each chapter is relevant to the book and in the right order, that each section or scene within each chapter leads nicely into the next, and that the reader is guided easily along from paragraph to paragraph.
   - ☐ During this phase, we may move large sections of text around or delete unnecessary material. Similarly, during a developmental pass, we may encounter areas that need expanding or expounding.

2. Copy edit or line edit
   - ☐ A copy edit can include proofreading, but it should be more focused on fine-tuning the language. This is the time to tinker with word choice, imagery, syntax, tone, and style. This is also the time to look for unnecessary repetition and redundancies. Omit needless words!

3. Proofreading:
   - ☐ This is when you deal with all the pesky rules of grammar, spelling, punctuation, and formatting.
   - ☐ I save proofreading for a day when I don't feel up to heavy lifting. If I am working on a different element and I see an error, I'll fix it, but I try not to get too precious about grammar and spelling because I know I will sort it out in a proofing pass. If I know I plan to tend to grammar later, I can focus my attention on other story elements.

4. Housekeeping:
   - ☐ A housekeeping pass focuses on details and continuity.
   - ☐ A continuity pass might simply be a speed-through to check that the characters' names are consistent throughout. Or, if you've reshuffled the sequence of scenes, a continuity pass is in order.
   - ☐ It takes singular focus to check accuracy, like making sure that a character's introduction happens when they actually enter the story.

5. Clarity:
   - ☐ It's helpful to make a focused pass on clarity. Take a break and come back with fresh eyes to see if the work makes sense. What's missing? What's confusing?

6. Characters:
   - ☐ It's worth taking time to tend to each character in a focused pass. When you are working with a one-hundred-thousand-word novel or a one-hundred-page script, it's helpful to isolate each character's journey to make sure there is continuity and a developed arc.

7. Research:
   - ☐ Don't fall down the research rabbit hole. Only research what you absolutely need to move the story forward.
   - ☐ Research can be a fun way to get inspired, but fixing factual details is often a way to procrastinate. Later on, you may make a dedicated pass to assess what needs more background.

RECAP: Drafting

In this chapter, we focus on the editing process and the different types of revision. We also break down the two main approaches to drafting: plotting and pantsing. To liberate ourselves from the conventional constraints of outlining, we look at the spine of your story.

Calibrate Your Compass

Tidy up: Declutter for ten minutes.
- ☐ Clear away debris, salvage scraps, and take inventory.
- ☐ One writer's trash is another writer's treasure. (Refer to the mosaic method.)

Tools and Techniques

- ◎ Pantsers and plotters
- ◎ The mosaic method
- ◎ Story spine

> . . . Setting out to write, if you have the idea of 'literature' in your head, is formidable, intimidating. A plunge in an icy lake. Then comes the warm part: when you already have something to work with, upgrade, edit . . . Let's say it's a mess. . . . As the statue is entombed in the block of marble, the novel is inside your head. You try to liberate it.
>
> —Susan Sontag

Chapter Thirteen Activities

The End
⏰ 20 minutes

Rather than thinking your way to an ending, try writing your way to it. Even if you have no idea how the piece will wrap up, give it a go. Make your best effort to bring the story to a close. Let go of pretty and simply try to resolve all the through lines. If you simply can't get words onto the page, try dictating an ending. Recording can free you up from getting it just right.

Step 1. Key into the emotional tone of the finale. 6 minutes

☐ Make a list of emotions that you'd like the audience/reader to feel. Consult emotion list from Chapter Five.

☐ Describe the tone of the ending.
  • Is it happy or sad?
  • Comedic or tragic?
  • Tidy or mysterious?

Step 2. Next, use list making or word clouds to brainstorm. 4 minutes

☐ Make a list of possible endings.

  • Challenge yourself to think of at least ten possible endings and be sure to have at least three really stupid ideas.
  • Consider what's lost, found, discovered, learned, revealed, destroyed . . .

Step 3. Pick an ending, set a timer, and give it a go. 5 minutes

☐ Sketch the ending. It can be a super messy brainstorm.

Step 4. Review and reflect. 5 minutes

☐ Read through what you've written and look for clues. Was there anything that felt close or important?

Repeat as necessary.

Timeline

Find your way to (or way back to) structure. Stories can span generations, or they can be contained to a single day. Before you sculpt the arc of your story, simply plot the key events. Then map out your story's events in chronological order.

- ☐ Use list making to brainstorm the events in your main character's journey and the key events in the story.

    For this exercise, include even events outside the timeline of the story like birth and death; milestones, like a graduation, a beginning or end of a romantic relationship, a marriage, a divorce, a new job, a move; hardships, like illness, injury, or loss; turning points, like a discovery, an epiphany, etc.

- ☐ After you've made the list, create a chronological timeline.

- ☐ Next, circle the section of the timeline covered in your story.

- ☐ Now look over the timeline and use freewriting to explore what you notice.

    - Are there surprises?
    - Is there a missing setup or payoff?
    - Is there something implied that needs to be included in the story?
    - Is there something in the story that could be implied instead?
    - Look for the peaks and valleys. What are the high points and what are the low points?

Tip: Make the process tactile and take up space. Consider using sticky notes or index cards. Spread out on the floor or use a whiteboard. This makes it easy to play with sequences and takes away the pressure of putting events in the perfect spot.

BEHIND THE SCENES: Endless Summer (A Cautionary Tale)

Veronica came to me with a rough draft of a pilot and a slew of episode ideas. After I read through the material, I was excited to work with her. The script needed work, but she had already amassed a good deal of material, and the concept was compelling. Veronica had a great sense of humor and was bubbling with ideas.

In our first meeting, after we discussed her script, we outlined a twelve-week schedule charting the road to finishing a new draft. Veronica was insulted that I thought it would take her "so long" to revise the draft. I told Veronica we could move faster but that it might take much longer.

At our following meeting, Veronica showed up empty-handed. She said she hadn't followed through on the assignments because she had done some thinking and had reconsidered the notes.

She had new ideas about her character's backstory and dramatic complications. The idea didn't seem wildly better, but she was excited about it, so we pivoted. We agreed on the next steps, but when our next session rolled around, she had dreamed up new plotlines and characters.

I was reluctant to switch courses again, and I gently explained that one of the biggest stumbling blocks is an addiction to ideation. I suggested that perhaps the reason she was spawning ideas was because the inner critic had taken hold. When we finally met up again—yep, you guessed it: she'd done no writing, and she confessed that all my assignments had been worthless. I knew it was no longer Veronica talking. The critic was running the show.

It was at this point that I suggested Veronica work with a different writing coach. She was hurt. She didn't understand. Weren't fear and doubt part of the process? Hadn't I been the one to warn her it would take time? Yes, and one must put pen to page. Writers write. Daydreaming is not writing. Thinking is not writing. Sometimes a bad decision is better than no decision. At a certain point, it's time to stop wandering and start writing. It's okay to make a wrong choice. Before picking apart your ideas, get the words onto the page. Don't get lost in the endless summer.

The Best Story Structure

Fall: Before the harvest, tend the garden. Weed and water.

Structure is a critical element of storytelling, but there isn't a one-size-fits-all approach. The best story structure is the one that feels right to you. The five sequences help the writer tease out the basic plot. We'll distill narrative to its core emotional beats. A story spine is essential, but the story comes alive with a beating heart.

FIRST THINGS FIRST: The Myth of a Universal Formula

Many teachers champion universal formulas, but before boxing yourself, consider the rich diversity of storytelling traditions around the globe. Both the content and the structure of a story reflect cultural beliefs and values. Not all narratives follow a linear track; stories can have multilayered plots, philosophical musings, and interconnected webs of stories.

Middle Eastern literature often features nested narratives in which stories within stories unfold. Many Asian traditions employ a cyclical or episodic structure with an emphasis on finding harmony with nature. Rather than centering a heroic individual, indigenous traditions from Australia and the Americas often elevate a connection to the land, animals, and cosmic forces.

In addition to cultural values influencing a narrative's architecture, stories are also shaped by the medium in which they are expressed. Stories can be shared in pictures, songs, dances, and games—and, of course, the written word. For instance, the griot, a West African story-teller, utilizes rhythm, repetition, and call-and-response patterns.

Western norms are shifting as we become more globally connected. There is a growing appetite for a more immersive experience, as evidenced by the video game industry—which is, in fact, larger than the film and television businesses combined. Conventional story structure is being tested by the advent of VR, AR, fan fiction, and TikTok. These mediums are interactive, personalized, and offer a more 360-degree experience.

We continue to spawn different ways to consume stories: e-readers, audiobooks, podcasts, Substack threads, online zines, and more. That said, in spite of the proliferation of video content, book sales are higher than ever. In addition to traditional publishing, self-publishing, eBook, and audiobook sales are steadily on the rise. The seemingly insatiable desire for content signals the enduring human need to partake in storytelling.

NARRATIVE STRUCTURE

Structure is a critical element of storytelling, but there isn't a one-size-fits-all approach. The best story structure is the one that feels right to you. A long list of writers have contributed to the tradition of storytelling. Scores of authors offer their take on story arcs, plot points, and beats. Experts like Syd Field, Michael Hauge, and Robert McKee provide excellent models. Blake Snyder's *Save the Cat* has been a game changer for many writers. Kurt Vonnegut outlines the basic "story shapes" in an entertaining lecture available on YouTube. In addition to Linda Seger's Story Spine, there are countless story metaphors. Rachel Stephen champions her "plot embryo," a method she developed based on the "Story Circle" introduced by Dan Harmon, creator of the TV show *Community*.

Author and television writer Ellen Sandler devised her own six-beat structure. In her book *The TV Writer's Workbook*, she likens the first beat of all stories to the question that kicks off the Passover Seder, "Mah Nish Tah Nah," or "Why is this night different from all others?" She distills this provocative question into a simple beat: "oh." Then describes the next beats as "The Little Uh-Oh!" "Ouch!" "The Big Uh-Ohhh!" "Oh, no!" (or "The Twist-a-Roo!"), and finally, the satisfying resolution of "Ah."

My favorite starting point comes from Joseph Campbell's *The Hero's Journey*. Specifically, I work with the "Hero's Journey" as outlined by author Christopher Vogel in his seminal book, *The Writer's Journey*. Vogler distills the seventeen stages of the hero's journey into twelve beats. While my stories usually feature a heroine rather than a hero, the hero's journey provides a sturdy structure: a hero goes on an adventure, learns a lesson, wins a victory with that newfound knowledge, then returns home transformed. Like many templates, the hero's journey can be broken into three parts: separation, initiation, and return. This is a fancy way of saying there's a beginning, middle, and end.

ACTIVITY: Your Cup of Tea   ⏰ 20 minutes

What's your cup of tea? What type of stories do you prefer? Sip and study.

- ☐ Make yourself a cup of tea.
- ☐ Use list making to jot down some of your favorite books, movies, or series.
  - It doesn't need to be your ultimate top ten. Simply list ten stories that you love or wish you had written.
- ☐ Use freewriting to explore what these stories have in common.
- ☐ Read and reflect.
  - Is there a common theme, genre, character, or narrative style that appeals to you?

When the structure isn't working, turn to character. Character is the heart of a story.

THE BEATING HEART

To find structure, identify your story's beating heart. Stories are intimate and personal, so one of the most reliable ways to find the narrative through line is to focus on the emotions of your protagonist. A story isn't just a series of dramatic events; action takes on meaning when we feel something. You will find the beating heart of the story by connecting to your main character.

Tip: You may need to return to the Cultivate Cycle to get to the root of the problem.

Understanding the character's desires and fears will help you refine your story structure. Instead of events happening to the character, events must happen because the character wants something they care about and struggles to get it. A story is held together by the dramatic question: *Will they achieve their goal?*

Your protagonist has something to lose or gain. In addition to identifying a tangible external goal, find the beating heart of your story by clarifying the internal drive. Consider how the problems they tackle will change them on the inside. By focusing on the beating heart, the writer taps back into the emotional world of the story.

> The story is about how what happens affects someone in pursuit of a deceptively difficult goal, and how that person changes internally as a result.
>
> —Lisa Kron, *Story Genius* and *Wired for Story*

To create dramatic tension, dig into the emotions, desires, and fears. This is where you'll find

the beating heart of your story. Clarify your character's goal by distilling the outcome driving the action. Once you simplify the goal, you can identify the human desire that's the beating heart of your story.

Four main character goals:

- *To win, to stop, to escape, to retrieve*

Three core desires

- *The desire to be loved*
- *The desire to belong*
- *The desire for meaning or purpose*

Tip: Deploy the filmmaker's secret weapon—the elevator pitch.

 Download
The Elevator Pitch

The Beats

Before getting tangled up in a fancy template, clarify the five key sequences of your story. First return to the three-act structure: beginning, middle, and end. Instead of trying to figure out all the twists and turns of your story, consider the three fundamentals: setup, complication, and resolution. Next, partition act one into two sequences, then break act two into 2A and 2B. Voilà, you have the beginning of the five sequences.

Each sequence is anchored by a key story beat. The word *beat* conjures a beating drum or a beating heart, a punch to the gut, walking a police beat, feeling beat, and the physical act of beating. In the film industry, we create a "beat sheet," a document with the significant

An effective story grabs your gut, tightens your throat, makes your heart race and your lungs pump, brings tears to your eyes or an explosion of laughter to your lips.

—Christopher Vogler

moments in the story. I like the term *beat* because it reminds us that a story's key moments are imbued with sensory power. Like Sandler's sensory-centered model, I use sensory triggers to kick off each of the five sequences.

We build the story beat by beat:

1. OUCH!
2. OH NO!
3. POP!
4. UH OHHH!
5. AAAAH!

THE FIVE SEQUENCES

Build the story beat by beat. First, the character's world turns upside down, and the story kicks into gear with *OUCH!* Then *OH NO!* Our main character's problem gets worse. Next, everything comes to a head, and *POP!* We hit the climax. Then everything falls apart and *UH OHHH!* The hero slides into what appears to be a place of no return. Finally, *AAAAH!* With the final denouement, we feel a release.

The first sequence kicks into gear with *OUCH!* The main character is in, or will soon find themselves in, pain. When we meet our character, it's probably not the beginning of their entire life story, but rather the first sequence begins just before our character's world turns upside down. This is sometimes called the "catalyst," the "call to adventure," or the "inciting incident." The first sequence pushes our hero into a new situation and takes them out of the familiar world. The audience wants to know what happens next.

In the second sequence, things start to get more difficult. Conflict builds into what is often referred to as rising action. The temperature is turned up, the stakes get higher, and the tension increases. Our main character's problem gets worse, their goal gets further away, and the quest becomes more difficult. Even though the main character keeps going after their goal, the prevailing sentiment is *OH NO!*

Tip: Keep raising the stakes.

 Download
Five Tips for Building Dramatic Tension

The next sequence explodes: everything comes to a head, and we hit the climax. The hero can no longer deny the problem, and there is nowhere to turn. Often the character will try to do the right thing, but it will end in disaster and climax with a *POP!*

The fourth sequence, sometimes called falling action, is when the wheels come off the bus and everything comes undone. Something happens to send the hero deeper into trouble and slides into what appears to be a place of no return. While things fall apart, the hero is filled with a terrible feeling, *UH OHHH!*

The fifth sequence is the denouement. Finally, the journey comes to an end. While every detail may not be wrapped up, usually there is some kind of resolution. There are many kinds of endings, but even if the story ends in tragedy or with unanswered questions, the character feels a release or revelation: *AAAAH!*

Tip: If even the five sequences feel elusive, it's time to go back to the development phase. Cultivate with discovery writing. Explore the three key parts: beginning, middle, and end.

ACTIVITY: Five Sequences   45 minutes

Identify five key sequences in your story.

   * See the end of the chapter for step-by-step instructions.

RECAP: Beat By Beat

In this chapter, we began with a brief survey of popular narrative structures, then explored an intuitive approach to structure with the five sequences. Each sequence is anchored in a sensory beat. We build the story beat by beat. Find a structure that works for you.

Calibrate Your Compass

Go nuts: When the Craft Cycle make you crazy, let yourself go nuts.
   ☐ Move your body: Crank some music and take a ten-minute dance party break.

Tools and Techniques

- ◎ The beating heart
- ◎ Story beats
- ◎ The five sequences

Chapter Fourteen Activities

Five Sequences ⏰ 45 minutes

To discover the spine of your story, first find the five key sequences.

1: OUCH!	Opening situation and catalyst
2: OH NO!	Hero faces life-changing obstacle
3: POP!	Challenges build to a climax
4: UH OHHH!	Challenges get worse, but protagonist continues to pursue the goal
5: AAAAH!	Success or defeat

Step 1: Where does the main character begin?

Use freewriting to explore where your character begins and what they want. What would your character's ordinary world look and feel like?

Tip: Identify the root action at the heart of their goal. Michael Hauge breaks all goals into one of these four categories: to win, to stop, to escape, to retrieve.

Step 2: What stands in their way?

Use list making or word clouds to brainstorm possible obstacles the character might face.

Step 3: What is at stake?

Use freewriting to explore these questions:

- What is at stake?
- What does the character fear losing?
- What will she gain or lose?
- What would amp up the tension?
- What might lock the main character in the predicament?

Step 4: Where does your character end?

Use freewriting, word clouds, or list making to explore where your character ends.

Consider these questions:

- How does the story end? Victory or defeat?
- What do they win or lose?
- What have they learned? What have they gained?
- How have they changed?

Step 5: Synthesize.

After exploring the four guiding questions, review your writing and do your best to sketch five key beats.

- You may not have unearthed the exact structure. Even so, take your best guess at identifying five starter beats.
- Bridge: What questions feel unanswered?
- Record insights about your process and any new takeaways about story structure in your Field Notes Writing Tracker.

Download
The Five Sequence Template

BEHIND THE SCENES: Denouement

I knew I should answer the call, but I let it go to voicemail.

After years of shooting, fundraising, writing, editing, and revising, we were at the finish line. The harvest had arrived, and finally, it was time to share the fruits of our labor. Yet, the closer I got to the finish line, the louder my critic got. I thought I would feel happy now that we were about to put the documentary into the world, but the prospect of sharing the story with an audience made my stomach turn. The stakes felt high, and soon I would face the ultimate test: watching the film with an audience.

The phone rang again. I ignored it. It was Hilary, the executive producer of the documentary and my sister.

Hilary had been an incredible creative partner. She's smart, honest, brave, and kind. She's the friend people call when they need help, a confidant, a cheerleader, or a pat on the back. In addition to being one of the kindest people I know, she is also the most tenacious. This combination of traits has made her a rockstar fundraiser. Yet, I hadn't fully considered what it would take to stand up to this force of nature.

We were in our fifth year of the project, out of money and patience. To make matters worse, my sister was unhappy with the final cut. I tried to explain we had "locked picture" and the time for changes had passed, but like me, she was freaking out.

I turned my focus to the business at hand.

Despite the stress and worry, I loved this immersive phase. I buzzed from one session to the next and crisscrossed the city. I went from the composer in the hills of Topanga, to the sound-mixing stage in Studio City, back to the westside for color correction in Santa Monica, then across town to the engineer to record the voice-over, and finally back to Silverlake to check in with the editor as she prepped final files. Running between multiple rooms felt exhilarating. I delighted in collaborating with these talented professionals, and polishing all the pieces proved wildly satisfying.

The phone rang again.

It was Hilary. I pulled over and took a deep breath. I needed to get centered before I answered.

Standing up to my older sister wasn't easy. Before making the movie together, we hadn't had much conflict. If differences came up, she let me do my thing or I deferred to her. Why wouldn't I follow her lead?

Our collaboration had gone great, but we'd hit a point of disagreement, and we couldn't see eye to eye. She objected to a sequence at the end of the film, but the time for making changes had passed. Picture edits at this stage weren't only cost prohibitive but also physically impossible, given that the premiere was in a few days, and we barely had enough time to finish the film. Trying to cut even ten seconds would be like asking a chef to just extract the sugar from a cake that's nearly done baking.

I tried to explain why the sequence worked.

During the previous sequence, the wheels had come off the bus and everything had come undone. Our grandfather is at the end of his career and loses his final re-election bid, thus throwing our hero into the place of no return. We feel a terrible sense of *UH OHHH!*

The final sequence begins with a clip of our mother's interview. She starts to tell a story about her father, but unexpectedly, our badass, bulletproof mom cracks.

Off camera, the viewer hears my sister and me trying to coax her to continue, but she declines. "Please," we push, but she can't finish her story. "Okay. Okay," I gently reply.

We then cut away to a series of candid mother-daughter moments with my narration. I pick up the story in voice-over and finish what our mother had been unable to tell.

The viewer hears the pain in her voice and mine, but then we cut to my Uncle Jerry being sworn in as governor.

Next, we cut to a shot of the audience, where our dignified mother is seated next to all the living governors of California (and one future governor). This was the section my sister was upset about. The image of our mother watching her brother on stage hit her in the gut. The editor had done a masterful job weaving it together, but my sister was having second thoughts.

It was the proximity of disappointment and victory that my sister adamantly objected to. I explained that returning to her defeat pulls the viewer back to the larger story, helping us tie up all the loose ends and bringing us back to the beating heart.

The scene highlights the emotional weight of our mother's gubernatorial loss. She thought it was too sad. I agreed the scene was emotional, but the emotion was intentional. It was the final *AAAAH!*

She felt that showing the moment of our mother's vulnerability was like revealing a shameful secret. I reminded my sister that everybody already knows our mother lost, and it's already mentioned in the film.

She countered that since our mother's loss was already mentioned, all the more reason to cut it.

I tried to explain that the juxtaposition of the painful loss with the jubilant inauguration was intentional. It pulls the audience out of their heads and into their hearts. Instead of being a dry history lesson, we see the father, the former governor who had dreamed his daughter would be governor one day too.

The sequence anchors the narrative in a story about a family: a story about a father and his son and daughter; a story about a sister and a brother; and, to a lesser degree, a story about me and my mother. This tender moment amps up and then releases the tension.

She still thought it was hurtful, spiteful, and unnecessary. I disagreed.

We went around and around.

We came to a compromise. I would consider modifying some of the voice-over, and before the premiere, I would be the one to tell our mom about the sequence. And I would let her know that my sister had objected, but I had insisted.

As confident as I was about the scene, the thought of telling our mother was uncomfortable. I put off the call until the day of the screening. Once I finally called my mom, she listened quietly as I recounted the final sequence blow by blow. There was a pause. Then she said, "Tonight's not about me. It's about the film. Don't worry about me. I can handle it."

That night, I placed a picture of my grandparents on my desk and lit a candle. I called in my muse and prayed for strength.

On the way to the premiere, we got stuck in traffic, so I barely got to speak with my sister before the movie played. Our smiles were tense as we took pictures on the red carpet. As the screen flickered to life, I held my breath. Within the first thirty seconds, the audience laughed, and the story unspooled. The final denouement flowed beautifully, and the theater erupted with applause. When the lights came up, I noticed that some people were dabbing away tears. I was pretty sure this was good, but nervously, I scanned the room for my mother. She was beaming with pride. My sister and I walked up to the stage for the Q&A. She gave me a big hug, and I could see her worries had dissolved.

CHAPTER FIFTEEN

Point of View

Fall: The Craft Cycle heralds the harvest.
Give thanks and honor those who have gone before.

In this chapter, we explore how the author can use voice to shape the reader's experience. In addition to how the character speaks, voice also refers to the author's signature style and point of view. A simple grammatical shift can reveal or conceal bias, enhance or destabilize reliability, and set the mood. We will turn to the masters for models that instruct and inspire.

FIRST THINGS FIRST: Signature

An author's voice captures their distinct way of seeing the world. When you bring your authentic self to the page, your fingerprints will be all over it. When an author develops a body of work with a recognizable voice, their signature style can even become a category in itself. For example, an author's work can be described as "Dickensian" because the style echoes the work of Charles Dickens. A moment can be described as "Proustian" when it captures the literary genius of Proust.

Study the masters but be sure to give yourself space for discovery. A writer's signature style comes from years of trial and error. It's easy to get tangled up in technique during the Craft Cycle, so be mindful not to hold yourself to unrealistic standards. Don't compare your first rough draft to a published novel. Measuring your work against the master is a recipe for failure. Rarely is an artist an "overnight success." Developing your craft happens over time. Finding one's voice requires experimentation and a willingness to make a mess.

Writers Read

Simply picking up a book is one of the easiest ways to inject a nourishing dose of cultivate energy into the Craft Cycle. Reading wakes up inspiration. My mentor Caroline calls this "medicinal reading," and she emphasizes that you shouldn't reach for challenging literature that you think you're "supposed to" read. Instead, pick something delicious.

Turn to books, movies, or poetry and consider targeting a specific element that you're struggling with. For example, if you're unsure what voice to use in a story, revisit your favorite books to see how those authors use first, second, and third person. You don't need to be a speed reader, nor do you need to read every book out there, but writers read. Medicinal reading is meant to nurture, not torture. I read slowly, so sometimes I listen to audiobooks when I want to cover more territory.

When I embarked on writing my first pilot script, it was a dose of medicinal reading that turned things around. I decided to rewrite one of my old feature scripts and reimagine it as a series. The original story had centered around the relationship between two brothers, but I changed the leads to sisters. The gender swap brought the story alive, but the deeper I got into the rewrite, the more unwieldy the narrative became.

I knew I needed to better understand the pilot structure, so I read books and articles, but studying wasn't helping. I decided it was time for a dose of medicinal reading. I tracked down the scripts of some of my favorite shows. As I read, suddenly, the pilot structure began to make sense. I devoured dozens of pilots and savored favorites like Vince Gilligan's *Breaking Bad* and Shonda Rhimes's *Scandal*.

There is a vitality,
a life force, a
quickening that is
translated through
you into action, and
there is only one
of you in all time.
This expression is
unique, and if you
block it, it will never
exist through any
other medium; and
be lost. The world
will not have it.

—Martha Graham

The format felt more accessible, and creative momentum returned. When I got tangled up in my story's twists and turns, I realized I needed to understand the inner workings of the mystery/thriller genre. So, I checked out a stack of Agatha Christy's books. Her novels are a master class in plotting riveting narratives. If you're writing a script, read scripts. If you are writing a book, revisit a book you love. Most of all, read, read, read.

Finding one's voice requires experimentation and a willingness to make a mess.

ACTIVITY: Story sip.   ⏰ 15 minutes

You don't need to reread a whole book or chew through an entire season's worth of scripts. Take sips. Study and savor.

Step 1. Pick a text.

☐ Pick a text that's interesting to you or pick one of the examples excerpted in this chapter.

Step 2. Focus your attention.

☐ Focus your attention on a specific aspect of the craft and analyze it.

  – You may examine how the author builds worlds, crafts character descriptions, makes transitions, uses dialogue, or shifts between perspectives.

Step 3. Review and reflect.

☐ Write about what you notice in your journal.

POINT OF VIEW

Point of view is a fundamental way authors shape the experience of the reader. POV can build tension, reveal or restrict information, create distance or intimacy, and even intentionally undermine reliability.

Let's start with a refresher on point of view: first, second, and third person.

First-person narration: *I go to the store. We see this. We do that.*
Second-person narration: *You did this. You see this. You go here.*
Third-person narration: *He did this. She went there. They did that.*

The writer can choose one of the three points of view or combine all three. First and third are commonly used in literature, and second person is a natural fit for self-help books and how-to nonfiction (like this book.) Literary classics often feature third-person narration like that of a character in the story.

First person

When the protagonist narrates, the reader is privy to all the character's innermost thoughts. The narrator's style of speaking informs the reader. First person also can reveal how a character thinks. First person is a natural choice for memoir, but it can be effectively used in fiction.

When an author successfully uses first person, the reader will feel pulled into the emotional world of the character, which establishes an intimate connection.

First Person in Fiction

Intimacies: A Novel by Katie Kitamura

> *It is never easy to move to a new country, but in truth I was happy to be away from New York. That city had become disorienting to me, after my father's death and my mother's sudden retreat to Singapore. For the first time, I understood how much my parents had anchored me to this place none of us were from.*

First Person in Memoir / Nonfiction

Eat, Pray, Love by Elizabeth Gilbert

> *I wish Giovanni would kiss me . . . Oh, but there are so many reasons why this would be a terrible idea. To begin with, Giovanni is ten years younger than I am, and—like most Italian guys in their twenties—he still lives with his mother.*

I Know Why the Caged Bird Sings by Maya Angelou

> *I don't think I ever saw Mrs. Flowers laugh, but she smiled often. A slow widening of her thin black lips to show even, small white teeth, then the slow effortless closing. When she chose to smile on me, I always wanted to thank her.*

Second Person

Second person can be tricky to sustain. These examples show how it can effectively engage the reader. You might find that second person draws you in and makes it feel as if the author is speaking directly to you.

Second Person in Fiction

How To Get Filthy Rich in Rising Asia by Mohsin Hamid

> *You keep thinking that with practice you will eventually get the knack of enjoying superficial encounters, that you will stop looking for the universal solvent, stop grieving. You will learn to compound happiness out of small increments of mindless pleasure.*

Second Person in Memoir/ Nonfiction

Undrowned: Black Feminist Lessons from Marine Mammals
by Alexis Pauline Gumbs

> *If you happen to be in the ocean and you see someone breathing, what do you do? If you see someone like you, a mammal, but unlike you not bound by boats*

and masks and land—you might wonder who they are, what are they doing, how do they do it. How do they live in salt and depth and motion? You might very well wonder in that case you would need a guidebook.

Third Person

You may have noticed in the previous examples that authors shift between voice and combine, for example, first- and third-person narration. Authors can use more than one approach in a single work to add tension and nuance. These next examples illustrate how, like first person, third person can get the reader into the head of the character.

Third Person in Fiction

Our Mutual Friend by Charles Dickens

Bradley Headstone, in his decent black coat and waistcoat, and decent white shirt, and decent formal black tie, and decent pantaloons of pepper and salt, with his decent silver watch in his pocket and its decent hair-guard round his neck, looked a thoroughly decent young man of six-and-twenty. . . . There was a kind of settled trouble in the face. It was the face belonging to a naturally slow or inattentive intellect that had toiled hard to get what it had won, and that had to hold it now that it was gotten. He always seemed to be uneasy lest anything should be missing from his mental warehouse . . .

In The Country of Others by Leila Slimani

The first time Mathilde visited the farm, she thought: It's too remote. The isolation made her anxious. He didn't have a car back then, in 1947, so they crossed the fifteen miles from Meknes on an old cart, driven by a gypsy. Amine paid no attention to the discomfort of the wooden bench, nor to the dust that made his wife cough. He had eyes only for the landscape. He was eager to reach the estate that his father had left him.

Turn to the masters for inspiration.

    * *Visit the end of the chapter for step-by-step instructions.*

WHO'S ON THIRD

There are a variety of ways to approach the third person. Here are some key variations:

- author or character (or mystery)
- omniscient
- objective or subjective
- unreliable narrator
- epistolary or authoritative

Voice of God

Many authors employ an omniscient narrator who sees everything because this gives the reader access to the characters' thoughts and feelings. This all-knowing "voice of God" narrator can move freely through time and space, allowing the author to give the reader their own opinions and observations as well as those of the characters.

Objective or Subjective

A subjective narrator makes no claims of neutrality; they embrace their bias and speak from their point of view. Memoirs rely on the subjective view to give the reader an inside experience. While the objective narrator is a fundamental principle valued by journalists and historians, everybody has a point of view, be it a conscious or unconscious bias.

Our experiences shape the ways we see the world, so can anyone really offer an objective point of view? When an author chooses a topic, they've subjectively focused the lens. They zoom in on specific areas and make decisions on what will take center stage. For example, in a news article, the reporter's premise assumes a point of view. Their bias informs what they pull into the foreground and what they shove into the background.

Our values frame our point of view, and in fact, some authors embrace their bias. For example, Rebecca Skloot wrote a nonfiction book about the ethics of science, but she shared details of her investigative journey. By including her experiences in the book, *The Immortal Life of Henrietta Lacks*, the author made the information more accessible and revealed how bias shapes information.

Reliable or Unreliable

A reliable narrator gives us the straight story. The unreliable narrator isn't completely credible and can even challenge our perception of reality. While some unreliable narrators intend to deceive, others might be ignorant or misinformed. An unreliable narrator could be a child, an outsider, or someone who is mentally ill. Christopher Nolan's entire body of work is focused on exploring the unreliable narrator. You don't know whom to trust or what is real in his hit show *Westworld*, his blockbuster *Inception*, and even back in his first feature, *Memento*.

Another way authors exploit voice is the tack of keeping the identity of the narrator a mystery. Usually, in this case, there will be some kind of twist, which can be satisfying if it pays off. For example, the older self might tell the story of their youth, or we discover it is the criminal who's telling the story.

One memorable use of an unreliable narrator is Mark Haddon's book, *The Curious Incident of the Dog in the Night-Time*. The story is told from the perspective of an autistic boy. What he notices differs from an average person. He focuses on unusual or small details and overlooks or omits key information. This disorients the reader, and we're not sure what he means or if he can be trusted. It's a brilliant book and an easy read. It was also turned into a play with inventive staging. Like third person, first person can be reliable or unreliable, objective or subjective. First person is by definition subjective.

Epistolary or Authoritative

Both the epistolary and the authoritative points of view offer first-person accounts. Authoritative perspectives draw upon historical documents like a captain's ship log or a scientist's field notes. Epistolary means it's written in the form of a letter.

One of the most well-known examples of the epistolary form is Mary Shelley's gothic novel *Frankenstein*. The immediacy of correspondence and private journals pull us into the story and create a sense of foreboding. The contemporary author Ocean Vuong uses the epistolary form in his book *On Earth We're Briefly Gorgeous*. Not only does this create an elegant nesting of stories within stories, but since the book is written as a letter to his illiterate mother, the impossibility of his mother reading the letter conjures a heartbreaking and unsettling intimacy.

On Earth We're Briefly Gorgeous by Ocean Vuong

> *Let me begin again.*
> *Dear Ma,*
> *I am writing to reach you—even if each word I put down is one word further from where you are.*

Breaking the Fourth Wall

Similarly, in theater, television, and film, actors sometimes speak directly to the camera, a narrative device called "breaking the fourth wall." The term comes from the theater and refers to the imaginary wall between the actors and the audience. The implied wall means that the characters are unaware that they're fictional characters and that an audience is observing them. When executed effectively, breaking the fourth wall creates an intimate connection with the viewer.

There are many examples of breaking the fourth wall in television like *The Office*, Issa Rae's *The Misadventures of Awkward Black Girl*, and Phoebe Waller-Bridge's *Fleabag*. In *Fleabag*, the eponymous main character, Fleabag, directly connects with the viewer throughout the series. She makes eye contact with the camera, pulls faces, and slips in sarcastic, witty quips. For example, when we meet her brother-in-law, Martin, after he says he's not drunk, she turns to us and adds, "He's always drunk." She continues, "He's one of those men who is explosively sexually inappropriate with everyone but makes you feel bad if you take offense because he was 'just being fun.'" Rather than disrupting the flow of the narrative, she heightens the comedy, gets us on her side, and makes us feel in the know.

Authors can also break the fourth wall in literature. In Lemony Snicket's *A Series of Unfortunate Events*, the narrator begins by asserting, "If you are interested in stories with happy endings, you would be better off reading some other book." Similarly, Rick Riordan kicks off *The Lightning Thief* with a warning. Percy tells the reader, "Look, I didn't want to be a half-blood. If you're reading this because you think you might be one, my advice is: close this book right now."

NEW POV

Instead of trying to figure things out by thinking, draw on the improvisational energy of the Collaborate Cycle. A great way to rekindle inspiration is to play with POV. Drop your character into an unexpected situation and spend some quality time with them. A shift in perspective can help us sneak past the critic and free up the imagination. By stretching your creative muscles, you regain plasticity, which allows you more freedom to shape your characters.

To mix it up, give your character the experience of seeing the world from a new POV, then explore the story world from this new perspective.

How does this new lens change your character's experience of the story world? Pay attention to both the character's emotional experience and your response as the writer. Does this situation trigger desire, fear, hatred, love, or sadness?

Throw the character into a challenging situation and see what they do. Insert your character into an unfamiliar or fantastical situation like an encounter with aliens, a visit to the Wall Street trading floor, or a mundane crisis like a burst pipe. How will your character deal with water flooding their space? The goal is to provoke a reaction that reveals more about your character. Observe their behavior in this new situation.

An Impossible Situation

Even when you've worked through multiple drafts, and you desperately want to finish, you may get genuinely stumped. It can be frustrating when the story just isn't coming together.

Sometimes we become so close to our characters that we resist throwing them into serious jeopardy. A common stumbling block is author-character entanglement or what my teacher Caroline Donahue calls "Protective Author Syndrome." Protective Author Syndrome is an affliction marked by the persistent need to protect our main character. The author unconsciously assumes a paternal attitude and treats the character like a child or a frail creature in need of protection. Shielding our characters from pain can be a fatal condition because writers must throw their characters into serious trouble.

When we dare to make trouble for our character, we may feel uncomfortable or overwhelmed. Sometimes this is a sign we've gotten muddled up with our character's drama. I recall working on a script in which the main character's son runs away. My hero tracks her son's trail into the desert, where night falls and a rainstorm leaves her trapped and worrying about her son's fate. I felt overwhelmed and hopeless. I had no idea how my character was going to find her son. I confessed to my

To see a World in a
Grain of Sand

And a Heaven in a
Wild Flower,

Hold Infinity in the
palm of your hand

And Eternity
in an hour

—William Blake

teacher that I didn't know how to get my character out of this situation. She responded gleefully, "That's fantastic!" At first, I was hurt by what I thought was an insensitive comment, but then she explained that putting my character in an impossible situation is exactly what a great story requires.

After a short discussion, I realized this was the perfect cliffhanger moment to end the episode. I set the script aside for a few days and spent some quality time with my own child. This calmed my nerves, and soon I felt refreshed. When I got back to the script, I shifted from the mother's perspective to the son's point of view, and new ideas began percolating.

If a character never wrestles with big problems, the story is not only boring, but it also is no longer relatable or believable. When a character struggles with something meaningful to them, the story hooks the audience. Affection for our characters is natural, but if nothing bad happens to them, the plot will stall or mindlessly meander into mushy, messy muck.

The act of writing can be a refuge, so it's understandable that when we experience real-world difficulties, we may feel reluctant to cause trouble for our characters. A great way to shake off Protective Author Syndrome is to play with point of view. When we look at the story from a new perspective, we can extract the character from the muck. There are countless ways to change perspective. We can zoom in or move further away. We can travel backward or forward in time. We can see the story from a different character's POV, drop an outsider into the story, or take our character out of their world.

ACTIVITY: POV Shake-Up   15 minutes

Spend quality time with your character.

> * See the end of the chapter for step-by-step instructions.

RECAP: Your Voice

Each writer has a unique voice. In this chapter, we review how point of view can shape the reader's experience. A story can be told from a variety of perspectives, and each angle triggers different emotions for the reader. The author decides whose eyes we see the world through. We look at examples because rereading our favorites illuminates how it's done.

Calibrate Your Compass

Back to school: Take a trip to the library and check out some books.

☐ Read around your story. Pick books related to the setting or your character's hobbies or emotional problems. Find stories covering the same time period or that are told in a similar way. Visit the young adult nonfiction section. How do authors explain your topic to kids?

Tools and Techniques

◎ Voice
◎ Point of view
◎ Breaking the fourth wall

Chapter Fifteen Activities

Mini Masterclass   ⏰ 45 minutes

You don't need to reread a whole book or chew through an entire season's worth of scripts. Take sips. Study and savor.

Step 1. Pick a text.

☐ Pick a text that is relevant to what you're writing (e.g., short story, essay, poem).
- Select a text that's interesting to you. If you're writing an essay, read essays. If you're penning a memoir, get your hands on memoirs. If you're writing a script, round up screenplays.

Step 2. Focus your attention.

☐ Focus your attention on a specific aspect of the craft and analyze it.
- You may examine how the author builds worlds, crafts character descriptions, makes transitions, uses dialogue, or shifts between perspectives.

Tip: Make it easy and use the text examples in this chapter.

Step 3. Review and reflect.

In your journal, write about what you notice.

☐ How does it make you feel? What do you experience?

Tension	Intrigue	Romantic
Intimacy	Immediacy	Immersive
Empathy	Comedy	Fear

☐ Here are other questions to consider:
- If you look at voice, ask:
  - Is it first person or third person?
  - Objective or subjective?
  - Is the narrator reliable?
  - Why do you think the author chose this point of view?

- What if the author chose to use first instead of third person? Third instead of second? And so on.
- How does the voice connect to the themes of the story?
- If you focus on the dialogue, ask:
  - Is this dialogue moving us forward? What would happen if the author had taken out this line of dialogue? How would this affect the rest of the narrative?
  - When and why does the author use dialogue?

Ready to go further?
☐ Study one specific element and compare authors.
- Study the first paragraph of different books and see how the author approaches beginnings.
- Read the last few pages of a book to see how the author wraps the narrative.

ACTIVITY: POV Shake-Up   15 minutes

A great way to find drama is to shift the point of view. Drop your character into an unexpected situation, explore what-ifs, or send them into a bizarre situation. Spend some quality time with your character.

Step 1: Warm-up   3 minutes
Freewrite from a different point of view. Goof around.
Select an animal or object. Write from that perspective.
☐ What do you want, fear, love, crave? Who are your friends? Enemies?
☐ Examples: a ring, a piece of trash, a streetlamp, a watch, a piano, a sock, an iPhone, a key, a dog, a bird, a pet, a bomb, a cake, a lake, a step, a closet, a ball, a superhero, a magical creature, etc.

Step 2: Pick a new POV.   1 minute
☐ Examples: a teenager, a detective, a criminal, your mother, a dad, a baby, a grandmother, a character from a movie

Step 3: Now describe a familiar event from this new POV.   4 minutes
☐ Examples: eating breakfast, driving to work, cooking, kissing, going to the gym

Step 4: Repeat step three, using your main character.   7 minutes
☐ Consider the following questions:
  • How does the world look from the new POV?
  • What does your character want?
  • Is there something they love that you hate (or vice versa)?
  • Is there something they fear that's ordinary to you?
  • How does the world look, smell, taste, feel, sound . . . ?
  • Who are the character's friends? Enemies?
☐ Bridge: Jot down takeaways from the writing session.
  • What did you learn about your character?
  • Did you discover a new secret or fear?
  • What surprised you?
  • Did you knock up against a new question?
☐ Field Notes
  • Did you learn anything about your process? What came up?

Note: The objective of this exercise might feel unclear. That's okay! If you feel disoriented, good! The point is to shake up your thinking so you can access the subconscious. Trust you will find insights into what the character is thinking and feeling.

For example, one student was struggling with a character that was silent and stoic. The momentum of the story was dragging. I suggested she force her characters to deal with an overflowing plumbing problem. This got the quiet character talking. Finally, the writer understood what was going on with him and how to move the story forward. This exercise revealed a betrayal he'd been hiding, and the drama took off. She even decided to keep the scene.

BEHIND THE SCENES: My Grandfather

When I embarked on making a documentary about my grandfather, it took a lot of trial and error to find the right voice for the narration. The stakes felt especially high because I was sharing a story about my family, and my proximity to the story made the task of crafting the narration especially tricky.

My grandfather had been in public office during a pivotal time in California history, and I intended to take a critical look at his tenure as governor. Even though I had great affection and respect for him, I didn't want to make a puff piece. I set out to make a journalistic biography, but it was impossible to be objective. Finally, after a lot of experimentation, I realized it made sense to tell the story from my point of view. I realized that, as his granddaughter, my insider perspective added dimension and emotion.

Reluctantly, I decided to narrate the documentary. I was more comfortable behind the camera, and it felt awkward to step into the limelight. It proved difficult to strike the right tone. My co-writer and I labored over each passage of the voice-over. The structure of the documentary was coming together, but it was difficult to stitch together a narrative that jumped through time periods, pivoted between characters, and combined historical events with intimate family moments. Each word impacted the meaning. When we discovered that it made a big difference whether we referred to the main subject as "my grandfather" or "the governor," we made a breakthrough. In the context of the story, switching between first and third person shifted the emotional resonance. At the time, it felt ridiculous to labor over each sentence of narration, but this experience taught me that when it's time to revise and complete, every word counts.

CHAPTER SIXTEEN

The Messy Middle

Fall: When the Craft Cycle arrives, it's time to dump the excess.
To complete, we must also let go.

Finishing is one of the most elusive aspects of the writing process. Countless books on writing offer valuable information about the technical aspects of craft, but an often overlooked part of this Story Cycle is learning to navigate the messy middle. More often than not, projects take longer than planned and invariably unexpected obstacles materialize. Even if you've diligently calibrated, carefully cultivated and thoughtfully collaborated, your project still may not be ready to harvest. When you find yourself in the muck of the messy middle, it's natural to look for a shortcut. Instead of looking for a way around, look for a way through. To weather this season, one must be open to transformation.

FIRST THINGS FIRST: Every Story Has a Season

The harvest arrives in its own time. If you've been working on something for years and years, it's easy to lose faith in the process or the project. It's true that not every idea will materialize into a completed project, but just because something hasn't come together yet doesn't mean that it won't. When you struggle, it is not a sign that your idea is a bad idea, nor is it a sign that you are incapable. It may simply mean that the timing isn't right.

Every project has a season, a natural arc. Just as your characters go on a journey, the process of each project is also a journey. Inevitably, there will be twists and turns on the path. Even when you make a perfect plan, you will encounter unpredictable weather and terrain. Life happens and sometimes life needs to unfold before the ending can be written.

Making my documentary took me deep into the messy middle. At a certain point, I shut down production and waited for this new chapter of our family's story to play out. While the story was about my grandfather, his son (my uncle) decided to run again for governor. Putting the production on hold was frustrating, and I worried I would never get out of the messy middle. Being in limbo was excruciating, but when my uncle won the governor's race, this unlikely turn of events generated interest in the topic. My uncle's comeback was a boost for the film, and I then had the material to craft the optimistic, uplifting ending that I'd hoped for. As it turns out, the project was just cycling through a winter. Every story has its season.

TRANSFORMATION

Stories can transport us to new worlds, bring people together, and reveal history. Words have the power to inspire people and disrupt the status quo. Think of the movies and books that have impacted you. Stories can make us feel as though we belong and that we matter. They can help us heal, make us laugh, open our minds, and spark joy. My mentor Caroline taught me that just as stories can transform us when we consume them, they can transform us when we create them.

A book or movie can be an act of resistance, and it can change how we see the world. So, it's natural that the experience of sharing your story will impact you. In fact, writing can be more potent for the writer than for the reader. The creative act can be a transformational process.

Just as stories transform us when we consume them, stories change us when we create them.

Most writers dream of sharing their work with the world, but this means stepping into the unknown and letting go of control. Being visible can disrupt the equilibrium. Just as dropping a stone in a lake creates ripples, releasing a story into the world makes waves. Even if the reaction is positive, the experience changes the writer.

As long as an idea is a work in progress, it stays in the safety zone. If something isn't done, then there is always the possibility of making it better. While the work is under lock and key, any perceived problems can be resolved. Rewriting is an essential phase of the process, but it can also be a way to maintain control.

As we near the finish line, we begin to change. Our understanding of the material deepens, and the desire to tinker can heighten. If you find yourself stuck in the messy middle, ask yourself, *Am I avoiding the changes the work will bring? Am I afraid of what will be revealed? Am I hiding from something or clinging to something?*

Sometimes an old trauma may be triggered, and it might be wise to slow your pace. But other times, the work doesn't feel ready because the inner critic fears change. The critic wants to keep us safe, so they tell us, *Not yet. Make it better.*

It's important to enjoy the fruits of your labor, but sharing sometimes means letting go. Usually, writers envision the rewards of completion, but we can't always imagine the changes it will bring.

LAND THE PLANE

It's natural for goals to evolve, but it will be impossible to reach the destination if your objective is vague or perpetually shifting. Without clarity, a vision is just a fantasy. If you slosh about without setting specific goals, the fantasy may become a nightmare.

The closer we get to being done, the more we need our critic's sharp eye and discernment, but if the critic is driving, you may not get very far. When the critic senses that the end is in sight, they might feel fear and just about any idea will seem like a "better" idea. The critic may trick us into moving the finish line, or they might convince us to abandon the project altogether. It's wise to have a few irons in the fire, but sometimes the critic steers us to a new idea because of fear.

How do we know the difference between worthwhile rewriting and pointless wordsmithing?

Are you stalling or making important changes? Is it time to ditch the project or stick with it?

It's fun to dream up new projects, but sometimes changing direction is a critic trick. Some projects are destined for the compost heap, but before abandoning your current project for a "better" idea, remember the inner critic is a sucker for a new shiny object. Without vigilance, you may succumb to the seductive loop of the endless summer.

Ask, *Why am I changing my goal?*

Before acting, take a moment to reflect and calibrate your creative compass. Slow down and reconsider the destination. Often, projects have extended time horizons, and while we set out with one destination in mind, we might discover that the story may take us some place unexpected. We may plan to write a feature film, but maybe it works better as a short story; perhaps we started writing an essay, but it's turned into a memoir; or it's possible that a television series works better as a novel. Periodically reconsider the end goal and take special care to look at the emotional landscape.

Writing is often a perilous journey. Low self-esteem or confusion about goals may be the Shadows that chill our work. An editor or one's own judgmental side may be the Threshold Guardians that block our way. Accidents, computer problems, and difficulties with time and discipline may torment us and taunt like Tricksters. Unrealistic dreams of success or distractions may be the Shapeshifters who tempt, confuse, and dazzle us. Deadlines, editorial decisions, or the struggle to sell our work may be the Tests and Ordeals from which we seem to die but are Resurrected to write again.

—Christopher Vogler

Declutter your mind and reevaluate the goal.
- ☐ Use freewriting and list making to capture what's floating around in your head.
  - Write down the questions, worries, and possibilities.
  - Include specific story questions, process issues, and outcome concerns.

- ☐ Make a question list.
  - Review what you wrote and identify the burning issues. Add questions and decisions to your question list.

- ☐ Read and reflect.
  - Did you change your goal without knowing it? And, if so, does that work?
  - Is it time to revise the goal? Do you need more time, or are you changing direction?
  - Does your goal still match your why?

ENOUGH

If you find yourself feeling like it's not "good enough," ask how you are measuring. A favorite critic tactic is to compare and despair. Don't judge your journey to someone else's and definitely don't compare your rough draft to a finished project. A published book looks so tidy but working your way through the messy middle is . . . messy!

Not only do we need to define what completion looks like externally, but it's worth considering how finishing will feel internally. Sometimes we don't *feel* like we've done enough, but we've done more than enough. *Is there something I hope to gain? Is there something I fear?* Even if you're not really done, let's pretend for an hour.

- ☐ Even if you haven't hit your original goal, it's important to acknowledge the work you have done, so let's practice.
- ☐ Even for just the next hour, decide it is time for you to walk away. Identify a marker or milestone and acknowledge your efforts.

ACTIVITY: I'm done!   7 minutes

Visualize what "done" looks like. What does being "finished" look and feel like?

* See the end of the chapter for step-by-step instructions.

Daydreaming is not writing. Thinking is not writing. Writing requires writing, so write it.

RECAP: Word by Word

One of the most difficult tasks for writers is completing a project. Finding the right way to wrap up a story can be genuinely baffling, but if you find yourself toggling between possibilities and stuck in a loop of endless pondering, the critic might be running the show. To make it to the finish line, the writer must be willing to change.

⊘ Calibrate Your Compass

Turn over a new leaf: Just because you haven't finished yet doesn't mean you can't finish. It may be time for a change. Calibrate with a pause.

☐ Reconsider your priority. What's the next best step?

Tools and Techniques

- ◎ The messy middle
- ◎ The mists of maybe
- ◎ Transformation
- ◎ Land the plane

Chapter Sixteen Activities

I'm done!

⏰ 30 minutes

Visualize what "done" looks like.

Step 1: Use freewriting to explore. Consider these guiding questions:

☐ What does completion look like?

- *What does "finishing" look like for me?*
- *How do I want to feel about it?*
- *What is enough?*
- *How will finishing change my life externally?*
- *How do I hope I will change internally?*

☐ Are there changes you fear or hope for?

- *What might I gain?*
- *What am I ready to let go of?*
- *How will this impact my relationships?*
- *Is there a transformation I'm seeking?*
- *Is there an experience I fear?*

Step 2: I am done!

☐ Congratulations! You did it!

- Even if you're not really done, let's pretend for an hour.
- Even if you haven't hit your original goal, it's important to acknowledge the work you have done, so let's practice.
- Even for just the next hour, decide it is time for you to walk away. Identify a marker or milestone and acknowledge your efforts.

Step 3: I have done enough.

Sometimes speaking can free up creativity.

- ☐ Say it out loud and see how it feels: I have done enough.

- ☐ Now write it in your journal: I have done enough.

- ☐ Use freewriting to explore the feelings that come up.

Step 4: Review and reflect.

- ☐ Read over your writing and record key observations in your journal or Field Notes Writing Tracker.

Step 5: Do something nice for yourself.

- ☐ How can you celebrate this milestone?
  - Leave something wonderful for yourself to come back to in your notebook. Write yourself an encouraging note, transcribe an inspiring quote in your Field Notes Writing Tracker, add stickers to celebrate progress, or place a flower on your writing desk. Schedule an artist date.
  - Give a gift to your future self. Challenge yourself to try a variety of rewards.
- ☐ Extra Credit: Give yourself permission to shine!
  - Brag to a friend and observe how it feels.
    - Enlist a trusted friend and ask them if they wouldn't mind listening to you talk about your writing process.
    - Talk about what's going well with your process. Celebrate that you've found tools and techniques that work for you. Claim your victories.
  - Use freewriting to explore the experience.

BEHIND THE SCENES: Mother Knows Best

Rachel's one of those people whose life seems charmed: she's talented, beautiful, successful, and happily married to a great guy. She's easy to smile and quick to offer a kind word. She's funny, smart, and energetic, but on the day we met to discuss her manuscript, she looked tired. She was still gorgeous, smiling, and stylish, but her characteristic glow had dimmed. We were meeting to discuss the first draft of her memoir, which detailed her journey to become a mother—a journey that had nearly killed her.

By the time Rachel was ready to become a mother, her biological clock was ticking, a pressure felt by many women at this stage of life. Her book begins like a fairytale. She and Joe fell in love the day they met. The two have been inseparable ever since. The perfectly matched rock and rollers dreamed of having a dog, two kids, and a home filled with music. Over the next ten years, life unfolded according to plan. They continued to perform and record music, and they doted on their rescue puppy. They gracefully translated their skills into good jobs. Joe had parlayed his technical smarts into a great IT gig, while Rachel turned her gift for singing into a voice-over career.

They had just bought a house, and still had jam sessions in the living room. They were still very much in love, and now they were finally ready to start a family.

As we walked through the story memo, I could see her eyes glaze over. Her manuscript was unfinished, but more importantly, her story was still unfolding, and she was emotionally raw. She is an excellent writer, and the draft was in good shape. I could see the path forward, but her perspective was still clouded by her lived experience. The book details her journey to becoming a mother, taking us through her struggle with fertility issues. She and Joe enlisted medical help and soldiered forward. She endured brutal rounds of IVF and poured staggering sums of money into the cause. Finally, Rachel got pregnant. It seemed that their dream was finally coming true, but then she was hit with sharp abdominal pains. Rachel thought it was nothing but figured she should get it checked. It turned out to be an ectopic pregnancy, and she was immediately rushed into emergency surgery. If she had waited a day, she would have died. It was a miracle she survived, but when she woke up from the surgery, she was dealt a heavy blow. She was informed that they had removed both her fallopian tubes, and it would now be impossible to carry a child.

Her manuscript takes us inside the heart-wrenching journey. The narrative sings with her characteristic optimism and describes how the resilient pair rebounded. She chronicles their way through the foster-adopt route: the arduous application process, maddening bureaucracy, nerve-racking home inspections, and invasive scrutiny. In her book, Rachel skillfully synthesizes the following eighteen months of struggle as the case churned through the court system. It was over a year before they finally got the call. Their baby had arrived.

She powerfully describes how they fell in love and how the journey all made sense now. The draft sparkled with powerful reflections on motherhood, filled with insights on navigating adoption. It seemed like a happy ending, but as I tried to guide her toward the priority for the next pass, I could see her face fall.

The manuscript needed revision, but first Rachel needed time to heal. Not only was she in the messy middle of writing her book, but she was also still slogging through a deeply painful experience. One day it would be part of the story, but she was still weathering the battering storm of trauma.

I reassured Rachel that the bones of the story were there, and I advised a developmental pass to massage the overall structure. I could see her wilt. She wanted to dive into a copy edit. She was eager to complete and put the book into the world, but while it was nearly certain the adoption would be complete, the legal process continued to drag on.

The final court date had been moved again. She was emotionally drained. I advised that a rewrite would be difficult while she was still navigating the adoption process, and the story was still unfolding. She admitted they were still holding their breath until the adoption was final. I explained that this event would inform her perspective and help her shape the overall structure. It was also important to recognize that telling the story was changing her. The process had led her to revisit her relationship with her mother, and writing about old wounds had sparked a profound personal transformation.

I realized she didn't need tips on how to polish and complete. I put the story memo aside and proposed she take a break. She resisted this idea. I recommended she take time to calibrate. Finalizing the adoption before finishing the book would not only make the ending clear but also give her more time to emotionally integrate everything she'd gone through. I suggested that, while she had intellectually let go of the dream of having two kids, there was likely grief she needed to work through. She wanted to push forward.

I could feel her desperation to complete and sensed that the desire was being stoked by the critic. I listened as she cycled through the hallmark firestorm of the Craft Cycle. She confessed she felt that if she didn't finish the book now, it would never get done. I reassured her that she was on track, and she had the skill to make it great, but I could see the all-or-nothing mindset take hold. I could almost hear her inner critic implore, *Jump ship!* Then she wondered aloud if it was even worth finishing. I reiterated that her story was not only compelling, but also that the book would be an invaluable resource for women who are struggling on the path to parenting.

A few weeks after we parted ways, we reconnected. She had decided to put the book on the back burner. She realized she needed to let the story play out. She also shared they had decided they would not adopt another child. They couldn't imagine walking through the adoption process again. She realized she needed to process letting go of this dream and the whole experience.

We met up about a year later. She had finalized the adoption but was dismayed she hadn't been able to complete the book. I pointed out that parenting a young child is a demanding and life-altering experience. It was understandable she had set the draft aside to devote her attention to the precious child she had fought for. She admitted motherhood was keeping her busy but confided that she was questioning her ability to complete the project. I challenged her assessment. It was a capacity issue, but perhaps it also needed a reframe.

What if she wasn't stuck? What if the material was still marinating? I asked her if her motivation for telling this story was the same as when she had set out to write the book. Upon reflection, she realized the experience of parenting was changing her. I reassured her the material would be there when she was ready. I also sensed there was more to the story.

As it turned out, the end of this story was still being written. Not long after we spoke, they were contacted by the foster agency because an infant was up for adoption. By some miracle, their second child had arrived.

She sent me a picture of their beautiful family of four and told me she now knew why she hadn't been able to finish the book. This new development had dramatically informed her story. Their adoption of their son worked its way through the court system, and she was finally able to dust off the draft. I have no doubt she will sail through a rewrite.

The Craft Cycle can be a minefield of critic tricks and traps. Honor your capacity and take time to calibrate.

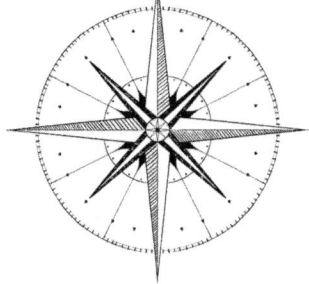

PART V

Dream to Draft

Story Cycles move in spirals.

Take a breath.
       Calibrate.
           Drop into the now.

      Make the plunge.
       Cultivate.
          Adapt, flow,
             swim through the seasons.

Turn up the heat.
      Collaborate.
        Cozy up to the critic.
        Call in the muse.
           Connect, care, create.

Get grounded.
      Craft.
        Refine, release, transform. Let go.
        Finally, finish . . .
or begin again.

Dream, dare, do, and draft.
           (Progress, not perfection.)

CHAPTER SEVENTEEN

Story Spirals

Dream, dare, and draft. Calibrate and begin again.

Calibrate, Cultivate, Collaborate, Craft. Are you finally finished, or is it time to begin again? Story Cycles move in spirals, so it's likely you'll circle through them again and again. To complete a project, we combine the distinctive forces of each cycle. Break through blocks by pulling techniques from one Story Cycle into another.

FIRST THINGS FIRST: Story Seasons

When you embrace the ebb and flow of the writing process, you will instinctively spiral through the Story Cycles. As the distinctive characteristics of each cycle become more familiar, you'll be able to adapt or call in the energy you need.

Call in the energy you need. For example, during the heavy lifting of rewriting, tap into the playful energy of the summer cycle. A simple activity like using markers to chronicle the critic's voice can bring their colorful comments to life, and the lighthearted approach provides relief from the critic's snarky rants. You can also invoke the Collaborate Cycle by connecting with your audience or calling in your muse. No matter what cycle you're moving through, continue to cultivate and nourish the process with an infusion of emotions.

Call in the Season

Story Cycles move in spirals. Circle back to the season whose energy you need.

- ◎ Calibrate with a wintry pause.
  - Include the bridge practice into your writing routine.
  - Invoke the Calibrate Cycle and reconnect with your *why*.

- ❁ Wake up by dipping into spring's well of mystery.
  - Plotting and planting take time, so move through the Cultivate Cycle by returning to the senses and emotions.
  - Calibrate with the question list and discovery writing.

- ☼ Restart by stoking your creative fire with collaboration.
  - Cozy up to your critic, call in your muse, and connect with your reader.
  - Spark the summer cycle with whimsy and play.

- ▲ Renew with radical self-care when the Craft Cycle tires you out.
  - The fall cycle offers a treasure trove of tools, but the harvest heralds transformation. To finally finish, you must be willing to let go.
  - Scaffold the process with radical self-care and enlist the kind critic.

BEING SEEN

One of the most thrilling parts of the writing is sharing our work. Being seen and heard makes us feel that we matter and that we belong. There are many reasons to write, but often the ultimate goal is publication, production, or an opportunity to perform. Yet, even if the writer dreams of putting their stories into the world, being in the spotlight can be uncomfortable. Receiving attention, even positive attention, may not feel natural. Often writers like to be behind the scenes; moving through the Story Cycles means being visible.

STORY CYCLES: THE BREAKDOWN

CALIBRATE
QUIET, REST

Reconnect to Your Why

Bridge

Pause

CULTIVATE
PLAN, PLOT

Emotions and Senses

Discovery Writing

Question List

Dream + Reflect

Develop + Draft

FALLOW

PREPARE

WINTER

SPRING

FALL

SUMMER

HARVEST

BLOOM

Refine + Release

Play + Explore

Kind Critic

Love List

Feedback

REVISE, LET GO
CRAFT

Be Visible

Celebrate

Warm-Up

CONNECT, SHINE
COLLABORATE

It's to be expected that the writer will experience rejection and even heartbreak. Be it from the inside or the outside, we must learn to cope with criticism. To weather the seasons of creativity, we must learn to manifest the "invincible summer" even in winter. Learning to celebrate success prepares us to be visible. Slow down and acknowledge what you've accomplished. Look back and give thanks.

YOUR FUTURE SELF

In addition to looking back, we can also look forward. Recapture a sense of wonder by writing a letter to your future self. The act of time traveling helps reset to a posture of play and reclaim a spirit of adventure. When we look at the project through the eyes of our future self, we imagine the work complete. This uplifting vantage point allows us to step back from the present and see the work in a new way.

This low-stakes writing assignment helps us renew intentions. Consider reminding your future self why you chose to tackle this project. You may want to suggest ways to connect with your muse and tips on managing the sneaky critic. You might offer hints on how to calibrate your creative compass. You might warn yourself about specific challenges or prescribe self-care. A little cheerleading can provide needed motivation.

Even after making great progress, it's not uncommon for writers to minimize their work. At one time, they thought a first draft was impossible, but as soon as it's complete, they diminish the accomplishment and criticize the imperfections. It's easy to lose steam before you reach the finish line, so when you reach a milestone, write a love note to your future self.

ACTIVITY: Thank You Note   ⏰ 30 minutes

Set aside time to write a thank you note to your muse. Sometimes it's hard to give ourselves credit for what we've done, so try looking at your writing from the point of view of your muse.

- ☐ In the letter, acknowledge what you've done and thank your muse for the inspiration and strength they provided to get you to this point.

- ☐ You can also ask for help putting your work into the world.

Put a Bow on It

When I completed the second draft of my first novel, I wanted to savor the moment. I was far from finished, but before I moved on to something new, I knew it was important to mark this milestone and my efforts. I knew that when it was time for revision, I would invite the critic to the party, so I decided I would take preemptive measures. I would write a letter to my future self.

While all the ups and downs of revising the draft were fresh in my mind, I wanted to reflect on the process. I leafed through my field notes, and I was struck by my diligent efforts. In my letter to my future self, I acknowledged the different areas I had worked on. I applauded my willingness to tackle tricky material. I reminded myself that it is important to value each Story Cycle. I gave myself words of encouragement and prescribed a bit of radical self-care.

I slipped the note into an envelope and wrote my name in curly script. Then I had the local copy shop print and bind the draft. The weight of it in my hands made it palpable, real. I wrapped the manuscript up and tied it in a white shiny bow.

After a few days, I started itching to dive into another rewrite, but when I looked at the draft wrapped up in a bow, it reminded me I needed to honor this milestone. Even though I knew what was inside, the pretty wrapping lifted my spirits and reminded me to savor this moment.

It was three months later when I opened my "gift," and I had forgotten what I had written to my future self. The letter was uplifting, empowering, and illuminating. It turns out my past self knew exactly what I needed to hear.

ACTIVITY: Dear Me   20 minutes

Write a letter to your future self.

> * See the end of the chapter for step-by-step instructions.

A new point of view helps you pull the work out of your head and into the world.

CONNECT WITH YOUR READER

Another great way to move from one cycle to the next is to look at the story from the reader's perspective. By tapping into the point of view of your audience, you experience the story with fresh eyes. When the puzzle pieces don't seem to fit together, a new vantage point helps you reconnect to the material and gives you a deeper understanding of the themes. Don't focus on gatekeepers like publishers or distributors; instead, envision your ideal reader. Who is the actual person you hope will read your book or watch your movie? It can be a friend, a relative, or an imagined person. Get super specific. This helps you pull the work out of the confines of your mind and into the world.

We can use letter writing to conjure a connection with the reader. This activity has helped me climb out of dark holes. The closer we get to the finish line, the louder the critic becomes. My critic starts piping up:

> *This story is so depressing and boring. The main character is such an idiot. Why did I think anyone would be interested in this story? Does this even make sense? Why did I choose this project? This is the wrong project to be working on. This is going to take forever. Even if I do pull it together, what's the point of putting this pathetic piece out into the world? Why would I want to share it? I don't want my parents to read this. I don't want my daughter to see this.*

I recall once when I was nearing the homestretch of a rewrite, the critic's complaints got darker and my outlook bleaker. Even though I diligently showed up, my progress slowed, and I got stuck in a whirlpool of indecision and shame. It was time to reconnect to the reader, so I ditched that day's writing goal and set out to work on a letter.

Without an audience, there is no theater. Everything done is ultimately for the enjoyment of the audience. They are our guests, fellow players, and the last spoke in the wheel which can then begin to roll. They make the performance meaningful.

—Viola Spolin

First, I decided I would imagine my ideal reader. She was twenty-one, just out of college, and working at a bookstore. She had only recently realized she was pretty, and she had just been dumped by a bad boyfriend. She volunteered at Greenpeace but was sick of her flakey coworkers.

In my letter, I explained my intentions and asserted what I hoped she would get out of the story. I tapped into my *why*. I wrote about why the story mattered to me and why I thought it would be valuable for a reader.

In a flash, I realized that at the core of my critic's fear was the worry that the story would traumatize the reader. In the same instant, I realized it was my own trauma being reactivated. At the center of the story was a fictional event inspired by a painful experience from my own life. The dark thoughts that had been slowing me down stemmed from my own shame and pain. I scheduled some extra self-care, and I decided it was okay if my pace slowed.

The act of imagining a reader took me out of my head and allowed me to connect with my younger self. To transform my real-life trauma into a meaningful story, I had healing to do, and part of that included having compassion for my younger self. I reminded the critic that we would decide later if we wanted to cut details, modify scenes, or even offer a trigger warning. This gave me new ideas on what my story needed, renewed my faith that the story had value, and cleared the way to move forward.

ACTIVITY: Dear Reader . . .   20 minutes

Imagine they just finished watching or reading your story. Consider their experience and what you want them to take away from your story.

  * *Visit the end the of chapter for step-by-step instructions.*

RECAP: Dare to Draft

To spiral through all the Story Cycles, remember to deploy the playful techniques of the Collaborate Cycle and the invigorating energy of the Cultivate Cycle. Employ letter writing to experience the world of the story from a fresh POV. A new vantage point helps you pull the work out your head and into the world. Letter writing can also help you connect to the character's inner world and your own psyche. By daring to dive into the river of emotions, you will be able to move from dream to draft.

Tools and Techniques

- ◎ Story spirals
- ◎ Connect with the audience
- ◎ Letter writing

 Download
All-Weather Playbook

> The story that comes calling might be your own and it might not go away if you don't open the door. I don't believe in writer's block. I only believe in fear. And you can be afraid and still write something. No one has to read it, though when you're done, you might want them to.
>
> —Melissa Febos

Chapter Seventeen Activities

Dear Me

Write a letter to your future self and tuck it away. Reconnect to curiosity, reset to a posture of play, and recapture a sense of wonder. Write a letter to yourself in your Field Notes Writing Tracker.

Consider these questions:

- ☐ What do you love about yourself that you always want to remember?
- ☐ When times are tough, whom can you reach out to?
- ☐ When times are great, whom can you celebrate with?
- ☐ What are telltale signs that the critic has shown up?
- ☐ If you had a secret message to yourself, what would it be?
- ☐ Clarify your why.
  - – Why do you want to tackle this story?
  - – Why you?
  - – Why now?

Add practical suggestions:

- ☐ Note three good places to write.
- ☐ Note the time of day that is most productive.
- ☐ Prescribe self-care, medicinal reading, or treats.
- ☐ Share inspiration: a favorite tip, mantra, quote, or insight.

Have fun with it. Try one of these suggested approaches:

- Make a request.
- Express appreciation.
- Reflect on your experience.
- Send an SOS to your muse.
- Write a love letter to yourself.
- Serve the critic a restraining order.

Shortcut: If you don't want to pen a long letter, make it easy.

- ☐ Jot down a few words in your Field Notes Writing Tracker.
- ☐ One word on a sticky note can be a bridge back to creativity.
- ☐ Dash off a postcard and pop it in the mail.
- ☐ Slip a sweet valentine into your journal.

Dear Reader . . .   ⏰ 20 minutes

Imagine they just finished watching or reading your story. Consider their experience and what you want them to take away from your story. You might tell the reader why you decided to write the story, why it's important to you, and what you hope the reader will connect to. You don't actually send the letter to a reader but rather use the activity to reactivate your why and reconnect to the value in your work.

Tip: This is not a disclaimer; instead, this is a way to remember why you care.

Step 1. Imagine your reader.

- ☐ Use list making to describe your imagined reader.
  - • Before writing take a moment to envision a specific reader.
  - • Consider these attributes:
    - • Age, gender, location, hobbies, dreams, challenges, secrets; what do they want, need, fear?

Step 2. Write the letter.

- ☐ As you write the letter, consider these questions:
  - • Why are you writing this story?
  - • Why do you care about these characters?
  - • What do you love about the world?
  - • What do you hope your reader learns from your story?
  - • What do you hope their key takeaways will be?
  - • What do you hope readers connect with and relate to?
  - • How do you hope your story will help the reader?

- Heal . . . move away from pain?
- Relief . . . move toward pleasure?

☐ Consider your approach:
- Share your enthusiasm.
- Make a request.
- Express appreciation.
- Send an invitation.

Step 3. Seal and reveal.

☐ Put the letter in an envelope, seal it, and tuck it away.

☐ Wait a few days.

☐ Make yourself a cup of tea and read it.

☐ Write about your observations. What did the activity reveal?
- Insights about your why?
- Revelations about blocks?
- Practical ways to navigate the next steps?

BEHIND THE SCENES: Kugel vs. Kugel

When I looked at the empty plate, I thought of the blank page. In both cases, I felt a mix of excitement and nerves. I craved the adventure that lay ahead, but the unknown could also feel dangerously anchorless. The New Year's Day brunch buffet brimmed with possibilities. It was the first day of a new year, so every choice felt extra important.

Before I could rejoin the party, I needed to tend to the serious business of kugel. Kugel, the Yiddish word for "noodle," is a cheesy, buttery baked casserole often served on Jewish holidays. It was a tradition at the annual gathering to vote on the favorite kugel. Will this year's story be sweet or savory? Light or heavy? A fantasy or a tragedy?

I wanted to start the new year on the right foot. I took a moment to do a body check-in. I have a complicated relationship with the buffet. I don't have great boundaries when it comes to a culinary cornucopia. I've been known to throw myself into eating with the same reckless abandon of a freewrite.

I eyed the creamy contenders. Would the champ be the sweet kugel or the savory? I'm partial to salty, so I sampled the savory kugel first. The delicate brine brought my taste buds to life, but to be fair, I would give its rival a chance. I cleansed my palate with a sip of coffee, then dug into the dessert doppelgänger. A surprising note of cinnamon swept me away. I swooned over the sweet slice. Before I could cast my vote, I needed a rematch. As the battle of bites continued, I wondered, is it even possible to compare sweet with savory?

One of the guests interrupted my buffet bewilderment. Thankful for the intervention, I set the kugel aside and listened as Meher spoke with breathy excitement. She had an idea for a book and wanted to schedule a session with me to talk it through. I was surprised and flattered that she wanted to enlist me as her book coach, as she's a successful curator, a respected art historian, and a published author. She explained that this book was different. It was personal. She described it as an "art memoir." I was hooked.

Over the course of the next few weeks, we charted a plan of action. She whipped up a list of chapters and set to work. Two months in, the pandemic hit. Work slowed. Then life dealt Meher another life-altering blow. Her father passed away. He was across the globe in Cambridge, England, and lockdown had complicated and compounded the loss. Understandably, the grief took a toll. A few months later, just as she had started to write again, another big event presented itself. She was up for a full-time gig. She recognized it was a good position, but she had some serious reservations. If she gave up her freelance lifestyle, she worried it would kill her writing project, but it wasn't just a job—it was a really great job: prestigious, well-paid, and exactly in her area of expertise. This wasn't a simple kugel vs. kugel debate; this was a serious opportunity. I counseled her to accept their offer.

I assured her the book would be here for her later and suggested that this experience would likely give her good material. Indeed, it was a rewarding experience, and it also intensified her desire to get back to writing. After two years, she resigned from the job and, sure enough, the book was waiting for her. As expected, the experience gave Meher new insights and even more determination. She cranked out an entire first draft. She sprinted through one chapter after another, all while juggling freelance gigs, parenting, and nursing an old injury that had reared its head.

Over the course of just five months, she completed the first draft. She wanted to jump into the rewrite. Instead, I encouraged her to celebrate this milestone and recommended she take a break. She was resistant to my suggestion. Meher was eager to begin the rewrite as soon as possible. I countered that she would benefit from refilling the well. She admitted she felt depleted. I reminded her it is natural for productivity to ebb and flow.

I suggested there were benefits to letting the ground lie fallow. She had raced through the Story Cycles, and it was time to calibrate. She was overdue for some radical self-care. She rejected this idea, but as fate would have it, she was destined for a pause. On the way home from our session, she got into a car accident. Miraculously, she was mostly fine. Meher took a much-needed rest from her writing.

Story Cycles wield their own power.

The pause is part of the process. It's hard to step away from the creative flow. Creative momentum is intoxicating, and it's tempting to stay spinning in your story, but there comes a time to put the kugel down. I reassured Meher that when the time was right, she'd come back with fresh eyes and new energy. Indeed, when she dove back into the second draft, Meher made great progress.

Every story has its season. Story Cycles move in spirals. Every season matters.

It's Elemental

Tune In: Drop into the now. Take a breath. Activate a wintry pause. Plunge into the potent waters of the spring cycle. Fire up inspiration with the summer season. Get grounded with fall's earth energy.

In this chapter, we harness the power of Story Cycles by wielding the elemental forces of air, water, fire, and earth. We break down the essential properties and identify the corresponding Story Cycle. This intuitive framework helps us calibrate and tackle creative challenges no matter what season we're cycling through. When you're unable to move forward, tune into the elemental forces.

- Air is associated with the power of the mind; wake up clarity: calibrate.

- Water taps into emotions; move into the mystery: cultivate.

- Fire ignites passion, imagination, and connection: collaborate.

- Earth roots us in practicalities; get grounded: craft.

FIRST THINGS FIRST: Brave The Elements

Working with the elements takes the Story Cycle Method to the next level. There are countless ways to use these forces to troubleshoot, adapt, and innovate. When you feel broken or out of control, the earthy act of being in nature can fortify the writing process. On the other hand, if the writer feels stuck, this is a sign that there may be an over-abundance of earth energy. If this is the case, we can lighten the mood with the airy act of calibration or unleash the combustible energy of collaboration. The fiery tactics of collaborating ignite inspiration and passion. Another approach might be to reinvigorate the process with the watery energy of cultivating. The elemental forces give us a new set of tools, free up creativity, and liven up the writing process.

One of my favorite ways to invoke the power of the elements is to use music. Specifically, music is a great way to tap into the watery nature of emotions. For example, writers can revitalize the process by creating playlists. I recall struggling to write a romantic sequence in a story. To get in the mood, I cued up the *Downton Abbey* theme song, put it on repeat, and let the score sweep me away. The sensory power of sound reliably reconnects the writer to the thematic undercurrents of a story.

ELEMENTAL

The elements provide writers with an organic metaphor that liberates us from self-judgment. The lens of the elements works as a helpful diagnostic tool because, instead of seeing an issue as a weakness, the writer can simply determine which elements are lacking or which are overabundant. A quick inventory of one's state of mind can reveal the elemental properties that are missing or in excess.

Let's break down each element's basic characteristics and show how the elements correspond to Story Cycles and seasons.

"All creativity is a cycle . . . a cycle that has that quickening and rising to a Zenith and begins to decline and falls into a death and then an incubation, a holding or waiting period, and once again a quickening and then a rebirth. And this process continues over and over again. And it is this cycle that is right, and proper and cohesive and sacred."

—Clarissa Pinkola Estés

◎ AIR: This element corresponds to the power of the mind.

- Air corresponds to winter and the techniques of the Calibrate Cycle.
- When a writer feels stuck, the airy act of calibration can lighten and open possibilities.
- Air wakes up clarity, communication, and expression.

🪷 WATER: This element is about emotion.

- Water energy is the hallmark of spring and the lifeblood of he Cultivate Cycle.
- When a writer feels disconnected, the watery nature of cultivating can activate emotion, intuition, and healing.
- Water brings the writer flow and adaptability.

🌅 FIRE: This element represents passion and creativity.

- Summer pulses with fiery energy, fueling the Collaborate Cycle.
- When a writer is unable to make progress, it's time to ignite creativity by unleashing fiery tactics.
- Fire acts as a cleanser to burn up negative thoughts, and the heat can rekindle connection.

⛰ EARTH: This element corresponds to practical and physical features.

- This grounding force is rooted in the Craft Cycle and heralds fall's harvest.
- The treasure trove of earthy tools gives both the writer and the project structure.
- Earth acts as a calming and grounding force.

THE ELEMENTS: A GUIDE

Harness the elemental forces. This quick guide highlights when and why to employ each cycle's corresponding element.

Calibrate: Activate the element of air: clarity.

LACK: Lack of air can lead to feeling stuck.

EXCESS: An excess of air can lead to overthinking, indecision, and disorientation.

Cultivate: Activate the element of water: emotion.

LACK: A lack of water makes the story, process, or mindset feel brittle.

EXCESS: An excess of water can result in a feeling of overwhelm or drowning.

Collaborate: Activate the element of fire: connection.

LACK: A lack of fire leads to a cold, lifeless, or flat story.

EXCESS: An excess of fire can lead to burnout or a dominance of anger and hate.

Craft: Activate the element of earth: grounding.

LACK: A lack of earth leaves a story without substance, meaning, or tangibility.

EXCESS: An excess of earth can manifest as perfectionism, fear of being visible, or an inability to take risks.

Download
The Elements: A Complete Guide

The Wheel Keeps Turning

There's a long tradition of tapping into the elemental forces as a way to understand the cyclical nature of life. Just as the seasons help us understand Story Cycles, the interplay of elements can help us navigate the dynamic process of creativity. Influential thinkers like Carl Jung employed the elements to describe psychological tendencies; astrologers use this model to categorize the zodiac signs; and around the world, the elements figure into spiritual stories. In the bhavacakra or "wheel of becoming," Buddhists employ the elements to symbolize liberation from suffering with the elements marking the path to enlightenment.

The elements are often used to describe nature's destructive and creative forces. In Central Africa, the Bakongo religion incorporates the four elements in a sacred symbol that shows a correlation to the life cycles, the four cardinal directions, and the seasons. Similarly, the Native American medicine wheel recognizes the elemental forces embodied in the four directions (east, west, north, south). Just as the elemental forces foster understanding, healing, and harmony, writers can invoke the elements to navigate the creative process.

CALIBRATE: SOMETHING'S IN THE AIR

The air element is immediate but invisible. Similarly, our thoughts are omnipresent and often unconscious. Like the atmosphere that surrounds us, it's difficult to harness this element. Just as atoms move quickly in a gaseous form, thoughts often race through the mind, and clarity can be fleeting.

While air helps us move through the process, too much of this element might make the writer feel restless and rushed. When creativity is dominated by air, you can develop ideas, but you might have a hard time emotionally connecting to the material and instead find yourself caught in contemplation.

You can activate the air element by creating breathing room: remove material and lean into minimalism. Another way to invoke this element is to seek new information and look at the work with curiosity. This element is especially important for nonfiction writers because these texts rely on accuracy, clarity, and thoughtful ideas.

When you feel confused or stuck in your head, it's time to calibrate and clear the air. When it's difficult to see the next steps, draw in a breath of fresh air. Pull back from the details and clarify the basics. For example, it may feel so obvious, we neglect to put it on the page. Articulate what you intuitively know and what you've already decided. Pause and get oriented. Sometimes, something as simple as remembering the story's genre can offer clues to the next steps.

CULTIVATE: TAKE THE PLUNGE

Water is often associated with emotions because of the element's shape-shifting nature. While we may think of water as characterized by its fluidity, it takes many forms: a vast, salty sea; a free-flowing river; a frozen lake; or a stagnant puddle. When your work has balanced water energy, the material will flow and feel authentic and believable.

Even though water can be healing and nourishing, if there is too much water, the material may not hold together or can dilute the meaning. When we are flooded with emotions, it might be time to balance our approach with a different element. If there is not enough water energy, the emotional current of the work will be hidden from the reader, or the audience may find it difficult to make emotional connections and empathize with your characters. To cultivate the missing element, spend time doing activities that stimulate your own emotions and empathy, such as watching a moving film or listening to emotionally charged music.

An infusion of cultivate's watery energy can help writers adapt to difficult terrain. For example, it's important to understand the core themes in your story, but sometimes identifying themes can be elusive. To access this important fundamental of craft, the writer must tap into emotions and plunge into the unconscious. Music can awaken our emotions and stimulate the senses.

There are many benefits of wielding this watery element. When I need to connect to the big idea at the center of the narrative's climatic crisis, I submerge myself in a sonic environment. The immediate and instinctive experience of music lets me soak in the emotional world of the story. I mine movie scores, sample orchestral recordings, grab grooves from lounge mixes, and pull in ambient nature tracks to build a surround sound experience. If I need to climb inside a character's scary secret, I conjure creepy vibes with a tense playlist.

Music not only can transport you into the mood of a scene, but it's also one of the fastest ways to shake off distractions and build the bridge back to creative flow. I like to jump-start writing sessions with an inspiring anthem that catapults me into the unconscious. Sometimes this can be as simple as finding music emblematic of a story's location. For example, when I am working on my novel set in Argentina, I turn to tango music. If your story is set in Cuba, perhaps listen to the Buena Vista Social Club.

COLLABORATE: TURN UP THE HEAT

When we feel uninspired, it's hard to know how to get fired up. One way to rekindle a connection to the material is to focus on desire. Fire's summery energy can spark ideas and shake up the mood. When you feel uninspired, turn to the tools and techniques of the Collaborate Cycle. Invoke the spirit of play with freewriting, word clouds, and improvisation.

Fire invokes passion and inspiration. Fire is both creative and destructive. Heat creates transformation and light illuminates. This element helps the writer bring ideas together and attract attention. When writers tap into fire energy, they feel enthusiastic, inspired, and joyful. A burst of fire energy can be purifying and illuminating. Fire helps us express from the heart even if sometimes too bluntly.

When fire dominates, the writer may feel impulsive, overly dramatic, or prone to pleasure-seeking. Too much fire can also make writers performative. It's a sign of too much fire when a writer has lots of energy and passion but lacks emotional understanding or mental clarity. The writer who finds they are dominated by this element can tame their fiery tendencies by calling in the other elements, especially water and earth. Fire energy is especially useful when the writing is dull or when the writer has lost inspiration. When this element is lacking, you may lose the determination to succeed. Great ways to activate the fire element are dancing, exercising, singing or even just conversing. The key to activating fire is to do things that excite you.

CRAFT: DOWN TO EARTH

When you don't know what element to activate, get grounded with earth energy. Earth provides stability. This element helps us get the job done. If you find yourself weighed down by worry or wanting, consider connecting to Mother Earth.

If you feel trapped or stuck, you might have an overabundance of the earth element. When earth energy dominates, the material might feel heavy or boring. Even when something is well written, if it feels laborious to the reader, it's time to tap into emotions and indulge in some watery exploration.

Too much earth energy fosters attachment, perfectionism, and resistance to change. If you find yourself stuck in a loop of rewriting, you don't need more earth energy. Instead, spark up some fiery, free-spirited play. Similarly, when you feel weighed down by responsibility or duty, it's time to rev the engine with fiery fun.

When earth energy is lacking, your process or workspace may be disorganized. Like air, earth can help one organize, but rather than drawing on the intellect, earth energy is more about practicality. Focus on order: declutter, organize, and make lists.

In this chapter, we use the elemental properties of each Story Cycle to infuse the writing process with new life. We invoke the elements to rekindle a connection to our story and to penetrate one of craft's more nuanced fundamentals: theme. When a writer is unable to find solutions, it is time to call upon the elemental forces.

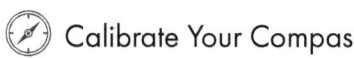 Calibrate Your Compass

Consult your creative compass.
☐ You decide how to calibrate.

Tools and Techniques

◎ The elemental forces
◎ Calibrate: air
◎ Cultivate: water
◎ Collaborate: fire
◎ Craft: earth

Chapter Eighteen Activities

In Your Element

25 minutes

Shift the energy. Use the elements to activate the power of Story Cycles. Follow your intuition.

Step. 1. Diagnose the condition that ails your story.   3 minutes

☐ Identify which area or aspect of the process you'd like to focus on.

☐ Use list making to brainstorm key characters, key moments, and/or important sequences. (List at least five but no more than fifteen.)

Step 2: Pick one area and explore with freewriting.   5 minutes

☐ What emotions does this facet of the story elicit?

☐ What emotions are you trying to invoke in the story and in the reader?

☐ How would you describe the tone and mood surrounding these details?

☐ Consider the senses:

• Is it sweet, slow, loud, soft, fast, funky, ethereal, or grand?

• Is it light, dark, silly, sad, patriotic, or mysterious?

Step 3. Describe what ails you and/or your story.   5 minutes

☐ Use freewriting to clarify the issue.

• How would you describe the problem?

• Use the senses to characterize the issue.

• Is there an excess or a lack?

Step 4: Pick which element can help energize your process.   4 minutes

Step 5: Pick the Story Cycle that's right for you.   8 minutes

Option A: Calibrate—Clear the Air
Take a field trip to the bookstore or do some armchair investigation.

Option B: Cultivate—That's My Theme Song
Use music to create a temporary score for your story.

Option C: Collaborate—Get Fired Up
Use freewriting to explore desire. Turn the heat up and give the desire a sinful spin.

Option D: Craft—Down to Earth
Come down to earth with a small act of self-care.

Option A: Calibrate—Clear the Air

Take a field trip to the bookstore or do some armchair investigation. The way other projects are marketed can help you clear the air. Go to the bookstore and see where books are shelved. Alternatively, look at a streaming service like Netflix and note how they describe shows.

Step 1: Find five books or shows that are in some way comparable to your story.

Step 2: Use list making to record your discoveries.
- What categories are you drawn to?
- Which sections might be where your book is shelved?
- Which area can you imagine your project fitting into?

You can look at online booksellers to see how they categorize books. For example, in the category of memoir and biography, one online seller lists these subcategories:

- Adventure
- Explorers & Survival
- Art & Literature
- Cultural & Regional
- Diaries & Memoirs
- Historical
- LGBTQ+

- Politics & Activism
- Professional
- Academic
- Religious
- Sports
- True Crime
- Women

On streaming services, notice how the mood is distilled into two or three words, like these examples:

- soapy, slow burn
- Surreal thriller, cozy mystery
- intimate, quirky
- cerebral, drama

Step 3: Use freewriting to clear the air.
- ☐ How would you categorize your project?
- ☐ What are three words you would use to describe your show or book?

Note: It's okay if there are multiple moods or categories. We're seeing more hybrid genres like horror-comedy, mystery-romance, or detective sci-fi.

Ready to go further?

Listen to the score of the television shows or movies you picked. Borrow their theme song!

Option B: Cultivate—That's My Theme Song

Just as filmmakers use music to cue the audience, we can use music to shift or heighten our emotional landscape. Tap into the vast body of music available and borrow a "theme song" or create a temporary score for your story. What if you had theme music for your story? Would it be light, dark, silly, sad, or mysterious?

Step 1: Pick comps.
Write down five comparable projects. Most importantly, think of comps that have a similar mood or tone. These can include a movie, a series, an opera, or even a video game.

Step 2: Research and pull selects.
Now scour the web for soundtracks and the musical scores of the titles you have identified. Pull large selections of possible tracks. Gather a grab bag of possibilities: consider your characters, specific scenes, or key sequences.

Step 3: Pick a theme song or soundtrack.

Pick a theme song or string together five or more tracks to create a temporary score for your story.

Option C: Collaborate—Fired Up

Use freewriting to explore desire. Turn the heat up and give the desire a sinful spin.

Step 1. Pick an emotion that drives your character's desire.

Consult the feelings list in Chapter Five to identify a core emotion at play.

Step 2. Explore the sinful side of their desire and write from the POV of your main character.

Prompt: *I want . . .*

Tip: *Consider the Seven Deadly Sins for inspiration:*

GREED: Characters want more.

LUST: Characters want sex.

ENVY: Characters want what other people have.

PRIDE: Characters value themselves and want to feel as if they're worth something.

SLOTH: Characters just want to do nothing.

WRATH: Characters want to cause suffering.

GLUTTONY: Characters just want to consume.

Step 3. Use freewriting to explore how this desire shows up in your story.

Prompt: *This story is really about . . .*

Option D: Craft—Down to Earth

Come down to earth with a small act of self-care.

Step 1. Consult your self-care cheat sheet from Chapter Two.

• Consider the eight realms.

Step 2. Pick a tiny, easy, free action.

- Stop and smell the flowers.
- Look at the moon, watch the clouds go by, or close your eyes and listen.
- Feel your feet on the earth; let the sun kiss your skin.
- Take a walk in the woods or sit in the shade of a tree.
- Get outside. Experience the elements!

Step 3: Now get outdoors and connect with Mother Nature!

Note: No need to drop money on a spa day. Steer clear of fancy and go for free.

Ready to go further?

Create a mixtape for your character.

- What songs would be on their mixtape?
  - For example, for a project set in the '90s, I created a playlist of pop songs my character would find on the radio during that period. Even if she didn't like the song, it provoked a reaction and revealed more of her personality.
- Is your story set in a specific period?
  - Find pop hits that transport you to the show's era.
- Is your story set in nature?
  - Ocean waves, desert wind, jungle rain . . .
    Cue up a soundscape!
- Need inspiration? Try a Story Cycle Playlist.

Story Cycle Writing Playlist

Desert Soundscape	Desert wind and critters
Search, Fight, Win	Driving, battle, triumph, grand, intense
Swoon Romantic	Hopeful, longing, romantic, heart strings
Dark and Stormy	Dark, intense, foreboding, looming
Moody Mood Music	Ethereal, moody, hopeful, possibility, mystery

 Download
Story Cycle Playlists

BEHIND THE SCENES: River Of Wings

It was a gorgeous Southern California day. The sun was shining, and the neighborhood gardens were blooming. As I headed to the café, I felt the exhilarating possibility of something new. For the last seven years, the details of my documentary had crowded my mind, but I was finally moving on to something different.

It had been almost three years since I had wrapped production on *California State of Mind*, yet the project had continued to dominate my attention. The creative work was wrapped, but the film kept me busy. After the festival run, I made a new cut for broadcast, and after I negotiated distribution deals, I created a companion curriculum. Even as I began archiving the project, I hadn't been able to get something new off the ground. I had dusted off an old script but couldn't rekindle the creative fire. For years, I had been in a serious documentarian mindset, and I was stuck in my head. I felt trapped in a wintry pause. I needed to shake up the elemental forces.

I craved the thrill of being in production, but I hadn't found directing work. I had considered making something small just for fun, but every time I tried to calibrate, my brain went into overdrive, and I'd get stuck spinning a cocoon of contemplation.

After years dominated by the earthy Craft Cycle, I needed to jump-start my creative engine with the fiery energy of collaboration. So, when I was contacted by a producer about directing a music video, I jumped into action. The project (if I even got the gig) was for an emerging artist, AKA a musician you've never heard of. This lowered the stakes and I appreciated that, unlike my documentary, a music video wouldn't be shackled to history and narrative. The genre's creative freedom was intoxicating.

Listening to the track instantly inspired my creativity. Writing the treatment was surprisingly easy. I surrendered to the song, invoking the elemental forces of Story Cycles. The music producer loved the concept, so I set to work putting together a budget. The biggest expense would be production design, so I had arranged a meeting with Marcelle, a brilliant production designer with well over a hundred music video jobs under her belt. She had worked with talents like Rihanna, Pink, Elton John, Lady Gaga, and Katy Perry. We didn't really know one another, but she was a fellow parent at my daughter's elementary school. For years, I had admired her ability to create spectacular haunted houses for our school's annual Halloween fundraiser on a shoestring budget.

It felt like a first date, and butterflies danced in my stomach. When I arrived at Broome Street, I smiled. When we had made the plan to meet at our painfully hip local coffee shop, Marcelle had called it "'z Broom Stick" in her thick Québécois accent.

Marcelle arrived at 'z Broom Stick wearing a stylish fedora. She looked like a female version of Indiana Jones, ready for adventure. Everything with Marcelle is laced with magic.

I laid out the basics of the music video as we sipped coffee and shared a pastry. I was nervous. I didn't want to insult her, but I admitted it was a low-budget project and sheepishly said I understood if this tiny project was not a fit. She brushed aside the talk of budget and dove into the details. She peppered me with questions. I felt my heart relax and my creative soul expand. She embraced the concept, and we talked about color and movement. She came back to the words on the page and praised my writing. She said, of course, she would do the job. Whatever the rate, she wanted to work together. I was speechless.

There was a lull in our conversation, and Marcelle looked over my shoulder. She pointed up toward the sky and said in her thick accent, "Look at 'z bud."

I was confused, but I turned to see a bird gliding overhead. I realized the "z bud" was "the bird." Her signature sparkle brightened as she described the city's many brilliant birds. She'd discovered "'z buds" on her daily bike rides along the Los Angeles River. I worked to decode her Canadian French accent as she rapidly slalomed through choppy grammar and disparate details: the varieties of birds and how the over fifty miles of river runs through the city and into the Pacific. She had an idea for an art project. I struggled to understand her heavily accented English. Did she just say something about flying bicycles?

Her passion was mesmerizing. Marcelle began her career as a costume designer with Cirque du Soleil, and she still exuded the thrill of the spectacular. As she spoke, I forgot LA River's reputation as a postapocalyptic concrete sewer.

It was unusual to be the one listening rather than the one pitching. I could see the vision despite the jarring gaps between a dream and reality. She apologized for her English and was frustrated with her difficulty describing her idea. She explained that she and her husband, also a production designer, had been working on it together and hoped to apply for a grant to fund the project. Her husband, an American, was supposed to do the grant writing, but he had been busy with his day job. The deadline was coming up, and she was stuck. She lamented the sorry state of her written English and sighed; she had all but given up on the grant. I offered to look over the proposal. Then, we realized it was time we both pick up our kids from school, so we agreed to meet up again.

I sent the budget proposal to the music producer. In the meantime, my mind buzzed with curiosity about Marcelle's bird project. She sent me a draft of the grant proposal. Indeed, the draft was filled with typos, sentence fragments, and large gaps in the narrative. That said, her brilliance shone through. I could see her vision. I asked to meet up so she could clarify certain concepts. She told me stories about the river in her hometown, a tiny rural village outside Québec. The river was where she found peace in the midst of our crazy city. I wrote as she paced and gestured wildly. She painted a vivid picture of a public art installation and a community project centered around the hidden gem of our city.

We moved through each section of the grant application. There would be fifty giant kinetic sculptures to celebrate the fifty miles of the river.

She explained how the project was meant to inspire a connection to the river and support efforts to restore it to its natural state.

She explained the birds would be herons because the blue heron was the established icon of the LA River. Her wish was that each sculpture would be personalized by members of the community. She described how each "perch" would be equipped with a solar light, illuminating not only the visually stunning birds but also transforming the bike path into a safe, welcoming environment for cyclists, pedestrians, and families. The goal was to disrupt the ordinary and make the moment extraordinary.

I asked if the project had a name. It did not. I told Marcelle I'd think about the name and rewrite the proposal. She asked me to keep her posted about the music video. That night, I got an email from the music video producer. They loved my proposal but didn't have the money for a shoot. Just like that, the project was dead. Like the leaves of autumn, some projects seem brilliant but fade, fall, and return to the earth.

I poured myself into Marcelle's arresting vision of avian-inspired sculptures. This wasn't what I thought would be next, but it felt right. It was accidental, easy, and free. After years of relentlessly pushing my documentary like a bolder up a hill, it felt liberating to not be the one leading the charge. I realized I didn't have the energy to be the general and the keeper of the vision. I had been trying to make my next project happen, but I needed to refill the well.

My fingers flew across the keyboard in service of Marcelle's brilliant vision. I embellished, moved sentences around, and cleaned up the copy. I detailed how the birds and bicycles would be equipped with sculptural elements that would create a sonic experience with chimes activated by the visitors and the natural forces of winds, light, and heat. The sculptures would be customized with words chosen by each artist or group. I described how the project would bring people together and lift up our dreams and hopes for the river.

The name came to me in a flash: RIVER OF WINGS or R.O.W. I sent the draft of the proposal to Marcelle and David. They were thrilled. How had I been able to synthesize the unwieldy vision into words? I realized that, like the music video, I had channeled the elemental forces and swirled through the Story Cycles. The calibration was a whirlwind of listening. The magic of speaking and scribing made the ideation airy. The watery exchange of ideas made the Cultivate Cycle fluid and fertile. Marcelle was my muse; I corralled her critic and fired up the Collaborate Cycle.

We won the modest grant and thus began a collaboration that renewed my spirit and gave birth to a cherished friendship. Over the next year, we marshaled dozens of volunteers to create what would be a carnival of delight. The "flock" was installed along a half-mile section of the bike path of the river for the local annual Frogtown Art Walk.

RIVER OF WINGS rekindled my creative fire. The project reconnected me with my community and reminded me how to invoke the elemental forces to activate inspiration. Shooting a music video would have been fun, but the magic of R.O.W. made me realize how much I loved helping others bring their visions to life. Thus began my journey as a grant writer, story consultant, and creative coach.

Collaborate with the Critic

Craft: During the hard work of the harvest, the critic likes to turn up the heat. When the critic stirs up fear and doubt, cycle back to summer and collaborate with the critic.

Sometimes my students recoil when I suggest they collaborate with the critic. It's natural to want to shut the critic up. I'm all too familiar with the critic's cruel complaints, but we need the critic when it's time to revise. The critic helps us make it to the finish line. So instead of being held hostage by the critic, we explore how the critic can serve the writer. We expose the critic's greatest hits and reframe their toxic narratives.

FIRST THINGS FIRST: Reassess Expectations

Setting unreasonable expectations is one of the most common issues writers face. The critic loves to make unrealistic demands and shames you when you don't meet their impossible goals. If you notice that you are chronically disappointed in yourself, instead of pushing yourself to do more, consider dialing back expectations and set more manageable goals. If you continue to ask too much of yourself, you will fail, then quit. Instead of beating yourself up or throwing in the towel, reexamine expectations.

Back to the Map

While the critic may demand independence, establishing a writing practice requires setting up a routine. Revisit your field notes and revise your writing schedule. It is the writer's responsibility to set limits, but often the critic doesn't like to be controlled. The critic may reject plans and rebel against structure, but here's the secret: deep down the critic craves order. Just as children challenge parents, the critic will fight boundaries and routines.

Tip: If your critic hates being bossed around, give yourself more options so the critic doesn't feel so hemmed in.

Critic's Complaints

We need to give the critic a seat at the table during the Craft Cycle, but their complaints can cripple our ability to move forward. The critic might start out with friendly suggestions and polite reminders, but what if the critic hurls zingers like: *Everything's wrong. You don't know what you are doing.* Or *No one wants to read that! Why bother?*

Consider the Critic's Point of View.

When the critic starts hitting below the belt, it's time to consider the critic's point of view. Being the critic is a thankless job. It's stressful and lonely to be on the lookout for danger 24/7. It's no wonder that the critic is a bit of a fear junkie.

Sometimes the critic freaks out about something that actually isn't a real problem. For instance, pace is one of the biggest worries I hear from my clients, but many talented authors don't churn out work at breakneck speed. Think of Pulitzer Prize winner Donna Tartt. There's a ten-year span between each of her three novels. Author Douglas Stewart spent ten years writing his award-winning novel *Shuggie Bain*. Another example is Min Jin Lee who spent over thirty years penning

It will never be perfect, but perfect is overrated. Perfect is boring...

—Tina Fey

her second novel, the best-selling *Pachinko*. Both Stewart and Min worked full-time jobs. These examples show that pace doesn't define a writer's talent, but logic is often insufficient to appease the critic. My mentor Caroline taught me to ask, *Why is that a problem?*

So, what if it's going to take you ten years! If the critic says, *You're too old*, or *You don't have a big enough vocabulary*, ask, *Why is this a problem?*

REFRAME

When the critic throws a tantrum, take a moment to reframe. It's often a sign we're tired and need to take a break. Maybe the critic feels unappreciated, neglected, or excluded. The critic needs to feel heard. By understanding what's driving the critic's panic, we reframe their complaint and uncover solvable stumbling blocks.

ACTIVITY: Suggestion Box   ⏱ 30 minutes

Let the critic know you're taking their concerns under consideration.

- ☐ Explore with freewriting.
    - Find out what's worrying them.
- ☐ Read and review.
    - What does the critic need?
- ☐ Make an adjustment.
    - Give them a treat, make an artist date, or assign them a job.
- ☐ Set up a "suggestion box."
    - Designate a spot in your Field Notes Writing Tracker for the critic to make suggestions.

FLIP THE SCRIPT: Five Reframes to Quiet the Critic

Turn the critic's complaints around.

1. Consider the possibility that you are exactly where you need to be.
   - What if the real problem is the critic's bad attitude?
     Reframe:
     > What if I am on the right path?
     > What if I'm not doing anything wrong?
     > What if my pace is perfect?

2. Challenge the veracity of the critic's complaints.
   - Is the content of the complaint the real issue?
     Reframe:
     > Why is this an issue?
     > Why is it a problem?

3. Look at what's driving the critic's panic.
   - What are they afraid might happen?
     Reframe:
     - Maybe the critic is worried you'll publish the messy first draft.
       - Promise you won't send out the work until you've brought them back for the revision process.
     - Maybe the critic feels unappreciated?
       - Give the critic a treat, make an artist date, or assign them a job!

4. Examine what you are making the critic's complaint mean.
   - What if the scary feelings you're having are actually good?
     Reframe:
     > What if I feel fear because I am sensitive and thoughtful?
     > What if I doubt the idea because I'm tired from working hard?
     > What if I feel worried because this matters to me?
     > What if I focus on faults because I care about the impact of my writing?

5. Get to know the critic's greatest hits.
   - Have you heard this story before?
     Reframe:
     > What if this is an old, toxic narrative?

THE CRITIC'S GREATEST HITS

The inner critic likes to replay old tapes of negative self-talk. The good news is by paying attention to the well-worn grooves of the critic's rant, we can excavate old, toxic narratives. The critic isn't always interested in the truth. The critic will attack talent, goals, and timing. That said, the critic cycles through some predictable rants. Let's look at their greatest hits.

Talent and Topic:

- The critic will say you're doing it wrong.
- The critic will inform you that you're not a real writer.
- The critic will bash your ideas and label them as dumb, bad, unoriginal, not funny, etc.

Goals and Vision:

- The critic sets unrealistic goals.
- The critic changes goals.
- The critic sets vague, unmeasurable ambitions.
- The critic picks a goal you can't control.
- The critic ignores the work on your stated goal and judges you on a different metric.

Timing:

- The critic never thinks it's the right time.
- The critic insists you need to do more research before you can start writing.
- The critic says you need to clean your closet, help someone [do xyz], get through [insert excuse], etc.
- The critic says you need more experience, training, and help.
- The critic says you'll never get there.

Watch out for the critic's bullying tactics.

- Globalizing with never, always, and every.
- Making ultimatums or proclamations filled with should.
- Dropping derogatory comments, resorting to name-calling, mocking, or making threats.
- Digging in with if-then logic.
    - *If you haven't finished this by now, then you're not really a writer.*
    - *If someone else writes about this topic, then there's no point in you writing about it.*
    - *If I don't accomplish X today, then I'll never be able to.*
    - *If I stop to take a break, then I am giving up.*

AGREE TO DISAGREE

When dealing with the critic, you may need to agree to disagree. Even if you play by the rules, the critic's wrath knows no bounds. Even if you play nice, the critic may strike back with blame and shame. The critic can be a drama queen, so watch out for histrionics and globalizing.

Once you learn to recognize their greatest hits, the critic will sing a new tune. The critic is a master of shapeshifting. No matter how adept one becomes at working with the critic, they'll find new ways to get your attention. Once you disprove one complaint, it won't be long before the critic pinpoints a new problem. The critic will bring up the past and make unfair comparisons, like comparing your first draft to a published book.

When we can't reason with the critic, we may not be able to stop our knee-jerk reaction, but we can agree to disagree. Stay curious and try these noninflammatory responses:

- *You might be right.*
- *I need to think about that.*
- *I'm sorry you feel that way.*

- *Could you say that differently?*
- *Tell me more . . .*
- *Tell me more about why you think x?*
- *Tell me more about why you think it is a problem to x?*

You can't edit something that doesn't exist.

Safe Space

Having feelings is part of the process, but if worry shuts down the process, it's time to create a safe space for generating material. You can't edit something that doesn't exist. If you find you're censoring yourself before you even get words onto the page, you might be dealing with a fear junkie.

INTERVENTION

Instead of being held hostage by the critic's thinking, it's time to stage an intervention. The purpose of the intervention is to encourage the critic to seek treatment and to offer support. It's an opportunity to set forth a vision of the kind of relationship you want.

The first step is to write an impact statement. The critic needs to know how their addiction to fear has impacted you. It's also important to express how much you value the critic. Support, compassion, and respect are essential ingredients to staging a successful intervention.

ACTIVITY: Impact Statement   60 minutes

* See the end of the chapter for step-by-step instructions.

RECAP: Moving Forward

In this chapter, we expose the critic's greatest hits and provide ways to reframe their complaints. Rather than hiding from the critic, we consider their point of view and focus on building a relationship with them. To keep moving forward on the writing journey, we reassess expectations, learn how to agree to disagree, and when to stage an intervention.

 Calibrate Your Compass

Consult your creative compass.
☐ You decide how to calibrate.

Tools and Techniques

- ◎ Reframe
- ◎ Agree to disagree
- ◎ Critic's tricks and greatest hits
- ◎ Impact statement

Chapter Nineteen Activities

Impact Statement

⏰ 60 minutes

Before you can really cozy up to the critic, take time to acknowledge how they've affected you. Write a letter to the critic that details how their attitude and behavior have impacted you.

WARNING: If you don't feel like you know the critic, go back to "Capture the Critic" (in Chapter Eight). Naming the critic is a prerequisite for this exercise. Especially if your critic is based on somebody you know, be sure you've separated them from the real person.

Step 1: Before writing your impact statement, use freewriting to get your feelings out.

Tip: This first draft is an uncensored rant that you don't "send."

☐ Detail how the critic's attitude has impacted you.

☐ Cite how the critic's messages have affected your mental and emotional health.

- Be honest but remember that the critic is not on trial.
- Remember, this is not about collecting evidence to prove your point.
- You are building a relationship.

☐ Focus on a few meaningful examples.

- If you find yourself condemning the critic or falling into self-pity, bring it back to specific messages from the critic.
- Don't get stuck in the past.
- Resist the urge to make an exhaustive list of every grievance through the ages. While you may have lots of examples, rehashing the past undermines your objective.

Step 2: Now cherry-pick the material for the impact statement.
- ☐ Let the critic know you understand that this is their job.
- ☐ Thank them for their care and concern.
  - Show love, respect, and gratitude.
  - Tell them you appreciate their interest in your writing.
  - If you have a tumultuous relationship, try to think back to a happier time when fear wasn't running the critic.
- ☐ List two or three specific traits or moments that exemplify their positive side. *(Don't be overly flattering or insincere; lack of sincerity will derail the intervention. The critic usually has a highly effective BS detector.)*
  - To encourage the critic to be more respectful, you need to demonstrate kindness and respect and be willing to hear out the critic.

Step 3: Make a request.
- ☐ Give them a job.
  - What's your critic's superpower? Is it research, proofreading, revision, analyzing, watching, or reading?
  - My critic loves tracking and ticking off items on a to-do list. I oblige but also make it fun for me with stickers and colored pens.

Step 4: Set the ground rules and clarify expectations.
- ☐ Offer the critic time and space to air their concerns. (Schedule it.)
- ☐ Define their area, (when, how, where, and what is fair game).
- ☐ Give the critic some love, like a treat, or schedule an artist date.

Step 5. End on a kind note.
- ☐ Reaffirm your love.
- ☐ Thank them for looking out for you.

Reminder: It's the critic's job to protect you, so you can set parameters, but you cannot—nor is it advisable to—eliminate all fear.

BEHIND THE SCENES: Garbage

Tensions were running high. Eileen's film was nearly done, but we were racing to meet a festival submission deadline, and our resources were dwindling. As a producer on the project, I could see how close we were, but the process of finishing is a moment that breaks many artists. We'd spiraled through the Story Cycles, and it was time to harvest.

The clock was ticking. Soon the editor would need to move onto another project. Winter was coming, and we needed to complete the Craft Cycle. I assured Eileen we were nearly there, but she was feeling worn down. This is the time when insecurities began to flare.

Basurero was Eileen's directorial debut, but she was already a seasoned writer. Drawing on experience as a television writer, and her top-notch training at the American Film Institute, she had written a short film about a fisherman wrestling with impossible choices. The script was a far cry from the Winnie-the-Pooh episodes she'd penned for Disney, but the script was captivating. She knew story.

The filmmaking journey had started the year before, and there had been many twists and turns. Eileen planned to shoot the film in the Philippines, but production had been derailed by a tropical storm. The village where we planned to film was directly in its path. Moving the shoot dates meant we lost our lead actor because he was already scheduled to return to the television series in which he starred. Finally, after months of delays, Eileen gathered the cast and crew and got the film in the can. The shoot had its challenges, but filming had gone brilliantly. Eileen stayed in Manila to edit the film so she could work with a local post team.

Eileen and the editor had done an exquisite job of weaving the story together, but she wasn't satisfied with the film's ending. They had tried different versions, but she didn't feel they'd hit the right emotional resonance. The story was a portrait of a character's unraveling, and Eileen knew that every scene should reflect that, especially the ending.

We lost the editor, and Eileen still hadn't found an ending that felt right. So, we needed to find a new editor, a task that wasn't a matter of simply swapping in a new technician. Like finishing a manuscript, editing is an important part of the craft phase. It requires thoughtful attention to the story. The editor makes hundreds of decisions that shape the story, so finding a new creative partner was important.

In the initial meeting with the new editor, Eileen explained it was a matter of locking down the ending. The new editor proposed a complete restructuring of the story as a way to land the ending. Eileen explained that she'd already tried that idea and that that wasn't the way she wanted to tell the story. After years of working in television, Eileen was an expert collaborator, and she understood any one story can be told a thousand different ways. So even though his comments had raised a red flag, she figured since she'd clarified her vision, he would listen.

Eileen reiterated the task at hand. At this stage, she'd already unearthed the gems, mined the material, and tried even the most implausible possibilities. She reiterated she wanted to stick with the current sequencing. It was not time for cultivating new ideas, but rather it was the final phase of finishing. Eileen had a gut feeling that he wasn't the right editor, but the clock was ticking. So, we moved forward and, as is customary, Eileen left the project in the editor's hands to take a crack at the changes.

I eagerly awaited news of the edit. It was after midnight in the Philippines, and back in California, I'd just finished driving the morning carpool when I saw Eileen's SOS. The new editor had ignored her instructions and had shuffled the scenes into an entirely different sequence. It's natural for an editor to infuse the Craft Cycle with the warm, playful energy of the summer cycle, but he had dropped a flaming collaboration firebomb.

Eileen's inner critic started stirring. At this juncture, Eileen had watched countless versions and, like all artists in the finishing phase, she was struggling to see the cut with fresh eyes. The inner critic roared to life. Eileen questioned her judgment. Her script had an unconventional narrative structure, but now she wondered if the previous cut made sense.

When I finally connected with Eileen on WhatsApp, she was beside herself. The editor was MIA. Like a new mother in her last trimester of pregnancy, the director felt wrung out and stretched to her limit. Eileen was ready to deliver, but the doctor had just gone golfing.

Eileen sunk into self-doubt. She worried the film didn't make sense, and she wanted to change its title, but that wasn't materializing either. I assured her that the story was close, and the new title would come to her. As a producer, I can help solve problems, cheerlead, counter the critic, and help clear a path forward, but it is the author who must walk the path.

She wisely decided she needed to pause and return to self-care. She took a day to sleep on it and let her mind settle. It was clear we needed to enlist yet another editor. While we looked for a new editor, Eileen played around with options on her laptop. After experimenting, she made the difficult decision to ditch two scenes from the film. She realized that the short called for a more subtle denouement. While the two scenes were powerful, it didn't make sense to end with cinematic fireworks. Rather than trying to manufacture a dramatic finale, she leaned into the main character's emotional turmoil. At last, an emotionally satisfying ending fell into place. As is often the case in the Craft Cycle, finishing means letting go.

Eileen worked with at new editor to clean it up and finalize. He embraced the story's organic climax. Then, instead of escalating the drama, the main character wanders aimlessly in the chaotic lights and frenetic traffic. We understand he feels insignificant and useless, like a discarded piece of trash.

As I watched the cut, I welled up with tears. Finally, the film felt complete. I had liked previous versions, but this new ending worked perfectly. The provocative ending was mesmerizing. Just as the film waded into political waters without being didactic, the more subtle ending effortlessly pulled the audience into the emotional heart of the character's journey.

The title for the film came to Eileen in a flash: *Basurero*. This Tagalog word roughly translates as "the one who throws the trash" (or "garbage"). When she had been struggling to finish the film, she had felt like garbage. This hadn't been a sign of artistic failing but rather keen attunement to the main character's pain. It had been a case of character-author entanglement.

Eileen's film went on to screen across the globe, win awards, and receive rave reviews. Most importantly, it was the story Eileen had wanted to tell. She had navigated the complexities of collaboration and the hazards of finishing. She'd faced her inner critic and stayed true to her instincts.

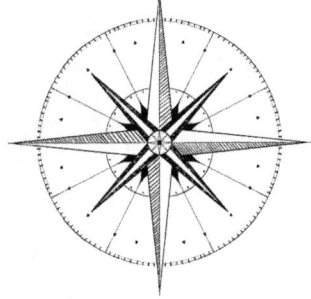

PART VI

That's a Wrap

It's time to complete and let go.

Welcome the in-between time.

Linger in the mystery.

Rest.
            Reflect.
                         Revive.

(Then begin again.)

Mulch More

Every Story Has A Season: Welcome the in-between time.
Progress, not perfection.

To the untrained eye, mulch may appear to be just a stinky pile of dirt, but the wise gardener knows this black gold makes the garden thrive. What does it mean to let the material mulch more? It means the writer must embrace the in-between time. Let the ground lie fallow. We've outlined tools and techniques to navigate the messy middle, but sometimes a project just needs to mulch more. We'll revisit the revitalizing power of radical self-care and return to markers and milestones.

FIRST THINGS FIRST: No Mud, No Lotus

The exquisite lotus flower needs the murky water—or, as the saying goes, "No mud, no lotus." I first heard this from Thich Nhat Hanh, the Vietnamese Buddhist monk, teacher, poet, and peace activist. He used this metaphor to explain that without pain and difficulty, there cannot be life. This also applies to the writing process. The murky middle is not something to avoid, but rather it can be a time of nourishment.

It can be uncomfortable to give a project time to mulch. It may feel as if you are abandoning ship. For example, after I completed the first draft of this book, I felt stuck. The idea of diving into a rewrite felt overwhelming. As an overwriter, I had amassed an excessive quantity of material. I didn't know where to begin. I was both sick of the project and clinging to every word. I also needed to turn my attention to generating income.

Reluctantly, I put the draft to the side. I focused on other projects and building my coaching business. In the intervening years, I wrote a new draft of my novel and the first draft of a pilot. Meanwhile, I also designed a course for my students. I based the curriculum on the material in the rough draft of the book. To accommodate the six-week time frame of the course, I cherry-picked material. After I taught the course, a lightbulb went on. I suddenly could see how to approach the rewrite of the book, so I dove into the editing process. Sharing the ideas helped me clarify the Story Cycle Method, but it was the in-between time that gave me a new perspective, restored my energy, and allowed me to nourish the foundation with layers of fresh new material.

Just as the magic of mulch revitalizes the soil, the writer benefits from sitting in the mystery and muck. Gardeners use layers of mulch to control weeds, retain moisture, and regulate temperature. Similarly, writers need rest to reinvigorate the process, nourish the imagination, and create conditions for inspiration.

FEED THE MUSE

No matter what Story Cycle you are moving through, it is important to acknowledge one's efforts and affirm one's commitment to the process. In addition to savoring success, take time to celebrate the seasons of creativity. Highlight new beginnings, create closure by honoring loss, mark transitions, and cultivate gratitude. By simply bearing witness, we reconnect to the ebb and flow.

Finishing your work demands patience. Marking milestones nourishes our muse, engages us in the process, and prepares us for what's next. When we release the work into the world, we let go of control, so this practice is a prerequisite to ready ourselves to share our writing.

If it feels uncomfortable to do something nice for yourself, then consider the treats as gifts to your muse. When I'm heading into challenging terrain, I call in my muse with a little luxury. A square of chocolate is sometimes all the muse needs. It doesn't need to be fancy, free-trade, single-origin, organic chocolate. I've been known to make a mocha by adding Swiss Miss to my coffee.

A celebration doesn't need to be a grand gesture. A simple treat might be to leave something wonderful for yourself in your journal or on your desk. Write yourself an encouraging letter in your notebook, transcribe an inspiring quote in your Field Notes Writing Tracker, or schedule an artist date.

When the milestone is big, mark it with something more significant. Choose something tangible. A concrete reminder provides proof that you did it. Buy yourself a fancy pen, an art object, or a new candle. Treats don't require you spend money. It's more about intention and making a real reminder of the progress. You might place a flower on your desk, pick up a pretty shell or rock, or press a flower in a book. The key is to make the process enjoyable.

ACTIVITY: Make an Offering   ⏰ 30+ minutes

While all exercises are optional, learning to acknowledge even little successes is essential.

☐ Honor your muse with a gift.

    – You might place a flower on your desk, go on an artist date, or break out that fancy journal you've been saving.

Note: For some, celebrating may feel highly uncomfortable, and for others, celebrating comes a little too naturally! It's worth taking time to observe your tendency.

Story Cycle Markers

When you map your journey, be prepared to spiral through the Story Cycles multiple times. Tune into the seasonal demands and include activities that celebrate the work of all cycles. Plot your course with markers that honor all of the seasons of creativity.

- ◎ Build in radical self-care, rest, and reflection. Calibrate with a pause.
  - Markers may include tasking yourself with freewrites that connect to your *why* and journaling to reflect on the process.
- ❁ Embrace the Cultivate Cycle's mindset of discovery. Track tasks centered on plotting and planning, like sowing seeds in the springtime.
  - Markers might include drafting an outline, reading a book on story structure, or doing research.
- ☀ Nourish your work with the spirit of play. The Collaborate Cycle reminds us to celebrate and connect to joy.
  - Schedule time for an artist date, connect with your muse, have tea with your critic, and celebrate a milestone.
- ▲ Go word by word, scene by scene. During the Craft Cycle, we revise and refine.
  - Count words and pages or liberate yourself from oppressive demands and simply track time spent. Focus on one element at a time: a scene, a character, structure, dialogue, etc.

As you sort through the fruits of your labor, it's easy to become disoriented and overwhelmed. Focus on one element at a time. A clear focus keeps the critic away.

STORY CYCLE MARKERS

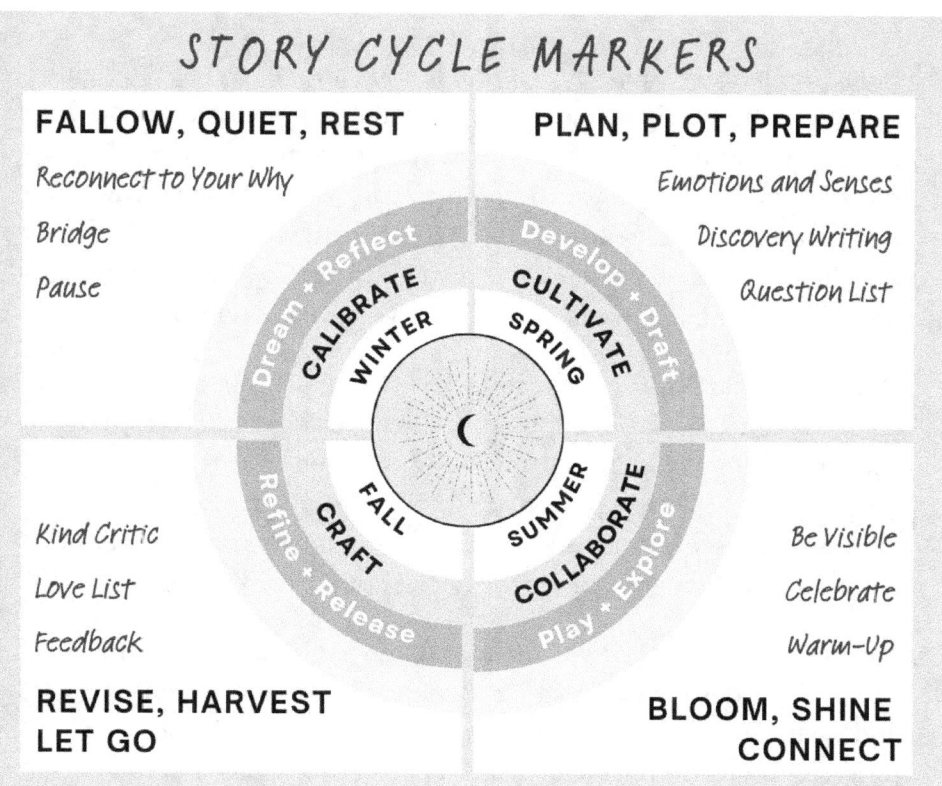

FALLOW, QUIET, REST

Reconnect to Your Why

Bridge

Pause

PLAN, PLOT, PREPARE

Emotions and Senses

Discovery Writing

Question List

REVISE, HARVEST LET GO

Kind Critic

Love List

Feedback

BLOOM, SHINE CONNECT

Be Visible

Celebrate

Warm-Up

Diagram labels: Reflect · Dream · CALIBRATE · WINTER · Develop · Draft · CULTIVATE · SPRING · Refine · Release · CRAFT · FALL · SUMMER · COLLABORATE · Play · Explore

ACTIVITY: Match Your Markers and Milestones   1 hour +

* See the end of the chapter for step-by-step instructions.

REST STOPS AND SCENIC VIEWS

Making a writing schedule is like planning a trip. The itinerary provides a helpful starting point, but it's important to be open to surprises. Be ready to reassess when faced with bad weather or unexpected opportunities. The road to a finished project can be long, and sheer will often isn't enough. To make it to the summit, you will need to acclimate to the change in altitude and adapt to the prevailing conditions, so why not marvel at the sights along the way? You set the pace. What's the rush? Often discoveries and aha moments happen in the pause, the time between the actual writing. Sleep is your superpower. Soothe the senses with self-care.

Enjoy the journey: stop to smell the flowers and marvel at the sights. When you hit the big milestones, do something special to acknowledge this victory. Even if you're the athletic type, remember it's a marathon, not a sprint. Have you ever been on a road trip with somebody who never wants to stop? Instead of a vacation, the drive becomes a forced march. Like a military general, the driver pushes forward: no bathroom breaks, no stopping for snacks, and no dillydallying to look at the view.

When you chart your course, include rest stops and treat yourself to rewards. It may seem unimportant to acknowledge little wins, but if you never pause to appreciate the experience, the critic is sure to crash the party and will stink up the place with fear. By regularly acknowledging your efforts, the critic is less likely to store up an arsenal of ammo. Even small actions work to deactivate the critic's fear bombs.

If you lose sight of the immediate goal, the critic shows up and stokes fear and self-doubt. So, instead of hoping you don't get derailed, track and treat. Tracking your process gives you concrete evidence of your progress. Your field notes can help keep the critic at bay.

Another important reason to recognize your progress is that it prepares you for completion. Sometimes, writers become so protective of a project, it becomes nearly impossible to release it into the world. A key part of finishing is letting go. You know the critic has taken control when you continuously set new or impossible standards. Keep moving forward inch by inch; fill the bucket drop by drop, bit by bit. Every droplet counts.

Rewards may feel self-indulgent, premature, or unnecessary, but make time. Celebrate before you move the goalpost forward. Each writing session is worthy of acknowledgment. Why keep showing up if you're not getting paid, and it's not fun? I'm not suggesting you throw a party every time you sit down to write, but why not make yourself an inspiring playlist, a special coffee drink, or a flower arrangement for your writing area? You might even put a dollar in a jar after each writing session. After a few sessions, you can treat yourself to a fancy coffee drink.

When we acknowledge our efforts, we are more likely to stay motivated. Did you ever have a boss who continually moved the goalpost and never acknowledged your hard work? Working for a bad boss is demoralizing and unsustainable. If you never feel a sense of progress, you will burn out. When a writer diligently shows up but hasn't identified markers, before long they will likely run out of steam or lose faith in the process.

Getting turned around is part of the journey. If you find you've gone off track, remember: Story Cycles move in spirals. Take a moment to calibrate. When you feel disoriented, check in with your markers and milestones. Have you lost sight of your intention? You may need to take a break, refuel, and refill your cup. When the feelings of doubt spike, it's just a sign to track and treat. (I'm saying *when* because it will happen.)

A writer is more likely to continue the journey if they can enjoy the process. Make a habit of celebrating wins.

You can do this! You know how to tell a story. We all know how to tell stories. We are, as the author Lisa Kron says, "wired for story," and, "we think in story." Even if you are a new writer, you've been experiencing stories since before you could speak. Story is how we make sense of the world. This is how we communicate every single day.

> Perfectionism is the voice of the oppressor, the enemy of the people. It will keep you cramped and insane your whole life, and it is the main obstacle between you and a shitty first draft.
>
> —Anne Lamott

Progress, not perfection

It's easy to lose confidence when we don't see the results we hoped and worked for. Learning to stay engaged even when we don't see results requires faith. The work needs time to develop. A seed needs time to grow and even before a new idea is planted, it's worthwhile to blanket the fields with nourishing mulch. During this critical phase of gestation, there's important work happening below the surface. Give yourself space to be incomplete and imperfect.

RECAP: Track the Process

A writer might be accustomed to tracking progress, but the Story Cycle Method illuminates the power of tracking the process and celebrating with treats. This chapter reveals the importance of feeding the muse and reiterates the importance of planning rest stops and scenic views.

 Calibrate Your Compass

Consult your creative compass.
☐ You decide how to calibrate.

Tools and Techniques

- ◎ Match your markers and milestones
- ◎ Rest stops and scenic views
- ◎ Progress, not perfection
- ◎ Feed the muse

Chapter Twenty Activities

Match Your Markers and Milestones

⏰ 1 hour +

Match your markers and milestones to the Story Cycle. Then, once you identify the next step on your writing journey, track the process, and then celebrate.

Step 1: Identify the major milestones and markers.

- ☐ Use freewriting to identify milestones. Explore these questions:
  - Consider your ideal vision. Where would you be with your writing in five years?
  - In light of your vision, what should you focus on first?
  - What's the most important goal for the next twelve months?
- ☐ Consider which Story Cycle you are moving through. Include actions that reflect all Story Cycles and set milestones appropriate to where you are in the process.
- ☐ Identify five mini milestones on the way to that bigger goal.
  - What are the concrete action steps to reach that goal?
- ☐ Identify the measurable markers to reach those milestones.

Reminder: When setting milestones, be sure they are something you can control. Milestones should match actionable outcomes. For example, perhaps you dream of being a best-selling author, selling a script, or winning an award. These goals are mostly out of your hands. It's okay to dream but set milestones that don't rely on outside recognition or gatekeepers. Instead, chart your course with milestones you can execute. For example, consider concrete accomplishments: complete a first draft, give a draft to beta reader for notes, send a script to an agent, or submit an essay to a contest.

Step 2: Write and track.

Now that you've identified markers and milestones, it's time to get to work.

- ☐ Write!
- ☐ Take time to regularly calibrate.
  - I like to use a writing tracker to chart the markers on the way to each milestone. The Field Notes Writing Tracker is also a good place to write down reflections, insights, and questions.

Step 3: Celebrate milestones.

Make time to acknowledge process.

Calibrate, then return to Step 1.

 Download
Story Cycle Markers

> We have lost touch with nature, rather foolishly as we are a part of it, not outside it . . .
>
> —David Hockney

BEHIND THE SCENES: Big Bear

My heart sank. The screening was scheduled to start in a few minutes, and the theater was nearly empty. What a letdown.

Just a few months earlier, we'd premiered to a sold-out house. It was a relief to finally be finished, and the screening had been a success, but the milestone hadn't felt like a celebration. The night of the premiere, I was exhausted from the last push to complete the film and disoriented after years of spiraling through the Story Cycles. Battling my critic had left me feeling raw, and the finish line seemed to be receding again. I'd delivered the film and landed the premiere, so hadn't I'd hit the mark? Yes, but now we had to look for distribution, apply to film festivals, and troll for reviews.

I'd been excited by the invitation from the Big Bear International Film Festival. They'd offered to put me up, and a weekend getaway sounded like the perfect way to celebrate. I was ready for some time in nature and a luxury hotel.

My husband and I made the scenic drive in two hours. It was delightful to be together. The sun was shining and the mountain air crisp. We picked up our festival passes and checked in. The log-cabin-themed motel wasn't the five-star accommodations I'd envisioned, but it was charming in a David Lynch kind of way. I welcomed the laid-back vibe and it felt good to be away from it all. I settled into the comfort of the low-stakes setting. I felt the prescreening jitters melt away.

When I'd envisioned an intimate affair, I hadn't imagined there would only be three other people in the audience besides my husband and me. Thankfully, it was a tiny theater. I squeezed his hand and told him we had to stay. We'd planned to duck out once the lights went down and sneak out to have a cocktail across the street. I had already watched countless cuts of my documentary, and he'd seen it several times too.

I slunk down in my seat as the movie started. A few latecomers settled in. I estimated we had six people in the audience. Things were looking up. As the movie unspooled, I closed my eyes. The audience chuckled in the right places. I opened my eyes and watched the years of work flicker on the screen. Somewhere along the way, a few more people straggled in, bringing us to eight people.

When it was time for the Q&A, I worried no one would stay and simultaneously hoped they all would leave. Normally, I love fielding questions, and I look forward to talking about the documentary, but having such a meager turnout was embarrassing. I was ready for that cocktail.

A festival volunteer quickly introduced me and rushed off to another screening. My husband smiled at me, and I remembered this was about having fun. Then someone asked a question, and a lively discussion unfolded. On the way out, I chatted with one of the moviegoers. I was taken by his insightful comments and before parting ways, I thanked him for coming and we introduced ourselves. I recognized the name. Was it *the* Christopher Vogler, the author of *The Writer's Journey: Mythic Structure for Writers*? It was. He was in town because he was on the jury and would be speaking on a panel. I was starstruck, thrilled to be meeting the author of my favorite screening book. I confessed I was a fan and that I had studied his book when making the documentary. He congratulated me on the structure of the movie. It felt surreal. We exchanged contact information, and the next week I sent him a picture of my copy of *The Writer's Journey*, covered with notes, dog-eared, and worn from use. It no longer mattered that the turnout had been terrible. I treasured the opportunity to connect with Mr. Vogler, and it reminded me that you never know who might be watching or reading your story.

The rest of the weekend was delightfully casual. Thankfully, the Big Bear screening was the smallest audience of our festival run. We went on to sell out shows at festivals, on college campuses, and for community organizations. Our California story even jumped the Rockies and packed the house in New York and Chicago. We secured a cable premiere on public television and then a run on Netflix.

The Big Bear screening wasn't as prestigious as our shows at the National Archives in DC or The Museum of Contemporary Art (MOCA) in Los Angeles, but it stands out as a highlight. That weekend was a much-needed rest stop on the long journey of making the movie. (I hadn't yet realized it was a journey that would continue on much longer.)

The Big Bear getaway was the perfect way to unplug, pause, and appreciate the view. It was the ideal treat after years of hard work. It is critical to mark milestones along the way.

CHAPTER TWENTY-ONE

Take Away

In Season: Trust the process. You're right where you need to be.

We are at the end of the book but perhaps at the beginning of your writing journey. There will always be more on the to-do list, so slow down and be in this moment. Calibrate and consult your inner compass. The next right action will become clear when you acknowledge which Story Cycle you're moving through.

FIRST THINGS FIRST: The Root of the Problem

Before you start trying to solve an issue, take a moment to get to the root of the problem. I've grown to love all phases of the creative process, but the Craft Cycle continues to be the most demanding phase. I used to think this was because I wasn't adept at sculpting structure, but then I discovered I excel at helping others map out their narratives. This made me realize that the perils of the Craft Cycle are less technical and more emotional. My biggest challenge stems from a fear of sharing my work. The Story Cycle mindset helped me get to the root of the problem. During the finishing phase, I pull in the playful energy of the Collaborate Cycle. Specifically, I call in my muse and work with my critic.

COMFORT ZONE

Take a moment to reflect on which Story Cycle feels most comfortable and which Cycle feels the most uncomfortable. There's no right or wrong answer. Rather, it's simply helpful information to know if you have an affinity for or an aversion to a particular cycle.

Are you attracted to calibrate's dreamy, reflective phase? Or do you avoid this phase because it feels like there's no forward momentum? If a writer becomes too cozy in the calibrate phase, they may get stuck in an endless loop of listening.

Many writers crave the combustible Collaborate Cycle, and it's easy to be seduced by the playful summer cycle. Are you happy to goof around and explore, or does this cycle seem like a waste of time? Writers can be stunted by spontaneity and get stuck in fantasy, but this cycle provides invaluable methods for connecting to your audience, enlisting your muse, and corralling the critic.

Do you prefer cultivate's expansive discovery phase, or do you find the abundant potentiality overwhelming? The Cultivate Cycle can feel exciting and free, but all that splashing and swimming around in possibilities can wear down confidence and sap motivation. A sneaky critic might lure the writer into a whirlpool of endless planning, planting, and preparing.

If you're like me, you may love to craft but struggle to complete. An overlooked obstacle is the habit of clinging to craft. When a writer fears the fall cycle's inevitable transformation, they may unconsciously postpone reaching the finish line. When darkness descends and the path is obscured, it's time to calibrate and check in with your creative compass.

To move forward on your writing journey, look at the elemental energies of the Story Cycles and identify the characteristic qualities needed during that cycle.

- ◎ The airy stillness of winter's Calibrate Cycle requires patience.

- ✤ The watery, fertile Cultivate Cycle calls for faith.

- ☀ The fiery Collaborate Cycle calls for spontaneity and surrendering to the unknown.

- ▲ Fall's earthy Craft Cycle demands dedication and decisive action.

ACTIVITY: In the Zone ⏰ 40 minutes

When do you feel in the zone? Explore your feelings about the different Story Cycles.

Step 1: Use list making to reflect on the Story Cycles.

For each cycle, write a love-hate list. This is like a pro-con list, but the focus is on what you like vs. what you don't like, what's comfortable vs. uncomfortable, difficult vs. easy.

- ◎ Calibrate Cycle . . .
- ✤ Cultivate Cycle . . .
- ☀ Collaborate Cycle . . .
- ▲ Craft Cycle . . .

Step 2: Review your lists and assess how you feel about each Story Cycle.
- Which cycles are comfortable?
- Which cycles are uncomfortable?

Step 3: Use freewriting to uncover the fear that might be driving aversion.

Prompt: The [X Cycle] is scary because . . .

Once you know your comfort zone, use this information to triage a situation.

TRIAGE

Challenges are part of the process, so learning to triage a situation is central to creative success. To bring a project to completion, writers can use the Story Cycle framework to diagnose problems and find a way forward. When in doubt, calibrate. This practice allows you to revisit intentions, clarify milestones, and chart your course with meaningful, measurable markers.

When you hit an obstacle, instead of muscling your way forward, take a moment to reevaluate. Acknowledge where you are in the Story Cycles and reconsider your approach. What tools and techniques are most appropriate? Have you slipped into another cycle? If so, is this where you need to be? Or do you need to get back on track? Is this an indication that you need to infuse the process with different energy?

Reminder: When identifying markers, count the time and attention given to understanding how you write.

If you find you're working hard but not getting anything done, it may be time to slow down and do less. Trying to juggle too many objectives at once is a common stumbling block. While narrowing one's focus may make the pace feel glacial, rushing is often a sign that fear has kicked in, and the critic is running the show. Speed can be exhilarating, but if you're not careful, likely you will crash and burn. It's critical to refill the well. It's natural for productivity to ebb and flow.

Tracking the cultivate phase can be frustrating. Sometimes, even after diligent planning, plotting, and planting, our efforts don't yield visible results. Yet, time spent developing structure or a character's background is invaluable. This type of writing yields potent fertilizer. What you nourish will flourish. It's satisfying to sort out structure or write a great scene, but it's also important to value the discovery writing along the way. Discovery writing isn't counted in pages or words, but rather these efforts are meaningful markers on the way to milestones.

The most counterintuitive aspect of the Story Cycle Method may be the principles of the collaborate phase. Conventional wisdom champions discipline, so it seems counterintuitive to goof around. During this cycle, we learned that meaningful markers also include activities such as reconnecting to your muse, going to a museum, or consuming inspirational material like books, movies, or music.

It can be demoralizing when we don't progress as planned, but instead of thrashing around in the dark, it might be time to calibrate. What does the journey demand? It's time to consult your inner compass. Do you need to rest, refuel, or check in with your *why*? It's normal to work through multiple drafts, but another common pitfall is perfectionism. To weather the spiraling nature of Story Cycles, strive for progress— not perfection.

Once you identify where you are in the Story Cycles, the next step is to choose the most appropriate tools and techniques.

Here's a reminder of the activities best suited to each Story Cycle:

◎ Calibrate:
- Reflect on and write about the process.
- Reconnect to your *why*.

✿ Cultivate:
- Research, study technique, corral questions, and wrangle them into the question list.
- Consider the big picture and rework the outline.

☀ Collaborate:
- Approach the work from a posture of play.
- Connect with your muse. Contain the critic.

▲ Craft:
- Refine a specific element, sculpt a scene, clarify character.
- Is it time to harvest? It might be time to share the work . . . to get feedback or submit for publication.

It is the function
of art to renew
our perception.
What we are
familiar with we
cease to see. The
writer shakes up
the familiar scene,
and as if by magic,
we see a new
meaning in it.

—Anaïs Nin

ACTIVITY: Pack Your Backpack   45 minutes

What discoveries did you make?
What will you pack for the journey ahead?

    * See the end of the chapter for step-by-step instructions.

TAKE TWO

It's easy to lose perspective or get turned around, so it's important to circle back and revisit intentions. At the beginning of this book, I asked you to complete a survey and to set forth goals. Before you set your sights on the next milestone, take time to renew your intentions. The instinct to keep the momentum going is valuable, but it is also important to periodically refresh and reconsider: assess and revise your goals if need be.

If you've hit the target, it may be time for a new aim, or it might be time to celebrate. When you fall short, it's critical to calibrate. You might be tempted to beat yourself up or throw in the towel, but instead, this is an opportunity to set forward a more manageable milestone or to make the markers more specific.

TROUBLESHOOT THE GOAL

When you fall short of the goal, it's time to calibrate. Here are three examples of how to handle common stumbling blocks.

Goal: Establish a writing practice.

☐ If you've successfully set up your writing practice, before taking aim at a new target, record what you've discovered about your process.

    – Now that you have a routine, perhaps you want to increase your writing time. Before taking more on, consider what's truly realistic. More isn't necessarily better. The paramount objective is to build a sustainable practice.

- What's working? How many hours a week is reasonable? What's the ideal length of a writing session? What's the best time of day to write? Is there a specific place that's most comfortable?

- If you haven't been able to get into a writing routine, take time to reflect. It's normal to get demoralized if we've set an unrealistic goal. Did you set unreasonable expectations? There are only so many hours in the day. Could you make the markers more manageable? Consider how the goal could be even smaller.

Goal: Identify a milestone.

☐ Once you've set a milestone, make sure to identify markers. Also, as you work toward the goal, consider how you feel. If this goal feels sustainable, great! Carry on. However, if you feel burned out, then calibrate and identify a milestone that's more achievable.

- Even if the process is going well, you may want to fortify your routine so you can keep up the momentum. Are you due for a celebration? Could you improve your tracking game?

- If you haven't been able to establish workable milestones and markers, it's time to reassess. Consider the landscape. Did life throw you a curve ball? Did you overestimate your capacity? Without shame or blame, calibrate.

Goal: Start writing X project.

☐ If you've been able to get started writing, consider what's working. Take note of your process and ask, *How can I keep the momentum going?*

- If you stalled before you even started, perhaps you need to make the milestones and markers more manageable, or maybe you'd benefit from making the goal more tangible.
- For example, instead of "start writing" make the goal very specific, like "write three times a week for one hour."
- If you hit a wall, try to identify when you got derailed. Did something change in your environment? Did you dip into some uncomfortable subject matter? Is your inner critic holding you hostage?

ACTIVITY: Take Two   40 minutes

Repeat the Story Cycle survey, then compare it with your initial survey answers.

See the end of the chapter for step-by-step instructions.

The novel will never be perfect and neither will you.

—Walter Mosley

THE LONG VIEW

As you move forward on your writing journey, it is also important to zoom out and take a look at the big picture. Just as projects spiral through Story Cycles, our lives also move through cycles. It's natural for our energy to ebb and flow. Just as a project moves through multiple drafts, we also go through different phases. When we are young, it may feel like we've mastered the summer season's carefree abundance, but inspiration may fade when adult responsibilities set it. It isn't the end of creativity. Instead, calibrate, consult your inner compass, and assess your capacity.

Even when we've set forward clear goals and diligently showed up, sometimes the universe has other plans. For example, you may feel desperate to harvest, but even after carefully tending to each Story Cycle, you find yourself trapped in a wintry cocoon of contemplation. When this happens, it's time to consider the prevailing conditions. Other areas of your life may need your attention. Another possibility is that you may get pulled into another project. An opportunity may come along and push you in a new direction. Even if it isn't your project or the one you wanted, it might give you important insights or provide needed experience with a specific Story Cycle. If you find you're unable to move out of your comfort zone, you may have healing to do or other business to take care of. Just as we can't rush the seasons, we can't rush Story Cycles. Take the long view.

The world needs your story.

RECAP

Remember, the closer we get to the finish line, the louder the critic might become. Writing can create powerful emotions for both the reader and the writer. When that negative self-talk kicks up, remember to translate the harsh words into the language of the kind critic:

This matters to you.

You care.

You care about the impact of your writing.

You are sensitive, thoughtful, and creative.

You are having an experience.

Your voice matters. Keep going.

Chapter Twenty-One Activities

Pack your backpack
⏱ 45 minutes

What discoveries did you make? What will you pack for the journey ahead? Use your Field Notes Writing Tracker to reflect and write. Use freewriting and list making to explore these questions.

- ☐ What are three things you learned?
- ☐ What are three favorite exercises?
- ☐ What is your biggest challenge at the moment?
- ☐ What are new insights about your process? About the craft? What writing routines worked and didn't work for you?
- ☐ What are good places to write? Time of day? Special treats?
- ☐ Any new rituals or routines?
- ☐ How has your framework for process changed?
- ☐ What measurable markers are effective or ineffective? Consider pages, words, time, a specific element.
- ☐ What have you discovered about your story?

Take Two
⏱ 40 minutes

- ☐ Repeat the Story Cycle survey (Chapter Four)
  - What is your current project?
  - What's the status of the project?
  - Talk about your process.
  - What is your intended outcome?
  - What would you like to accomplish?
- ☐ Now look back at the initial Calibrate Your Compass answers from Chapter One.

- How do your answers compare?
- How has your project evolved?

☐ Did you take a different direction?
- If it has changed, how so?
- How do you feel about this?

☐ What discoveries have you made?

☐ What questions have come to the surface?

☐ Did your initial assessment match the reality?
- If not, how was it different?

☐ What was the intended outcome?
- If you achieved this outcome, does it feel the way you expected?

BEHIND THE SCENES: Empty Nest

The hulking young man smiled at me, and I burst into tears. How could this six-foot-tall gentle giant be my son? I wasn't prepared for the flood of emotions. It seemed like yesterday he was a toddler playing with Legos and yet, there he was, graduating from high school. He looked so grown up with his hands folded, attentively listening to the graduation speakers. He wore a dapper suit his grandmother had purchased and a colorful tie borrowed from his father. His curly hair fell past his shoulders.

I loved seeing those delightful ringlets. During middle school he'd grown to hate his unruly mane, and ever since he'd kept his hair short, but in tenth grade, he lost a bet with a friend. The prescribed consequence was a moratorium on haircuts. I wasn't privy to the nature of the bet, nor the reasoning behind the restrictive grooming mandate. He was eighteen, and—as to be expected—I was no longer the center of his universe.

A mix of feelings and thoughts fueled more tears. Intellectually, I understood that nothing blooms forever, but something about looking at my son in that suit put a spotlight on impermanence, and I wasn't ready for him to leave the nest. I felt untethered. This rite of passage for my son was also a turning point for me. Until that moment, I thought I was ready for the change. Hadn't I been looking forward to having more time to write and pursue filmmaking? Plus, my daughter still had four years of high school, so our home wouldn't technically be an empty nest.

Even though I champion the wisdom of the Story Cycle Method, the magnitude of this moment woke up the critic. I thought back to that spring break trip when he was a toddler. I wondered what my career would have looked like if I had chosen to get on that plane to London for the film festival.

Over the last nearly two decades, I'd never fully stopped pursuing my creative dreams, but I'd stepped back from the front lines. I spiraled through the Story Cycles and completed projects, but the pace felt glacial. I was struggling to break back into the business, and I thought about my contemporaries who now had extensive IMBD credits. I had sometimes experienced pangs of envy, like when a former assistant got hired as a staff writer and when another won an Oscar. I reminded myself that these colleagues often were the ones who either didn't have children or had wives who took the lead on looking after the children.

I blew my nose, and my daughter rolled her eyes. My mother whispered, "Are you okay? Are you having allergies?"

Her question made me laugh. She's never understood my emotionality, and I didn't try to explain. She's one of those high-powered women who built an impressive career while raising children. I admired her and often wish I'd managed to manifest the same kind of success, but her question also reminded me of how different we are and that we each must follow our own path.

Looking back to that aborted trip to London, I realized I wouldn't have made a different choice. There's nothing that I'd trade for the time I spent raising my kids. Being a mom has been the best part of my life. I quieted the critic and remembered I am exactly where I am supposed to be.

My journey isn't over. I have stories I want to put into the world and more to discover about Story Cycles.

As I looked at the graduates, I wondered how their journeys would unfold, and I mused on what was next for me. Little did I know, in less than a year's time, a pandemic would make the whole world pause and calibrate.

As I make the final revisions on this book, my daughter has just graduated from high school and in the fall, she'll set out on a new adventure. My mother keeps asking me what I'll do when both the kids are out of the house, and I have an empty nest. There seems to be the promise of more time, and I imagine this new phase will expand my capacity, but there's still so much mystery ahead.

Maybe I'll make another movie, sell a screenplay, or publish my novel. I also know, with certainty, that inspiration will ebb and flow, productivity will wax and wane, and the Story Cycles will keep turning.

Just like yours, my story is still unfolding.

Acknowledgments

To my family and friends, thank you for believing in me. A special thank you to Mom for showing me how to enjoy the journey, and to Dad for giving me a love of storytelling. Thank you to Van for asking good questions and listening attentively, and to Nancy for giving me permission to choose the artist's path.

To my muse, Miss Samara May, you're a rockstar copyeditor and you light up my life. Thank you for giving me the confidence to shine. To my big bear Chazen, you bring joy into the world and my heart. Thank you for giving me the courage to choose my own path and to take the time that I need.

I couldn't have written this book without the love and support of my cherished BFFs: Pamela, Katie, Aizita, Nicole, Marla, Suzanne, Sarah 941, and Eileen. I am especially grateful to the brilliant book group women. You've made me a more thoughtful reader and a more courageous writer. To the Joy Buck Club, Dreamy Drafters, and the Step-sisters, thank you for being a refuge.

I'm deeply grateful to my teachers, especially Caroline. Thank you to Paper Raven Books and my editors Kate, Avalon, and Colleen. To my designer, HR. Thank you to my beta readers, most especially Kat.

To my clients and students: It's a privilege to be on the creative journey with you. Thank you to those who granted me permission to be included in the behind-the-scenes stories: Dan, Meher, Nandi, Kaili, Rachel, Marcelle, and Karen. Thank you to the Central Valley Community Foundation, CMAC, and the Big Tell.

Thank you to my siblings and in-laws Hilary, Zeb, Sarah, Jen, Jeremy, Mark, Bruce, Nina, Dave, Rebecca, Julia, Andrea, Eirik, Luke, and all your cool kids. To the Auntourage: Delia, Miranda, Bernadine, and Fran. Thank you for embracing me. Thank you to my grandparents, aunties, uncles, and my cousins—the Kellys, Caseys, Benzians, Rices, and Cunninghams. An extra shout-out to my SF cousins for always cheering me on: Tricia, Cynny, Carol, and Kathleen.

An extra-extra special thanks to my sister Hilary for being my cheer-leader and making everything more fun.

I am grateful to my dear friends Traci and Brian, Joaquin, Eric P. Buk, Jessica, Scott, Annabeth, Gia, and Jennie G. To my walking buddies: Stephanie, Tracii, Marjorie, and Sarah F., thank you for keeping me moving. And to my creative comrades: Aretha, Sarah B., Sara S., Tchaiko, Rae, Liz, and Marnie, thank you for lighting up the artist path.

Thank you all for understanding when I ducked out early from gatherings and disappeared into the writing cave.

Lastly, but most of all, a big thanks to my husband, Joe. Your unwavering confidence in me made all the difference.

Index of Exercises

denotes the activity instructions are within the chapter

Index of Tools and Techniques

All Season (Chapters 17 -20)

Story Spirals
Connect with the Reader/Audience
Letter Writing
The Elemental Forces
Calibrate: Air
Cultivate: Water
Collaborate: Fire
Craft: Earth
Reframe
Agree to Disagree
Critic's Tricks and Greatest Hits
Impact Statement
Match Your Markers and Milestones
Rest Stops and Scenic Views
Progress, Not Perfection
Feed The Muse

Recommended Reading

Writing and Creativity

The Artist's Way: A Spiritual Path to Higher Creativity by Julia Cameron

Bird by Bird: Some Instructions on Writing and Life by Anne Lamott

Body Work: The Radical Power of Personal Narrative by Melissa Febos

Improvisation for the Theater: A Handbook of Teaching and Directing Techniques by Viola Spolin

Manifesto: On Never Giving Up by Bernardine Evaristo

On Writing: A Memoir of the Craft by Stephen King

Story Arcana: Tarot for Writers (book and course) by Caroline Donahue

Writing Down the Bones: Freeing the Writer Within by Natalie Goldberg

Wired for Story: The Writer's Guide to Using Brain Science to Hook Readers from the Very First Sentence by Lisa Cron

Women Who Run with the Wolves: Myths and Stories of the Wild Woman Archetype by Clarissa Pinkola Estés

Screenwriting and Filmmaking

The TV Writer's Workbook: A Creative Approach to Television Scripts by Ellen Sandler

Making a Good Script Great by Linda Seger

Shooting to Kill: How an Independent Producer Blasts Through the Barriers to Make Movies that Matter by Christine Vachon and David Edelstein

The Writer's Journey: Mythic Structure for Writers by Christopher Vogler

Mindset

The Art of Money: A Life-Changing Guide to Financial Happiness by Bari Tessler

The Creative Habit: Learn It and Use It for Life by Twyla Tharp

The Four Tendencies: The Indispensable Personality Profiles That Reveal How to Make Your Life Better (and Other People's Lives Better, Too) by Gretchen Rubin

No Mud, No Lotus: The Art of Transforming Suffering by Thich Nhat Hanh

Citations

Part I

The Audre Lorde Project. "Breaking Isolation: Self Care and Community Care Tools for Our People," January 27, 2017.

University of Idaho Library. "Bhavacakra: Wheel of Becoming/Wheel of Life," n.d.

Watt, Jeff. "What's in a Symbol? Bhavacakra." Tricycle: The Buddhist Review, October 29, 2022.

"Turning of the Wheel Humanities Colloquium 2011-2012 - Digital Initiatives - University of Idaho Library," n.d.

Part II

Ang, Alvin. "10 Legendary Writers & Their Daily Word Counts - The Writing Cooperative." Medium, September 3, 2022.

Charney, Noah. "How I Write: Margaret Atwood." The Daily Beast, July 11, 2017.

Write The World. "Amanda Gorman's Advice to Young Poets," July 21, 2023.

Ned Hayes. "Writer Tip: How Many Words Do Famous Writers Create Every Day?" Novel Doctor, November 2, 2020.

Viola Spolin. "Viola Spolin Biography," n.d. www.violaspolin.org/bio.

Part III

Snowden, Ruth. *Jung - The Key Ideas: Teach Yourself. Teach Yourself*, 2018.

Griffith Review. "Acts of Reckoning - Griffith Review," March 15, 2023.

"The Seven Lessons of the Medicine Wheel | SAY Magazine," n.d.

Gompertz, Will. *What Are You Looking At?* National Geographic Books, 2013.

Rae, Casey. *William S. Burroughs and the Cult of Rock "n" Roll*. Hachette UK, 2020.

Donahue, Caroline. "Dream to Draft" and "Story Arcana." Courses.

Conway, Susannah. "78 Mirrors." Online course by Susannah Conway.

Part IV

PublishersWeekly.com. "New Report Puts Online Sales of Books, Audio at $12.13 Billion in 2022," n.d.

Yoon, Kim. "Worldwide Story Structures." Tumblr, February 1, 2021.

National Geographic. "Storytelling," Encyclopedic Entry. n.d.

Rouse, Rebecca, Hartmut Koenitz, and Mads Haahr. *Interactive Storytelling*. "The Myth of Universal Narrative Models" (pp. 107-120). Springer, 2018.

Part VI

Hanh, Thich Nhat. *No Mud, No Lotus: The Art of Transforming Suffering*. Parallax Press, 2014.

Text Excerpts (Chapter 15)

Kitamura, Katie. *Intimacies: A Novel*. Random House, 2021.

Gilbert, Elizabeth. *Eat, Pray, Love*. A&C Black, 2007.

Angelou, Maya. *I Know Why the Caged Bird Sings*. Random House, 2009.

Hamid, Mohsin. *How to Get Filthy Rich In Rising Asia*. Penguin UK, 2013.

Gumbs, Alexis Pauline. *Undrowned: Black Feminist Lessons From Marine Mammals*. AK Press, 2020.

Febos, Melissa. *Body Work: The Radical Power Of Personal Narrative*. Catapult, 2022.

Dickens, Charles. *Our Mutual Friend*. National Geographic Books, 1998.

Slimani, Leila. *In the Country of Others*. Penguin, 2022.

Vuong, Ocean. *On Earth We're Briefly Gorgeous*. Random House, 2019.

About the Author

Sascha Brown Rice is an award-winning filmmaker, writer, coach, and teacher. Her Emmy-nominated documentary *California State of Mind* and her feature rom-com *Mango Kiss* both won multiple honors, screened internationally, and were broadcast (on Netflix, public television, Logo, and more). Producing projects include the feature film *Solace,* the web series *Black Kungfu Chick,* and the short film *Basurero.* In her role as consulting producer for the Central Valley's Big Tell, Rice has mentored dozens of filmmakers and shepherded over seventy short docs to completion. As the Global Marketing Director for Eastman Kodak's motion picture division, she amplified Kodak's visibility with innovative collaborations, strategic partnerships, and community engagement. Rice supported marketing initiatives for an array of projects including commercials, music videos, fine art museum pieces, and notable television and feature films: blockbusters like *Star Wars: The Force Awakens*, and *Batman v Superman*; hit shows like AMC's *The Walking Dead*; indie favorites like *The Hateful Eight* and *Carol*; and Academy Award-winners like *La La Land.*

Rice is driven by a passion for making art and making a difference. As the granddaughter of California's former Governor Pat Brown, niece of four-term Governor Jerry Brown, and daughter of former State Treasurer Kathleen Brown, Rice is committed to carrying on her family legacy of civic engagement and serves on the Board of Advisors of the Pat Brown Institute, which is a nonpartisan public policy Institute at Cal State LA. Other notable projects have included

The Audience Awards' Women's Film Challenge and R.O.W. (RIVER OF WINGS), a public art installation of interactive kinetic sculptures aimed to bring awareness to LA River revitalization via giant bird sculptures personalized and reimagined by local schools, community groups, and artists.

With over twenty-five years in the industry, Rice offers clients a wealth of practical, strategic, and creative insights. She mentors both experienced writers who seek to rekindle their creative fire and emerging storytellers just beginning their writing journey.

Additional Publications by Sascha Brown Rice

The Companion Journals:

The Compass Notebook: A Story Cycle Guided Journal

The Field Notes Writing Tracker: A Story Cycle Process Journal

The Story Cycle Companion Workbook: Writing Prompts and Activities

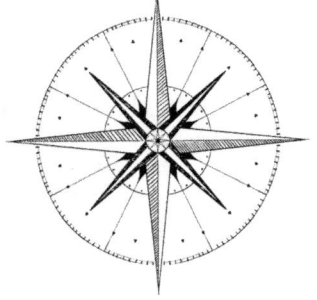